T4-AIK-811

Modification of
Child Behavior

Garth J. Blackham
Arizona State University

Adolph Silberman
Tempe Elementary Schools

Wadsworth Publishing Company, Inc.
Belmont, California

To:

Our children and our child clients–who have taught us so much and have made our efforts so rewarding.

© 1971 by Wadsworth Publishing Company, Inc., Belmont, California 94002. All rights reserved. No part of this book may be reproduced, stored in a retrieval system or transcribed, in any form or by any means, electronic, mechanical, photocopying, recording, or otherwise, without the prior written permission of the publisher.

L. C. Cat. Card No.: 79-134365

Printed in the United States of America

1 2 3 4 5 6 7 8 9 10—74 73 72 71

Preface

In the past ten or fifteen years striking changes have been taking place in concepts and applications of theory in counseling and psychotherapy. Well-established systems have come under critical review, and many principles of behavior and therapy once accepted as truisms have been subjected to searching assessment. Controlled experimentation with both animal and human behavior has led to the demise of some cherished notions, has modified others, and has led to important new developments. While these changes are apparent in many areas of theory and practice, they are most dramatic in the application of learning theory to promoting behavior change. Articles and research reports are rapidly growing in number, and applications to human problems are steadily increasing. Behavior modification seems to be coming of age.

However, even though reasearch in and applications of behavior modification are increasing, their reports are scattered throughout a number of journals. The applications of behavior modification in dealing with specific child problems are still not extensive. Consequently, to assess the utility of these procedures for effectively modifying child behavior and learning problems is often left to the ingenuity of the practitioner. If the practitioner does not have ready access to the journals or is not sophisticated in the basic theory and methods, he may not be effective in utilizing them.

The present volume has been formulated and written with these problems in mind. First, the theoretical concepts and principles of behavior modification are precisely presented to provide the reader with the necessary background. Second, as we have reviewed pertinent literature and clinically tested some of the principles and procedures, we have attempted to cull and describe some of the more useful applications for working with teachers, parents, and specific child problems. Third, we have attempted to sensitize or alert the potential practitioner to some relatively common application problems. Consequently, the practitioner has in a single source the theory, procedures, process, and applications that are useful in a variety of child-behavior and learning problems.

The first four chapters outline the theory essential to understanding and use of behavior-modification principles. Chapter 1 introduces the reader to essential learning-theory concepts, ways of identifying behavior that it is desirable to change, and value questions inherent in the alteration and control of behavior. The principles and procedures relevant to the process of strengthening or enhancing adaptive behavior are discussed in Chapter 2. Methods by which nonadaptive behavior is altered or eliminated are described in Chapter 3. The use of observation, recording, and measurement of behavior in which change is desired is considered in Chapter 4. Since observing and recording behavior are such integral parts of behavior-change procedures, methods that may be used in studying a variety of problem behavior in different settings are reviewed.

The remainder of the book (Chapters 5-8) is devoted primarily to a translation and application of theory in changing nonadaptive behavior in children. Chapter 5 presents the necessary steps involved in identifying and analyzing problem dimensions, determining behavior-change priorities, specifying the client(s) to whom treatment is most appropriately directed, and formulating strategies (or models) for modifying the client's behavior. Methods or individual intervention strategies that promote change in a variety of child-behavior problems are discussed in Chapter 6. In Chapter 7 the applications of behavior modification to child problems in the classroom setting are considered. The final chapter describes the principles and procedures by which parent-child problems may be conceptualized and appropriately modified.

It is impossible to identify all of the influences and people who have been helpful in the process of writing this book. The references at the end of the book clearly reflect our intellectual debt to a number of people. Two of our colleagues, Dr. H. D. Richardson and Dr. Tom Cummings, read the first draft and raised questions that led to elaborations, reformulations, and additions. Several doctoral students in the Department of Counseling and Educational Psychology at Arizona State University were helpful in making constructive suggestions. Among those students we are especially indebted to Donald Tobin and Marshall Chatwin.

For permission to paraphrase or adapt material, we wish to thank the following authors and publishers: Josef Cohen, *Operant conditioning and operant behavior,* Chicago: Rand McNally, 1969; and Robert Havighurst, *Human development and education,* New York: David McKay Company, Inc., 1953.

The effort and time that was required in writing the book necessitated our being often absent from our wives and children. For their understanding and gracious acceptance of these absences, we are sincerely appreciative.

Barb Barmore spent many hours proofing and typing the final manuscript. Her dedication to the task and her thoughtfulness in performing it were far beyond the call of duty. We sincerely and gratefully acknowledge it.

Contents

Chapter 1

Introduction

Everyone who has the responsibility for socializing, training, and educating children is involved in the process of enhancing or changing behavior. And everyone who is involved in that process has implicit or explicit notions regarding how it may be done and what kinds of growth or change are desirable. These notions, or "theories," vary greatly in their completeness and validity. Typically, it appears, these notions are handed down from one person to another, generation after generation, without critical examination. But, interestingly enough, these poorly articulated and infrequently examined views continue to be acted on as if they were correct. Apparently, these time-worn but relatively untested views work well enough on the basis of some criteria to stay firmly implanted in the individual's belief system.

There are many examples in everyday life that illustrate the point. For one, many people explicitly hold and act on the assumption that people will behave desirably if they are told what they ought to do and are given logical reasons for doing so. Basic to this unverified assumption is that if you give people the facts, basic changes in their attitude and behavior will follow. If the person to whom the "good advice" is given does not change his behavior, the failure to change is usually attributed to some personal idiosyncrasy. The basic assumption, "facts change a person's behavior in desirable ways," is rarely examined.

There are commercials that frequently appear on television describing the ill effects of cigarette smoking. The assumption of the advertisement appears to be that this description will in fact make people terminate the habit. Yet, personal observation of people who are smokers watching the commercial seems to suggest that it does not promote that behavior. Rather, what it appears in fact to do is to develop avoidance behavior in people who watch the commercial. They simply stop watching it and continue their smoking.

If desirable behavior acquisition and change are to be promoted in predictable ways, clear and valid conceptions of change must be carefully formulated. Stated in its simplest terms, by the socialization, training, and education of children we strive to accomplish two basic goals: (1) to facilitate acquisition of desirable behavior that is not present in the individual's repertoire, and (2) to change behavior already acquired that is socially undesirable or self-defeating. While both types of behavior acquisition involve a form of learning, they are somewhat different in type, for in the first instance, the acquisition of previously unattained behavior, one basic step or phase is involved, while in the second instance, two basic steps or phases are involved: (i) the unwanted or undesirable behavior must be unlearned; (ii) new learning must occur that allows the person to function effectively. The second type of learning or behavior change is usually more complicated because the undesirable behavior often has some functional utility. That is, the behavior is useful in reducing anxiety or promoting some other satisfying state. But despite its functional value, because it is in some way undesirable or self-destructive, this behavior must be extinguished and a new behavior must be encouraged in its place. Thus it is apparent why it is desirable to have the person learn the appropriate behavior in the first place.

If the task of those who are charged with training, educating, and socializing children is essentially promoting desirable behavior acquisitions and changing undesirable and self-defeating behavior, how does one identify the forms of behavior to be enhanced and those to be changed or unlearned? These are the specific concerns to which we now direct our attention.

Identifying Behaviors To Facilitate and Change

Upon cursory examination, it may seem that it is relatively easy to identify behaviors that might be appropriately changed. And in part that is true. It is certainly not difficult to determine that a child who exhibits an unnatural fear, or is excessively inhibited or aggressive, or is unable to adequately attend to learning, or is doing failing work in reading or arithmetic is in need of some assistance in changing his behavior. These behaviors cause distress to the child himself, create alarm reactions in others, and ultimately deter adequate and healthy personality development. That is, the behavior acts in a circular way. The behavior of the child causes others to react negatively to him, and this results in devaluation of the child.

There is an inherent caution that should be noted. The fact that a child's behavior is distressing to a parent or teacher may not be an adequate criterion for effecting a change. The behavior exhibited by a child may not be the "real problem," but instead it may be the person who so labels it. For example, a parent may not be able to feel comfortable until all expressions of competitiveness or aggression are completely submerged or stricken from a child's behavior. In this instance the "real problem" resides with the parent and not the child. Obviously, a certain amount of competitiveness is necessary to adequately adapt in our society.

The decision to change a child's behavior should involve at least three criteria. First, the behavior presumed to be maladaptive must occur with sufficient frequency; for example, an occasional fight might be typical for most children, but when they occur daily the behavior is maladaptive. Second, the behavior, if continued, will ultimately end up being hurtful to the child and/or the environment; for example, a child who has a severe reading disability cannot be kept idle in the hope that he will "outgrow the problem." Adequate reading facility is basic to progress in most academic areas. Third, the behavior impedes subsequent adaption and healthy development; for instance, excessively dependent or infantile behavior poses serious problems at later ages and developmental periods.

Some may object to the terms "healthy" or "maladaptive" because they are thought to imply an absolute standard of what is desirable behavior. Or the terms may be criticized because they are related to a medical concept of disease. Another objection may arise because the cultural relevance of the desirable behavior is not clearly specified. Each of these is a quite valid criticism according to a particular view of the nature of man. If one assumes that ultimate development is primarily a function of the stimulus events to which one is subjected in his lifetime, the nature of the stimulus events are obviously determinant in the ultimate outcomes of development. However, if one assumes that ultimate development is primarily influenced by the unfolding of the genetic givens, stimulus events and their consequences assume a lesser importance in determining human behavior. At the present time, the state of our knowledge in the behavioral sciences does not make it possible to conclude that any one view of the nature of man is completely valid.

We recognize also that different environmental, cultural, and social-class circumstances promote quite different behavior as being desirable. Each society, social class, and subculture values, sanctions, and emulates very different behaviors. Acceptable behavior in one society may be socially or legally condemned in another. Adaptive behavior must be socially relevant. Behavior that is not socially relevant evokes all manner of negative consequences and ends up punishing to the offender. However, there is a limit to the application of this criterion. Individuals who learn the approved social behavior in one group may find their behavior quite alien in another social context. For example, a "good hippie" is a social outcast in polite middle class society; but the opposite is also true. So what is indeed appropriate social behavior is a moot question.

What is considered maladaptive or deviant is obviously related to one's theoretical orientation (Bandura, 1969). If one is psychoanalytically oriented, one conceptualizes deviancy in terms of the functioning of Id, Ego, and Superego processes. Rogerians tend to formulate deviant behavior in terms of alterations or deficiencies in the self concept and the "necessary and sufficient conditions." Skinnerians are likely to formulate their conceptions of ineffective behavior in terms of the stimulus-response-consequence relationships. If behavior-change measures are implemented and they prove ineffective, the hypothetical terms peculiar to the theoretical system are used as explanations. Rogerians are prone to explain ineffective therapeutic movement by the lack of empathy, congruence, and positive regard in the therapeutic relationship. Similarly, Skinnerians may explain the lack of behavior change by inappropriate conditions of reinforcement. The major difference in the way in which adherents of the different theoretical systems formulate these problems is the degree to which the explanations are verifiable. Those systems that attempt to state the variables in terms that are testable or refutable will ultimately be more helpful in promoting and defining successful change strategies.

Perhaps one useful way to conceptualize what is considered adaptive behavior (beyond the three criteria we have previously mentioned) is to determine the extent to which a person is successfully meeting the realistic expectations and demands made on him in broad areas of living. If his behavior is ineffective or inappropriate, he is likely to manifest it in disordered cognitive processes, the kinds and intensity of emotional reactivity, utility, and appropriateness of motor behavior and in his physical and/or physiological functioning. Ultimately, adaptive behavior may well be determined by the capacity to appropriately discriminate among the stimulus and response requirements in the context of one's life that lead to satisfactions without our suffering unsought or negative consequences.

We will have more to say about ineffective or nonadaptive behavior in a subsequent section. Attention is now directed to the problem of identifying those behaviors that it is desirable to facilitate and enhance. The problem cannot be ignored even though what may be identified as the ultimate goals of human development have not been clearly delineated. Most children go to school to learn something, and that "something" cannot be determined after the fact. Some definable goals have to be specified. The plaguing question, "Education for what?" is still relevant.

What Behavior Should Be Enhanced?

What type of person do we ultimately wish to develop? What are the desirable end products of one's becoming? What learning or developmental steps and acquisitions are necessary to get there?

We could easily escape the complexity of these questions and provide an immediate answer by indicating that our goal is the self-actualization of every child. And, after Maslow (1954), we can enumerate the characteristics of such a person briefly as follows:

1. An efficient and clear perception of reality.
2. The capacity to accept self, others, and nature.
3. Spontaneity, naturalness, and lack of artificiality in behavior.
4. Capacity to problem center and interest in and acceptance of responsibility for the solution of problems outside ourselves.
5. Capacity for objective detachment and affinity for privacy and solitude.
6. Autonomy and independence from the culture and environment for basic and extrinsic satisfactions.
7. A richness of subjective experience.
8. A deep feeling of identification and sympathy for mankind.
9. Capacity to commit, invest, and enjoy deep interpersonal relationships.
10. A democratic personality structure.
11. Ability to make clear distinctions between right and wrong and to discriminate between means and ends.
12. A philosophical and noninjurious sense of humor.
13. Creativeness.

These are important and noble goals. In a general sense, they do provide some direction for considering the types of behavior we wish to enhance. But, because they are general, not longitudinally charted or sequentially arranged, they are difficult to translate into the successive developmental steps. To promote their acquisition, they must also be operationally defined. Others have made significant developmentally ordered contributions regarding the essential developmental acquisitions. The most notable contributions are Havighurst's (1953) developmental tasks and Erikson's (1963) eight developmental epochs or stages of man. These contributions are briefly summarized in Figure 1.

The Havighurst and Erikson formulations are useful because the developmental acquisitions considered essential for complete development are sequentially arranged. Consequently, more specific direction is given for those who wish to facilitate crucial behavior acquisitions. Of course, these formulations are not exhaustive. A more detailed and comprehensive formulation of other crucial developmental acquisitions is desirable. We can only hint at some of those. For example, all of the following additions seem equally important for complete psychological differentiation.

1. Learning to give to others and accept from others affectional responses without expressing feelings of anxiety, guilt, embarrassment, or unworthiness.
2. Learning to express, assess, and consider one's feelings in relating appropriately to others as judged by peers and self-perception.
3. Learning to accept responsibility for one's behavior as determined by the acceptance of consequences following an act, making necessary psychological or material reparation.

4. Developing satisfying self-reinforcement patterns so that one feels comfortable with one's physical appearance, accomplishments, and ability to perform.
5. Learning appropriate social roles required as a participating member in a variety of groups.
    a. Developing the capacity to perform roles related to being son or daughter, boy or girl, pupil, leader or follower as evidenced by being able to carry out responsibilities required in each role.

Havighurst	Erikson
0-6 Years	Developing a Sense of:
Learning:	1. Trust (feeling a sense of safety and predictability in relationships with others)
1. To walk	
2. To take solid foods	
3. To talk	2. Autonomy (a sense of independence, freedom to explore, developing self-control without excessive loss of self-depreciation)
4. To control elimination of body wastes	
5. Sex differences and sex modesty	3. Initiative (developing effective ways of acting on the world, striving to reach self-determined goals, perseverance and persistence)
6. Achieving physiological stability	
7. To distinguish right and wrong and develop a conscience	
8. To relate emotionally to others	4. Industry and/or Accomplishment (learning a great variety of skills)
9. To form simple concepts of social and physical reality	
6-12 Years	5. Identity (a sense of who one is and his role in society)
Learning (or Developing):	6. Intimacy (learning to make deep emotional investments in persons of the same or opposite sex without strain, anxiety, or fear)
10. Physical skills necessary for ordinary games	
11. Wholesome attitudes toward oneself	7. Generativity (feeling a sense of fulfillment in producing and caring for children)
12. To appropriately relate to age mates	
13. An appropriate masculine or feminine role	8. Integrity (being at peace with oneself and others, accepting responsibility for one's life and what one is)
14. Fundamental skills in reading, writing, and calculating	
15. Concepts for everyday living	
16. Conscience, morality, and a scale of values	
17. Personal independence	
18. Attitudes toward social groups and institutions	

FIGURE 1.   Essential developmental acquisitions as suggested by Havighurst's developmental tasks (infancy to 12 years) and Erikson's eight stages of man. (Adapted from Havighurst, 1953, by permission from David McKay Company, Inc., and from Erikson, 1963.)

Besides extending the list of essential developmental acquisitions, the formulations listed above have an additional dimension. They are stated in terms that more closely approximate the observable behavior considered desirable. An operationally stated outcome has two essential ingredients (Mager, 1962). First, the desirable terminal behavior must be stated in terms that are overtly observable and hence measurable. Second, the behavioral outcomes must identify behaviors to be performed and the exact conditions in which they are expected to occur. For example, if we were considering the acquisition of the social role of "son," we would have to specify all of the behaviors the parents feel he should perform (actions and verbalizations) as well as behaviors developmentally desirable in a psychological and societal sense for "sons." When it is so stated, we know the exact behavior we wish to promote. However, if developmental outcomes are not stated in behavioral terms, we simply do not know when the child has made the acquisitions.

When we consider the facilitation of the desirable behavior outcomes that might result from learning, education, and socialization, we must also sequentially order them. An excellent job of sequentially organizing educational objectives is contained in two volumes, by Bloom (1956) and by Krathwohl, Bloom, and Masia (1964). They have attempted to formulate a hierarchy of educational objectives in the cognitive and affective domains. Although they have not stated all behavioral outcomes that are presumed desirable in each of these areas, they have specified the general nature and levels of attainment that are desirable in each domain.

Because the Bloom *et al.* formulations provide useful guidelines to thinking productively about important developmental acquisitions, it is desirable to briefly describe the general structure of the cognitive domain. The taxonomy in the cognitive domain is a hierarchy of six levels with each level being foundational and, to some extent, prerequisite to the attainment of the next higher level. Starting with the most basic and the simplest level of attainment and moving sequentially to the next higher level, we identify them as: (1) knowledge, (2) comprehension, (3) application, (4) analysis, (5) synthesis, and (6) evaluation.

Knowledge, the first level, consists of facts and/or information in each discipline that it is considered desirable to know. It is divided into subclasses involving knowledge of terminology, conventions, trends and sequences, classifications and categories, criteria, methodology, principles and generalizations, theories and structures. If a person knows (is able to recall) the facts specific to each of these subclasses in a discipline, it may be said that he knows all there is to know about that discipline. The first level represents the simplest level of cognition and is, to some extent, prerequisite to the attainment of the other levels. The other levels of the cognitive domain essentially represent ways in which knowledge may be employed or various types of cognitive operations that may be utilized in dealing with problems and materials.

The second level, *comprehension,* refers to the lowest level of understanding of the knowledge that one has. For example, the first subclass under comprehension is translation, which essentially involves the paraphrasing of a communication from one language to another. At the highest level of comprehension, one is able to extrapolate by going beyond the given data (oral or written communication) and determining implications, consequences, and effects and even making predictions. Obviously, the extent to which one comprehends something that is known is exemplified by the degree to which he can make inferences beyond given data.

Application, the third level, is indicative of the extent to which a person is able to apply an idea, principle, rule, or method to a specific situation. For example, when a teacher has taught—and a child has learned—a phonics principle, the extent to which the child exhibits this level of cognitive activity is demonstrated by his capacity to apply the principle to new words in his free reading.

Analysis is the fourth level of the cognitive domain. Cognition at this level consists of the capacity to break down the components of a statement or communication into its parts and order them in a hierarchy. This may involve identifying the major elements or principles and recognizing the relationships among them. Characteristic of this level of cognitive attainment is the capacity to distinguish facts from hypotheses, to validate hypotheses from given data, or to analyze principles underlying a communication.

Synthesis, the fifth level, denotes the capacity to amalgamate many elements (ideas and varied data) into a new structure. It is the creation of something new (a product or conceptualization) that has not existed previously. Perhaps the simplest way to describe this type of cognition is to suggest that it is a type of intellectual activity that is popularly described as creativity. It is the construction of a unique communication, plan, or set of abstract relationships.

The final level of the cognitive domain is *evaluation.* Cognition at this level is exemplified by the ability to make appropriate judgments regarding the utility or value of certain formulations, methods, and materials for specific purposes. At the lowest level, evaluation may be illustrated by the ability to identify fallacies in arguments. At its highest level, evaluation is expressed by the ability to compare major generalizations and theories for their utility in conceptualizing certain phenomena.

The Bloom *et al.* contributions represent a commendable attempt to systematically and sequentially organize the types of cognitive attainments considered important as outcomes. As such, it serves as a useful model for thinking about outcomes that may well deserve some emulation. Until we have refined and systematized other human-development goals in some similar type of classification, we are likely to suffer from a sense of indirection. Of course, we may never be able to state or order them all (and it is probably not entirely desirable), but such conceptions have much to offer.

Another conception of some basic learning goals (or abilities) that have been systematically and sequentially organized is that of Valett (1969). He has identified and operationally defined 53 basic learning abilities in six major areas of psychoeducational development. These 53 basic learning abilities are divided among the following developmental areas: (1) gross motor development, (2) sensory-motor integration, (3) perceptual-motor skills, (4) language development, (5) conceptual skills, and (6) social skills. A particular virtue of the Valett formulations is that he has operationally defined each basic learning ability, developed appropriate ways of measuring their attainment, and identified instructional activities and approaches for promoting their acquisition.

Theoretical and Value Questions about Behavior Change

Before concluding our introductory remarks about the enhancement and change of behavior, it is appropriate that we discuss some of the inherent value questions. The most basic issue is sometimes stated as follows: "In a democracy, where individuality, freedom of choice, the right to self-determination, and dissent are highly cherished values, it is not 'right,' or may even be 'immoral,' to manipulate, change, or control another's behavior." Certainly, almost everyone can subscribe to some of the values inherent in this challenge. However, the *real* problem is that a person's ability to make choices and the freedom with which he can make them are restricted by the environment and by other men. As Skinner (1966) has suggested, behavior is controlled by its consequences. Thus, that a choice that initiates a certain behavior has a certain probability of reoccurrence depends on the consequences of the action. A person jumps from too high in a tree, injures himself, and seriously restricts his future behavior choices. A man commits an illegal act, is caught and punished by the law. His freedom and his choice are seriously curtailed. Apparently, a person has freedom of choice to the extent that he does not violate physical laws, man-made laws, or the mores of his social group.

From these simple examples, one readily observes that behavior is subject to restrictions and controls. But let us extend the analysis further. The society-at-large has little question about the "rightness" or "justness" of the manipulation and control of socially undesirable or destructive behavior. And when such acts are committed, there is no dearth of opinion on the appropriateness of severe punishment or aversive control. On the basis of actual examples such as those above, one infers that it is "right" to manipulate some behavior and not others. And we should also note that the more behavior dramatically deviates from the socially acceptable, the greater the sentiment for punishment or aversive control and the sterner the punishment invoked (for example, the death penalty for certain actions is still law in most states). It is not very difficult to find people who proclaim the justness of the death penalty but who aggressively protest the immorality of behavior manipulation and control.

One of the problems inherent in the question of control versus freedom of choice is that few people realize how widespread the use of various forms of behavioral control is. A teacher may object to giving material rewards (such as candy or trinkets) for a certain performance, yet freely utilize stars, awards, punishments, or smiling and frowning faces on the pupil's papers. If the teacher's attention is directed to the fact that he or she is manipulating and controlling the pupil's behavior by these methods, the defense is often that the difference is in the "rightness" of the methods used. Yet it is difficult to subscribe to this logic. Empirically, it is difficult to validate the argument that punishment is more effective than positive reinforcement in changing behavior.

Apparently it is not widely recognized that child training and socialization, education, persuasion, and moral discourse *are* forms of manipulation and control. All of these methods have as their aim the changing of a person's covert or overt behavior in ways consistent with the values and beliefs of those in authority. In achieving this aim, various forms of negative manipulation, coercion, and control are frequently used. Often, however, these forms of control are acceptable because they only partially control a person's behavior, not because they recognize the individual's freedom or right of dissent. The inherent freedom recognized by those who protest manipulation and control is from severe or coercive forms of control (Skinner, 1966). What is often being questioned by objectors is the amount of control; "a little control is good, a lot is bad." That is, if the form and amount of control do not completely restrict one's choices and independence of action, it is often viewed as acceptable manipulation. It is analogous to a situation in which the infliction of a little pain is all right ("A little swat never hurt anyone"), but a lot is very bad.

The issue, then, of the desirability or rightness of behavior manipulation and control seems to revolve around several questions. What behavior is it desirable to change? How much should we change it? What methods of behavior change are right and who should change the behavior? As one ponders the issues carefully, most of them seem to revolve around what is considered to be the appropriate or "right" values.

Our position may be stated simply. Everyone has the right to exercise freedom of choice in living and regulating his own life. It is recognized, however, that this freedom is relative, depending on one's age, the mores and laws of his social group, one's maturity and psychological health, and the extent to which one is aware of and able to control the influences that affect his life. The enhancement of an individual's ability to make meaningful, responsible, and wise choices is one of the ultimate educational goals. When an individual seeks psychological assistance, he should be given the choice of what behavior he wishes to change and be informed of the method(s) by which it might most effectively be promoted. It does not seem appropriate, either because of whim, social, economic, or political gain to change a person's behavior without his participation or consent. If the subject is a child and he is not equipped from the point of view of experience or ability to determine his own best welfare, his parent or legal guardian must make the decision.

After Skinner (1966), we will conclude the controversy with the following statements. Perhaps the best protection against tyranny and abuse is the widest dissemination and discussion of techniques of manipulation and control. For it does not seem logical to suppress the empirical findings that move us closer to a science of man. Rather, we should use the science to construct a cultural design that wise men have sought for a thousand years.

Basic Concepts and Definitions

We have previously discussed behavior acquisitions that it seems desirable to enhance, ways of thinking about and identifying behavior that it may be desirable to change, and some questions relating to the manipulation and control of behavior. It is appropriate, therefore, to discuss some terms that we will use as central concepts. In a subsequent section, the concepts will be more completely examined.

Respondent Behavior

A person's behavior may be classified into two categories: respondent (unlearned) and operant (learned) behavior. Respondent behavior is sometimes thought of as being reflexive, since it occurs automatically in response to a specific stimulus. The shedding of tears in response to peeling onions, the knee jerk in response to a tap on the patellar tendon, and the contraction of the pupil of the eye in response to changes in light intensity are all examples of respondent behavior. Respondent behavior is always elicited automatically to a specific stimulus; it is not under voluntary control and appears when a specific stimulus condition is present. The capacity for this type of response is part of the innate equipment of the human organism (Keller, 1954; Reese, 1966). The role that respondent behavior and conditioning assumes in influencing behavior, the ways in which respondent conditioning takes place, and its importance in human affairs will be completely discussed later.

Operant Behavior

Operant behavior, in contrast to respondent behavior, is under voluntary control. It is influenced and controlled by events or consequences that follow its occurrence. Operant behavior includes all behavior that "operates on," changes, or affects the outside environment (Keller, 1954). Almost any movement under the voluntary control of an individual may be appropriately classified as operant behavior. Picking up and bouncing a ball, writing a letter to a friend, and conversing with an associate are examples of such behavior.

Because higher animals, including man, are much less instinct-controlled, they exhibit more emitted (operant) behavior than elicited (respondent) behavior (Cohen, 1969). Consequently, operant behavior and operant conditioning assume a more decisive role in the manipulation and control of human behavior, and we shall give more complete attention to it.

Operant behavior is determined by the conditions or consequences that follow it. Consequences of a response that increase the probability of its occurrence are referred to as *reinforcers* (Keller, 1954). A reinforcer may be something edible, a smile, a reassuring word, or a friendly pat on the back, if it increases the probability that the response it follows will be emitted again. The response is strengthened by increase in the frequency of its appearance. And when the consequences that follow a response have increased the frequency of that response, conditioning has occurred. The strength of a response decreases when reinforcement is terminated. If reinforcement is completely withdrawn for a period of time, the response rate tends to return to the preconditioned rate or *operant level*. The decrease in response strength is referred to as *extinction* (Reese, 1966).

Positive and Negative Reinforcement   Reinforcers are often classified as either positive or negative according to the state of the organism after they have been employed. Hence, a positive reinforcer is sometimes described as a type of rewarding stimulus that leads to comfort and a desire to repeat the response. However, some behavioral scientists object to the use of terms such as "comfort" or "desire" because they are subjective states which must be inferred and cannot be precisely measured.

Operationally defined, a positive reinforcer is any stimulus that acts to strengthen the response (behavior) it follows, while a negative reinforcer may be defined as any stimulus which by its removal strengthens the response (behavior) it follows (Keller, 1954; Skinner, 1953). It is apparent that in positive reinforcement the response is strengthened by the addition of something. In the example referred to previously, the use of something edible or a reassuring word is a positive reinforcer. In negative reinforcement the response is strengthened because something is removed or withdrawn (Skinner, 1953). The removal or withdrawal of almost any aversive stimulus after a response is made typically acts as a negative reinforcer. Suppose, for example, that you are sitting listening to the radio and it suddenly emits a very loud noise that continues. You reach up and turn the radio off. This act terminates the noise (aversive stimulus) and increases your comfort. You have been negatively reinforced.

Let us consider another example. Suppose you have just placed your four-year-old child in her room for some misbehavior. After she is isolated in her room, she begins to cry. You respond to the crying by saying: "When you stop crying, I will let you come out of the room." If you follow through immediately upon the cessation of the crying and allow the child to come out of the room, you have employed negative reinforcement. The response "to not cry" has been strengthened because you have removed an aversive condition (being confined in a room). We should note, however, that these acts may not have any desirable effects on the earlier misbehavior. To enable you to do something to strengthen appropriate behavior, the child must make the desirable response before positive reinforcement is administered.

It can be seen, then, that negative reinforcement produces its influence by removing a host of aversive stimuli. That is, we act to terminate an aversive stimulus or we act to remove it by performing an avoidance or escape response. When we act to remove or terminate a loud noise, a bright light, or even a disturbing thought, negative reinforcement is operating. Under certain conditions, and depending on how it is defined, punishment may be negatively reinforcing. However, this appears to be so *only* when it is withdrawn and not when it is administered. If the use of punishment acts to *strengthen* a response, it would have to be defined as negatively reinforcing. However, as Travers (1963) has indicated, punishment is seen as *reducing* the strength of a response by the application of an aversive stimulus. Moreover, we should note that the effects of punishment are not predictable.

The distinctions that are made from a behaviorist point of view among positive reinforcement, negative reinforcement, and punishment are illustrated in Figure 2 (Cohen, 1969). This table should make the differences clear as well as introduce some possible uses of positive and negative reinforcement. In a later section on operant conditioning, the use of reinforcement in changing behavior will be discussed at greater length.

Primary and Secondary Reinforcement Reinforcers may be further classified as *primary* and *secondary*. Primary reinforcers are stimuli having reinforcement properties because they have biological significance and/or satisfy a physiological need (Lundin, 1961; Travers, 1963). Thus, we may designate as primary reinforcers water, food, and sexual release. Secondary (or conditioned) reinforcers refer to stimuli that have acquired reinforcement properties by being associated or paired with primary reinforcers or stimuli that have established reinforcement power (Skinner, 1953; Travers, 1963). The types of stimuli that may function as secondary reinforcers are incalculable, since any stimulus that is *paired with and precedes a primary reinforcer* may acquire such properties. Consequently, a sound, a light, a word, and a gentle touch may all function in this way. What stimuli do in fact acquire secondary reinforcement properties are related to a person's life history.

Some stimuli that have been paired with more than one primary reinforcer acquire the attributes of a *generalized reinforcer*, that is, stimuli that have reinforcement property regardless of the conditions operative at the time (Skinner, 1953). Generalized reinforcers are secondary reinforcers that have been paired with a variety of primary reinforcers. However, not all secondary reinforcers are generalized reinforcers. Perhaps the best illustration of this is money. It can frequently be demonstrated that money has reinforcement strength even though the amount given has no notable economic significance to the person who receives it. Indeed, a person may be financially very solvent but increasingly performs responses that are reinforced by small amounts of money.

Other stimuli may also function as generalized reinforcers, since they have frequently been paired with more than one primary reinforcer. Particularly significant stimuli of this type are attention, approval, and affec-

Behavior Desired	Verbal Prompting Statement	Method of Reinforcement	Type of Reinforcement
1. Completion of homework	"Complete your homework and I'll give you a quarter."	Reward presented	Positive
2. Completion of homework	"If you don't do your homework, you will lose your allowance."	Reward withdrawn	Punishment
3. Completion of homework	"Do your homework and you can leave your room."	Punishment withdrawn (aversive condition terminated)	Negative
4. Completion of homework	"If you don't complete your homework, I will spank you."	Punishment presented	Punishment
5. Termination of thumb sucking	"If you don't suck your thumb, I will give you a toy truck."	Reward presented	Positive
6. Termination of thumb sucking	"If you suck your thumb, I will take away your toy truck."	Reward withdrawn	Punishment
7. Termination of thumb sucking	"If you don't suck your thumb, you may leave your room."	Punishment withdrawn	Negative
8. Termination of thumb sucking	"If you suck your thumb, I will spank you."	Punishment presented	Punishment

FIGURE 2. Illustration of positive reinforcement, negative reinforcement and punishment. (Adapted from J. Cohen, Operant Behavior and Operant Conditioning, © Rand McNally, Chicago, 1969, with permission.)

tion. Each of these stimulus conditions appears to acquire these reinforcement properties by their position as preludes to satisfaction of a physiological need. For example, in a typical feeding situation, attentive and/or affectionate behaviors are directed by the mother toward the child before feeding. The giving of attention and affection prior to the satisfaction of many other infant needs probably takes place thousands of times in the early months of the child's life. Consequently, these generalized reinforcers acquire great strength that is maintained in subsequent years because of their constant association with primary-need gratification.

With the exception of primary reinforcers, stimulus conditions have no inherent capacity to reinforce. The capacity to reinforce is acquired. Therefore, one cannot assume that certain stimulus conditions will automatically reinforce a person's behavior. The only sure way of finding out is to carefully study the individual's past history and observe those stimulus conditions that increase the response rate.

Generalization Behavior that is learned in one stimulus situation tends to be expressed in other situations. Consider, for example, a very young child who has learned to fear the neighbor's dog. This fear is not likely to be restricted to the neighbor's dog but directed to many if not all dogs. As a matter of fact, the fear of the neighbor's dog may spread to toy dogs. The spreading or transfer of a learned response to one stimulus (or stimulus complex) to other similar stimuli is called *generalization*. The more similar the two stimulus situations, the more likely the response is to generalize.

The process of generalization in learning does provide some dividends, but it may be advantageous or disadvantageous depending on the situation. In the example described above, the generalization of the child's fear of the neighbor's dog greatly restricts the child's desire to explore the environment. To the extent that the fear generalizes to many similar objects and situations, the child is likely to be very inhibited in exploration of unfamiliar situations.

Generalization is also advantageous. Behavior learned in one situation may be readily employed in other similar situations in which it is appropriate. Consequently, in each new situation, one does not have to resort completely to trial and error to know how to behave. Once a child has learned to relate to a teacher in an acceptable manner, he may employ the same manner of relating to other teachers and be assured that his behavior is acceptable.

Discrimination and Differential Reinforcement However, there could be occasions when this would get him into trouble. In the situation described involving our hypothetical pupil, if he responds to a teacher with strict discipline in the same manner that he responds to a permissive one, he is likely to find his behavior inappropriate. If he is to spare himself some discomfort, he will have to learn to *discriminate* between the expectations of each and behave accordingly.

We learn to make appropriate discriminations when behavior is reinforced in the presence of one stimulus situation and is not reinforced in another. Thus, the teacher with strict discipline noted above may help the child behave according to her expectations that no one talk without permission by reinforcing the pupil for remaining quiet when it is desired and reinforcing him for asking permission before he talks. In this way, through the use of *differential reinforcement*, the child soon learns to make appropriate discriminations of the situations in which talking is permitted. However, if the teacher is not consistent in enforcing her own rule of no talking without permission, the discrimination is more difficult for a pupil to learn.

Teachers often use *verbal reinforcement* to help children learn appropriate talking or nontalking behaviors. For example, in the situation described above, when the teacher says to a pupil, "I am certainly pleased with the way Johnny raises his hand and gets permission before he talks," she is helping Johnny to distinguish the time when it is appropriate to talk by being approving of him when the response is appropriately made.

Reese (1966) describes an experiment in which a pigeon was taught to execute appropriate behaviors in response to the visually presented stimulus words "peck" and "turn." Initially, the pigeon was taught to peck at a circular pattern presented in a window. When that behavior was occurring at an appropriate rate, the letters "peck" were inserted in the window. The bird continued to peck at the window. The pecking at the window containing the word "peck" was reinforced (by raising and lowering a feeder with food) until an appropriate response rate had been established. At this point, the sign in the window was turned so that the word "turn" appeared. Differential reinforcement was begun so that pecking was not reinforced when the word "turn" appeared in the window. Subsequently, the two words "peck" and "turn" were presented randomly with reinforcement following pecking in the presence of "peck" in the stimulus window. By this procedure, a differential response was established. The pigeon pecked in the presence of the stimulus word "peck" and did not when "turn" was present.

When the pigeon had been conditioned to make an appropriate response to the word "peck," additional conditioning was attempted. The bird was conditioned to make a turning response by the following procedure. He was first reinforced when he turned his head slightly. When he turned his body, he was further reinforced. Subsequently, he was reinforced for making a quarter turn, then a half turn and so on, until he had executed a complete turn. Ultimately, he was reinforced for making a complete turn in the presence of the word "turn."

Several important concepts can be illustrated by the experiment just described. Reinforcement of pecking in the presence of the word "peck" and the absence of reinforcement of pecking in the presence of the word "turn" is *differential reinforcement*. *Shaping* was demonstrated by the differential reinforcement of the pigeon for step-by-step approximations of turning. The behavior was finally shaped by differential reinforcement of pecking to the stimulus word "peck" (and not when the word "turn" was exposed) and differential reinforcement for turning when the word "turn" was presented in the window.

In the reported experiment, the word "peck" is a *discriminative stimulus* for the pecking response, as is the word "turn" for the response of turning. We may define a discriminative stimulus as a stimulus with which an operant response has become associated as a result of reinforcement (Cohen, 1969). The discriminative stimulus does not elicit the operant response. Rather, when the stimulus is present, it serves as a cue and triggers the response. The stimulus does not cause the response. Discriminative stimuli, in a sense, prime the organism to respond or not respond, depending upon the presentation or withholding of reinforcement.

Before we proceed to discuss ways of enhancing or modifying behavior, we should pause momentarily to comment on the application of learning theory in promoting behavior change. We make the assumption that many of the psychological problems and the deviant or distressful behaviors that plague children are products of learning. And if so, they may be modified by properly establishing the conditions for "unlearning" (Dollard and Miller, 1950; Skinner, 1953). This presumes that human behavior is a function of certain lawful relationships (Grunbaum, 1966). And, while all of the laws that govern man's behavior have not been discovered, many learning-theory-based principles have now been demonstrated to have utility in altering human behavior.

Most of the principles that we will utilize are laboratory-derived. Yet the applications that we will make in promoting behavior change are based primarily on their use with human subjects reported in the literature. In addition, the authors have utilized these principles in their own clinical work with children. Consequently, we are cautiously optimistic, hoping that future research and clinical applications will extend as well as validate their utility.

Methods for Promoting Behavior Change: Enhancing or Strengthening Desirable Behavior

Historically, two basic propositions have served as theoretical cornerstones for promoting behavior change—that is, behavior is learned for two reasons. First, behavior is learned in order to terminate a condition that is noxious, distressing, or painful. Second, behavior is learned in order to induce positive sensations or lead to some satisfying state (Ford and Urban, 1963).

When we say that behavior is learned in order to terminate conditions that are noxious or distressing, we mean that responses are performed that reduce anxiety or enable us to avoid physical or psychological pain. There are many examples of this in everyday life: A burnt child avoids a hot stove; a child with a hypercritical parent stops "hearing" the parent; a soldier rapidly forgets (suppresses or represses) a terrifying combat experience.

The second proposition, that behavior is learned in order to induce positive sensations, satisfaction, or pleasure, is a familiar notion, since it is involved in reinforcement. It is simply another way of indicating that we learn behavior that is positively reinforced.

Each of these principles will be illustrated and applied in a variety of ways in the material that follows. To do this, we will want to discuss again respondent and operant conditioning as it applies to behavior change. Other forms of learning that are useful to enhancing or changing behavior will also be discussed.We will also give careful attention to procedures that can be used to translate theory into practice. At appropriate points, practical applications will be made and studies reported that illustrate the concepts, principles, and procedures.

Respondent Conditioning

Respondent behavior, we indicated, refers to behavior (involuntary muscle reactions and glandular activity) elicited automatically by a particular stimulus. Respondent conditioning utilizes these stimulus-response relationships by greatly extending the range of stimuli that will elicit a particular response.

Respondent (or classical) conditioning involves stimuli of two types and an involuntary response. One of these stimuli is not sufficient to elicit a response, while the other does so automatically on its occurrence. The stimulus that is not sufficient to elicit the response until learning has taken place, that is originally neutral, is referred to as the conditioned stimulus. The stimulus that is adequate to elicit the response is referred to as the unconditioned stimulus; that is, learning did not have to take place before a response occurs. The response is designated in two ways: Prior to conditioning, it is appropriately called the unconditioned response; once conditioning has taken place, it is called the conditioned response (Gladstone, 1967).

As is well known, Pavlov (1927) was the first to report systematically on classical (respondent) conditioning. He discovered that by presenting a bell (conditioned stimulus) followed by food (unconditioned stimulus) a salivary response was elicited in a dog. After repeated pairings of the two stimuli, the bell alone elicited salivation. By this experimentation, he demonstrated that a neutral stimulus (bell), not originally adequate to elicit a specific response (salivation), could in fact do so if paired appropriately with an unconditioned stimulus (food). It can be seen that Pavlovian conditioning essentially involves the pairing of a conditioned stimulus and an unconditioned stimulus periodically (eight to ten pairings, usually) until the response is elicited by the conditioned—although originally neutral—stimulus. Thus, Pavlovian (classical) conditioning consists primarily of substituting one stimulus for another. Consequently, a great range of neutral stimuli, not originally adequate to elicit a response, will evoke the reflexive behavior. This is why Pavlovian conditioning is referred to as *stimulus substitution*. Some of these relationships are illustrated in Figure 3.

It is well to note that the extent to which and the rate at which a neutral stimulus may be conditioned to elicit a response is governed by *when* it is presented in relationship to the eliciting (unconditioned) stimulus. The neutral stimulus must be presented *before* the eliciting (unconditioned)

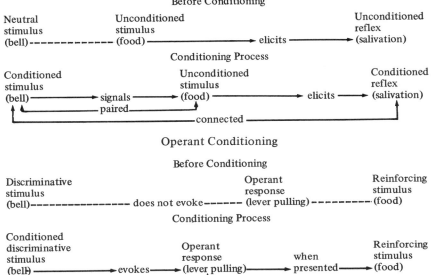

FIGURE 3.   *An illustration of respondent and operant conditioning before and after conditioning has taken place.*

stimulus. Moreover, for most rapid conditioning the neutral stimulus must be followed by the eliciting stimulus within seconds.

One of Pavlov's important discoveries was the process of *extinction*. He observed that if the unconditioned stimulus was omitted in a series of conditioning trials, the conditioned response began to decrease and eventually disappeared. As we described above, in his conditioning experiments with dogs, a bell (conditioned stimulus) was sounded a short time before food (unconditioned stimulus) was presented. As we can predict, the dog salivated when the bell sounded. However, if the bell was rung repeatedly without food present, salivation decreased and ultimately stopped. Although the food may appear to act as a reward, Pavlov did not conceptualize it in those terms. He considered the food as the evoking stimulus and as a "reinforcing stimulus" in that it was a "strengthener," but he did not speak of it in terms of its rewarding properties (Bugelski, 1964).

Even though a response has been extinguished, after a period of time it may reappear. The return of the previously extinguished response, referred to as *spontaneous recovery,* explains why an undesirable behavior in a child, thought to have been extinguished, makes a somewhat mysterious reappearance after the initial extinction. Also, as we will indicate later, spontaneous recovery may have other practical implications when conditioning procedures are used to change behavior.

Pavlov's experimentation and discoveries did not end with the ideas we have already presented. He experimented extensively with the process of *generalization*. He found that once a response had been conditioned to a particular stimulus, it was unnecessary to present that exact stimulus for the response to occur. Slight variations of it and/or similar stimuli would also evoke a response. This tendency to give a specific response to similar stimuli is called generalization. Pavlov was able to demonstrate this by conditioning a dog to salivate to a metronome. After a dog had been conditioned to respond to a metronome beating at 60 times a minute, the rate was accelerated or decreased and the dog would still respond (Bugelski, 1964).

Pavlov did rather extensive experimentation with discrimination learning and discriminated stimuli. It was in this connection that Pavlov discovered he could induce *experimental neurosis* in dogs. A dog was first conditioned to salivate when a luminous circle was presented on a screen. The animal was then trained to discriminate between a circle and an ellipse. When appropriate discrimination had been established, the ellipse was gradually changed to more closely approximate the circle. The dog continued to make appropriate discriminations, but as the two stimuli began to more closely approximate each other, discrimination became poor. At this point, the dog began to get very restless and to struggle and squeal. Ultimately, the dog became violent and resisted going into the experiment room (Deese, 1958). The dog had developed an experimental neurosis.

The experimental neurosis developed because of the dog's inability to know when to respond and when the response was inappropriate. Conflict apparently developed because the discrimination problem was too difficult for the animal. Deese (1958) has also indicated that similar conflict may develop if an animal is required to delay a conditioned response too long after the presentation of a conditioned stimulus.

Respondent conditioning has been demonstrated in dogs, sheep, worms, cockroaches, and humans. In humans, this type of conditioning influences reactions mediated by the autonomic nervous system. Hence, smooth-muscle and glandular response, and activities which they influence, such as changes in heart rate, blood pressure, stomach and bowel activity, adrenal secretion, perspiration, and salivation, may all be involved. Since some of these reactions are intimately involved in the experiencing of emotional states—*i.e.,* anxiety, fear, etc.—it is readily apparent how respondent conditioning may influence many aspects of our emotional behavior (Lundin, 1961).

The process by which emotional reactions are conditioned is illustrated by the classical study of Watson's and Raynor's (1920). An eleven-month-old boy who displayed approach reactions to a white rat was taught to fear it by the following procedure. A white rat (neutral or conditioned stimulus) was presented to the child, and at the moment his hand touched it, an iron bar was struck. The striking of the iron bar created an unexpected, loud noise. The noise (the eliciting or unconditioned stimulus) evoked a start and what appeared to be a fear response in the child. The pairing of the noise with the presence of the rat was repeated seven times. A strongly conditioned (fearful) emotional reaction to the rat had been established. Albert's fear generalized (spread) from the rat to a rabbit, a dog, a Santa Claus mask, a fur coat, and even Watson's hair.

In much the same manner, a first grade teacher (originally neutral stimulus) may present noxious stimuli (adequate to elicit fear) and come to be feared by first graders. And, in accordance with the principle noted above, the fear of the first grade teacher may generalize to other teachers or to any stimulus or object in the school situation. Indeed, some first graders' aversion to reading might well be explained on the same basis. Obviously, a first grade teacher should erect those conditions (by the way she behaves) to ensure that she is regarded with positive feelings. Then first graders are more likely to generalize this positive feeling to learning and stimulus objects in the environment of the school.

An experience that occurred with one of the author's children illustrates the principle equally well; it demonstrates the effect of generalization of stimulus words rather than objects. The event occurred when the author's daughter experienced her first practice fire drill at school. When the teacher announced to the class that they were going to have a fire drill, the child became very frightened. She rose from her seat and quickly ran out the back door of the classroom. The teacher was perplexed and later discussed the incident with the author. Upon investigation of the incident with his child, several interesting facts emerged. His daughter apparently had associated the words "fire drill" with a dentist's drill that shot flames of fire. She had assumed that all children in the classroom would be subjected to tooth repair with the fire drill. Recognizing the pain previously associated with the dentist's drill, she found the added element of fire indeed a frightening prospect. A brief discussion with her regarding various types of drills helped her to quickly discriminate the difference. Subsequent fire drills at school created no further fear reactions.

In this episode, the pain from the dentist's drill might be considered the eliciting or unconditioned stimulus, and the words "fire" and "drill" (once neutral stimuli) became associated with pain and now evoked fear. Consequently, any stimulus that is labeled "fire" or "drill" may now evoke a fearful response. It can be seen, therefore, how words themselves may evoke fear by having been associated with stimuli adequate to elicit fear. Indeed, thinking itself may evoke considerable fear.

It is apparent from these examples that any stimulus that precedes and is appropriately paired with an eliciting stimulus adequate to evoke fear (or any negative affect) may acquire the capacity to automatically provoke certain emotional states in a person. The pairings may take place without the person's awareness. Yet, on subsequent occasions, in the presence of the conditioned stimulus, the person may experience the emotional state without understanding it or knowing why. This has been labeled clinically as free-floating anxiety. If the conditioned fear is intense, avoidance of situations involving the conditioned stimulus may be complete.

Noxious stimuli (stimuli adequate to elicit pain, avoidance reactions, and negative affects) have been utilized ingeniously to assist people with certain types of problems. Typically, a noxious or aversive stimulus (such as electric shock) is paired with another stimulus that symbolizes or relates to the undesirable behavior.

A study reported by Kushner (1965) illustrates the procedure very well. Using the following procedures, Kushner treated a thirty-three year old man for a fetish of twenty years' duration. A history of the complaint, the fetish, was first taken. The history revealed that the fetish had begun to develop when the patient became sexually aroused watching girls slide down a sliding board with their underpants exposed. At about the same time, the patient experienced similar sexual arousal from masturbation. On subsequent occasions, he experienced fantasies of the girls and their panties when engaging in masturbation.

The treatment consisted of the attachment of electrodes to two fingertips, to which an electric shock could be administered. At each session, stimuli related to the fetish were shown and immediately followed by a shock. The patient terminated the shock by uttering the word "stop." Approximately twelve stimuli related to the fetish were presented during each session. As each stimulus was presented, a shock was administered, a minute interval followed, and the next stimulus was presented.

The stimuli used involved three major elements. First, a rear-view picture of a woman from the middle of the back to the knees, wearing panties, was presented. Second, at the same time the picture was presented, a pair of panties was placed in the patient's hands. Third, the patient was encouraged to imagine himself wearing the panties, think about a clothesline with panties on it, and fantasy himself standing in front of a lingerie shop window. Each session involving these elements lasted approximately twenty to thirty minutes, and sessions were held three times a week.

The treatment continued for forty-one sessions during a period of fourteen weeks. The treatment was terminated at this point because the patient indicated that he was no longer disturbed by the fetish. However, approximately one month after the termination of the shock sessions, spontaneous recovery of the fetish occurred. Consequently, two "booster sessions" were given. It should be noted that spontaneous recovery is not uncommon when a behavior is being extinguished. However, the behavior that reappears can usually be quickly extinguished.

Subsequent to this, a new treatment phase was begun to help the patient with his sexual impotence. Desensitization, as advocated by Wolpe, was undertaken. (Since desensitization will be discussed in a later section, it will not be reported here.) The use of these procedures with the patient quickly relieved the impotence. Adequate heterosexual adjustment was subsequently established. A return of the fetish occurred once more, apparently due to stress, upon the advent of the patient's appearance in court for a driving offense. One more booster session was given. At follow up, some eighteen months after the patient's appearance in court, he apparently had no more trouble with the fetish.

The methods used in treating the fetish illustrate clearly the application of aversive therapy. The aversive stimulus (an electric shock) is paired with stimuli of the undesirable behavior (the fetish) in order to inhibit conscious thought leading to sexual arousal. Although the clinician does not discuss the importance of saying the word "stop" to terminate the shock, the utterance of this word would presumably become associated with anxiety relief. Subsequently, saying the word "stop" would act to inhibit thought and images leading to sexual arousal.

The other important aspect of the case is the reappearance (spontaneous recovery) of the fetish after original success in aversive conditioning. Such a recurrence is not surprising and may be predicted from respondent-conditioning theory. The subsequent "booster shots" appeared to complete the treatment task.

Operant Conditioning

The conditioning of an operant response is achieved when positive reinforcement immediately follows the appropriate execution of the response. Three major steps are generally involved in the conditioning of the operant response. First, a measurement of the operant level or baseline is taken. Second, a reinforcer is presented each time the response is performed until the operant rate has clearly increased. Third, the reinforcer is withheld to permit the conditioned response to become extinguished. If the conditioned response is extinguished, then there is some certainty that appropriate variables have been identified (Reese, 1966).

Although these three sequential steps may appear to be very simple to perform, this appearance may be deceptive. Therefore, it is desirable to elaborate on the additional procedures that are required in operant conditioning.

Basic Procedures in
Conditioning Operant Behavior

At least six basic procedures are considered essential in conditioning operant behavior. Each of these is stated below (Reese, 1966).

1. *Define and state operationally the behavior to be changed.* This initial step seems obvious, but beginners have a tendency to attempt to reinforce a behavior that is vaguely defined. For example, a teacher may attempt to reinforce "good student behavior" without specifying exactly those observable behaviors that comprise "good student behavior." But unless the exact terminal behavior is identified, the student may be inappropriately reinforced for performing a variety of behaviors that may or may not be related to good student behavior.

2. *Obtain a baseline or operant level of the behavior that it is considered desirable to promote or change.* Before a specified behavior is reinforced or treated, its frequency or magnitude must be noted.

Subsequently, after treatment is instituted it is possible to determine its effects and whether procedures need to be changed. Methods of observing and recording behavior in a variety of situations are thoroughly discussed in Chapter 4.

3. *Arrange the learning or treatment situation so that the desirable behavior will occur.* Before reinforcement is implemented, it is essential to determine whether the individual can perform the response that is desirable. A child's arithmetic-calculating behavior cannot be enhanced unless he has the necessary skill to do the calculations. The arithmetic must be graded to his attained skill level.

Working with children, one can often prompt the desirable response by a verbal request. Or a situation may be arranged so that the desired response has a high probability of occurrence. For instance, if you want to increase a child's tendency to say "Thank you," set up a situation in which he is given something he desires, and the "Thank you" will most likely follow. An excellent example of a relatively ingenious prompting of a desired response is discussed in the section "Fire-Setting," in Chapter 6.

4. *Identify potential reinforcers.* Before most people will *do* something, they must *want* something. With the possible exception of primary reinforcers and some aversive stimuli, a stimulus has no inherent reinforcement property. We must determine the reinforcement property of a stimulus (that is, its capacity to increase response probability). Although it is possible to increase the probability that a stimulus will tend to be reinforcing by first depriving a child of something (say, extend the length of time since he last had something to eat), such a procedure is not desirable. It is more feasible to capitalize on the conditions operating at the moment. For example, if a child has been sitting at his desk for two hours with little or no opportunity to move around, the possibility of participating in a "fun game" may have great potential reinforcement value.

Fortunately, some stimuli—for example, attention and affection—function as generalized reinforcers and may often promote the type of response that is desirable. Such generalized reinforcers may not function equally well with all children, and it may be desirable to establish their reinforcement properties by pairing them with primary reinforcers (see Chapter 1).

Perhaps the most useful method of all for identifying potential reinforcers is to observe a child (or person) in his free-choice activities. What a child does when he has the opportunity to do what he wishes usually reveals the type of stimuli or events that have reinforcing properties for him. In a subsequent section, the authors will present the products of their attempts to identify potential reinforcers.

5. *Shape and/or reinforce the desired behavior.* If a child is able to perform the desired response, reinforce it on its first and every subsequent appearance until it has assumed appropriate strength. Once the response is being performed with high frequency, the reinforcement schedule may be changed to ensure its durability. As we will discuss later in this chapter, both variable-ratio and variable-interval schedules promote behavior that is resistant to extinction.

If a child is unable to perform the terminal (desired) behavior, successive approximations of the behavior must be identified and appropriately reinforced. Since the reader will be introduced to this concept in the "Shaping" section that follows, we will not discuss it here. It is sufficient to indicate that shaping essentially involves identifying and reinforcing step by step the responses that ultimately lead to the desired behavior.

Finally, it is important to mention that as the terminal behavior is being shaped and/or reinforced, a variety of reinforcers must be used to avoid satiation. Popcorn may be very reinforcing for making a response the first ten or twenty times; after that, one's appetite for popcorn greatly diminishes.

6. *Maintain records of the reinforced behavior to determine whether response strength or frequency has increased.* To determine whether the reinforcement contingencies have been effective, longitudinal records must be kept. Comparison of each experimental or treatment session with the baseline rate quickly reveals whether the reinforcement has promoted the response considered desirable. If the reinforcement procedures are not producing the desired result, it is necessary to determine why and to make appropriate adjustments.

When operant conditioning has established the desired behavior, procedures are reversed and extinction is begun. Such a procedure allows one to determine what has promoted changes in response, but in clinical or school situations, this is often not practical and may not be implemented.

This presentation serves to give the reader an "advanced organizer" for the material that follows. Several of the elements and concepts in the basic operant procedure will be elaborated upon in subsequent sections.

Shaping

The steps enumerated above are typically employed when the operant behavior occurs with fair frequency. If it does not, another procedure called *shaping* must be used. By shaping, a desired behavior is evoked by reinforcing successive approximations of that behavior. Essentially, it involves a careful analysis of movements or responses that approximate step-by-step the final desired behavior. The experiment previously reported in which the pigeon was taught to read is an excellent illustration of the shaping process. Using such procedures, Skinner and his associates taught pigeons to play ping-pong and to play *Take Me Out to the Ball Game* on the xylophone (Cohen, 1969).

At first glance, shaping would appear to be amazingly simple to use; however, it is not that simple and requires that certain cautions be recognized. First, the desired approximation must be reinforced immediately upon its execution. Otherwise, the wrong response will be reinforced. Cohen (1969) has indicated that in some instances a delay of one-twentieth of a second may lead to the reinforcement of the wrong response. Second, the successive approximations of the desired behavior must be appropriately reinforced. If an approximation is reinforced too long, it may become too well established. Other approximations that must be performed in order to establish the desired behavior may not occur. Moreover, if the shaping process is too slow, the subject may become satiated. Third, if shaping proceeds too rapidly, the earlier shaped behavior may begin to become extinguished (Reese, 1966).

It is apparent that effective shaping involves appropriate selection and reinforcement of responses as well as determining the length of time to reinforce each approximation before advancing to the next. Thus, the experimenter or clinician must have clearly in mind the response sequences that are most likely and necessary to get the desired behavior.

Chaining

From the discussion of operant conditioning, the reader may have gleaned the impression that behavior is a simple matter of learning separate stimulus-response units. In part that is true, since stimulus-response units must be first learned before more complex learning can take place. However, most human behavior is characterized by a series of stimulus-response (S-R) units connected together in a sequence. The connection of two or more previously learned S-R[1] units in a sequence as a result of learning is called *chaining*. These chains of connected S-R units may involve both motor responses and verbal responses or verbal chains (Gagné, 1965).

An example may help clarify the concept of chaining. One of the authors has a small, lovable dog of pekingese and poodle parentage. The dog has been taught a number of tricks involving the chaining of separate motor response units. For example, when prompted by the request, "Give me a love, Ebbie," she will jump up into your lap and lay her head on your shoulder. In the performance of the trick, it is apparent that at least two separate S-R units are involved. The initial learning of the S-R units demonstrates clearly how the process of chaining takes place.

The dog was first taught to jump into the trainer's lap when the command "jump" was accompanied by the trainer's patting of his knee. Since the dog was accustomed to jumping into the trainer's lap, this was relatively easily executed by the dog. When the action was performed, she was reinforced.

Once the first S-R unit had been learned, the next S-R unit was taught. After the dog had executed the first S-R unit, and while still on the lap of the trainer, the request was given to "Give me a love, Ebbie" while the trainer was patting his shoulder. As the dog performed an appropriate approximation of the desired response, he was reinforced. After

---

[1]Stimulus-response units are typically designated as Ss - R to denote that part of the stimulus complex is proprioceptive or internal, resulting from muscle activation. In chaining, a symbol is added to designate response-produced cues as each response is performed sequentially: A small s is added to the R. Thus, it appears Ss - Rs - Ss - Rs, etc. For ease of presentation, the S-R is used in the text.

a series of training sessions, the dog was able to perform the appropriate terminal behavior upon verbal command. With this accomplished, the dog had chained (or connected) two separate S-R units in a sequence.

As the reader will note, in the initial learning sessions, two types of stimuli were presented: (a) verbal stimulus (statement) and (b) a visual stimulus (the trainer's patting of his knee and later his shoulder). However, as the dog began to perform each S-R unit with high frequency, only the verbal stimulus was presented. Consequently, the dog learned to execute the two S-R units in sequence only to the verbal command "Give me a love, Ebbie." The verbal command now appears to function as a discriminative stimulus.

The reader may be wondering how chains of S-R units get to be connected. In some instances, the connecting of the S-R units may be explained by contiguity—that is, because the stimulus is rapidly followed by a response, the two become associated. In other S-R chains (much like the example cited above), reinforcement appears to be operative (Staats and Staats, 1963). There are additional explanations, among them this: It is quite generally accepted by experimental learning theorists that the response element in the S-R unit produces stimuli which may serve as a cue for the response that follows. Each stimulus produced by a response is referred to as a *response-produced cue or stimulus*. It seems to function in the following manner. When a motor response is performed, the sensory receptors in the muscles and tendons are activated. The stimuli accompanying these movements, proprioceptive stimuli, appear to cue or trigger the next response in the chain (Staats and Staats, 1963).

In human beings, the learning of response chains is greatly facilitated by external stimuli, particularly by verbal instructions that direct us to perform certain behaviors in sequence. For example, consider how such instruction facilitates learning how to kick a football. We may direct our young learner to perform the appropriate sequence of acts by saying, "Extend the football with both hands as far as you can in front of you. As you begin to drop the ball, move your right leg into the air in front of you to meet the football as it falls." After our young learner has had a few practice trials (and if he can perform the separate motor acts involved in the sequence), he will have learned motor response chains. Besides the proprioceptive stimuli produced by the motor responses, he may self-instruct his own actions—that is, he may talk to himself as he sequentially performs the motor responses. He engages in thinking responses which also produce stimuli. Such thinking-produced stimuli become involved in verbal chains. For example, the child who is learning to kick a football may instruct himself to (1) "hold the football in front," (2) "drop the football straight down," (3) "raise your right foot as the ball drops," and (4) "kick the football before it hits the ground." However, once the chains of motor responses have been learned, the response-produced stimuli allow him to execute the response chain with ease. With the forming of the response chain, the actions may be performed independent of the original evoking stimulus (Staats and Staats, 1963).

The role of response-produced stimuli in learning response chains is clearly seen by the difficulty people have in performing certain learned responses in reverse order. A dramatic test of this is to try to recite the alphabet backwards or to count in reverse. The central importance of the response-produced stimuli in cueing each of the S-R units in the chain is clearly revealed by the difficulty a person has in starting at the middle of the sequence and performing the remaining responses from that point on. It is difficult indeed, but if asked to go back to the beginning of the sequence, he performs the responses with much greater ease.

Children must acquire hundreds or even thousands of response chains to approximate the complex behavior characteristic of adults. In the primary grades of elementary school, skill learning requires the acquisition of many motor-response chains. Examples of simple motor chains are buttoning a coat or dress, tying one's shoes, and using scissors. More complex chains are involved in learning to print or write. In the higher elementary grades, the learning of response chains involving various types of procedures is required (Gagné, 1965).

The Conditions for Learning Response Chains

If it is true that much of the behavior people exhibit in daily life is composed of response chains, it is important to know the basic conditions for learning them. Gagné (1965) describes five essential conditions. First, the separate S-R units or links must be learned before they can be chained. In the example of the child learning to kick a football, he must be able to (1) hold the football in front of him, (2) simultaneously drop the football and begin to raise one leg, (3) make contact with the football before it hits the ground, and (4) kick the ball in the right position to increase distance.

The second essential condition is that the learner must execute each link in the proper sequence. Perhaps the most effective way to achieve this is to prompt or verbally instruct the learner in the proper execution and sequence of response, as in this example of the child learning to kick the football.

The third condition requires that S-R units (or links) be performed in "close time succession" to ensure that the links are chained together. If there are long delays between the execution of each link, it is difficult to establish the chains.

The fourth condition requires that the sequence be repeated until the desired learning has been achieved. Since one cannot always assume that the individual links have been adequately mastered or that the instructional prompting has been entirely effective, it is generally necessary to repeat the sequence. Repetition tends to polish the performance into a smoothly executed sequence. Also, the better it is learned the more resistant it is to being forgotten.

The final condition is that reinforcement must be present in the learning of chains. The execution of the final link must lead to the proper effects. The reinforcement must be immediate. If reinforcement is not given upon the execution of the final response unit in the chain, the terminal link is extinguished, and the chain is not maintained.

While the discussion of chaining may appear to have little relevance to the practical tasks of initial learning or behavior modification, it is quite relevant. Too often, one suspects, we attempt to teach children a response chain without knowing whether the child can perform the S-R units involved. If such is the case, it is important to break the chain into performable S-R units and help him master those first. Even more important, it may be well to make such an analysis before any instruction is attempted to help the child acquire response chains (or skills).

An Application of Operant Methods

The use of operant conditioning with children who do not complete school assignments is well illustrated in a study done by Dickinson (1966). A child who had a history of turning in almost no school assignments was invited into the experimenter's office. The procedure was initiated by simply asking the child to solve some arithmetic problems. Ten problems were presented which the child was able to solve. When each problem was solved correctly, candy corn, a poker chip, and verbal reinforcement were presented. After the series of ten arithmetic problems were solved, frequency of reinforcement was changed from presentation for each correct solution to presentation after a series of five problems had been calculated correctly. When this type of reinforcement had continued for a short period of time, reinforcement was transferred to and administered by the teacher. The teacher reinforced the child for completing arithmetic assignments by using poker chips and verbal reinforcement. Poker chips were traded for candy after school. After three weeks, poker chips were discontinued, but a chart was kept indicating the number of poker chips earned. Thus, the check marks could be redeemed for candy.

Conditioning was terminated by the experimenter after eighteen days, at which point the child's performance dropped sharply. But during the third week after termination, performance began to increase; during a twenty-week period, the child failed to complete arithmetic assignments only six times.

Besides illustrating the potential value of operant methods to a child's school problem, Dickinson's experiment demonstrates other important operant features. He began by using primary reinforcers with reliable reinforcement properties. But, since he also presented poker chips and gave verbal approval simultaneously with a primary reinforcer, they acquired reinforcement properties. When the desirable behavior was fairly well established, immediate primary reinforcement was delayed. Also, once the desirable behavior was being performed at a higher rate, the schedule of reinforcement was changed. Reinforcement was given for the correct solution of five problems (fixed-ratio reinforcement) instead of one (regular reinforcement). This type of schedule establishes behavior more resistant to extinction. Finally, to get a transfer of the appropriate response to the classroom, the teacher maintained reinforcement in the classroom where school assignments should be done.

Schedules of Reinforcement

The quickest way to increase the frequency or strength of a response is to reinforce it each time it is performed. That is, the response is reinforced regularly or continuously. However, once responding has increased to an acceptable rate and if one wishes the response to endure, a different type of *reinforcement schedule* is desirable.

There are two basic ways in which reinforcement can be administered: (1) *ratio* schedules and (2) *interval* schedules. When a ratio schedule is used, a certain number of responses must be emitted before reinforcement is given. If the ratio is *fixed*, a response is reinforced after a specified number of responses are performed. If the fixed ratio is 5 (FR 5), reinforcement is given immediately after every fifth, tenth, fifteenth, etc., response. When a *variable* ratio is employed, the number of responses that must be made varies; that is, reinforcement could be given after the third, seventh, eighth, eleventh, etc., responses. The reinforcement on a variable schedule is not entirely predictable (Reese, 1966; Cohen, 1969).

Reinforcement based on an interval schedule is primarily a function of the passage of time. When a *fixed-interval* schedule is used, a specified amount of time must pass between each reinforcement. If the fixed interval is 4 (FI 4), an interval of four minutes must transpire before reinforcement is given. When a *variable-interval* schedule is used, the length of time varies from one reinforcement to another.

Ratio Schedules Behavior, as we have noted, is maintained or changed as a result of its consequences: that is, behavior is a function of reinforcement. Ratio schedules, like interval schedules, tend to promote a patterning of response peculiar to them. Thus, knowing the basic features of each type of reinforcement schedule assumes considerable importance in promoting certain types of response and extinguishing or decreasing others. Failure to develop a certain pattern of response through inadequate knowledge of reinforcement schedules occurs with considerable frequency. For example, more than a few parents have been dismayed to find that offering a dollar for every "A" on a report card often fails to promote the "A" getting behavior. The long delay between one reporting period and another makes this offer an ineffective way to utilize reinforcement for a low-probability behavior (behavior that occurs infrequently). Hundreds of appropriate responses have to be made between the two reporting periods to attain the desired achievement level. Only a few of those responses, near goal attainment, can be influenced by this type of reinforcement.

Ratio schedules are generally characterized by a high rate of respond-ing—if the ratio is reasonably low: that is, if the number of nonreinforced to reinforced responses is small (*e.g.,* nonreinforced, 15:1 reinforced). With variable-ratio reinforcement, responding is maintained at a high rate. This also tends to be true with fixed-ratio schedules, but typically there is a pause following reinforcement with a somewhat sudden change to a high, stable rate of response (Skinner, 1953; Lundin, 1961).

When one employs a fixed ratio, and the ratio is low and then in-creased slowly (from 5:1 to 10:1 to 15:1) a very high ratio may ultimately be used (400:1). Response usually diminishes immediately after reinforce-ment, but rapidly builds up as the next reinforcement is about to be given. Fixed ratio has demonstrated superiority over both continuous-reinforcement and fixed-interval schedules (Lundin, 1961).

Extinction under fixed-ratio schedules is characterized by a high rate of response for a short period of time after termination of reinforcement, followed by a somewhat sudden drop. Sometime after the drop, respond-ing may again increase for a while but is subsequently characterized by rather sudden termination.

Fixed-ratio schedules operate in many areas of human activity. Since reinforcement is contingent upon the number of responses given, any work paid according to quantity produced illustrates this type of schedule. Money paid for piecework completed, arithmetic problems successfully solved, or errands performed are excellent examples of fixed-ratio sched-ules. It can be seen that when reinforcement is administered for a number of behaviors properly executed, incentive to stick to a task is high.

Variable-ratio schedules are characterized by a relatively steady rate of responding without sudden or marked changes. Because reinforcement is not exactly predictable, an animal or a person is likely to continue to respond in anticipation that the reinforcement will be given at any time. The anticipation of reinforcement on variable ratios is aptly illustrated by the persistent interest in and involvement of large numbers of people in games of chance or gambling. And even though the spacing of the vari-able reinforcement is wider than the gambler would like, he continues to entertain the notion that he will be lucky and win a large sum of money.

A remedial reading teacher with whom one of the authors is ac-quainted used variable-ratio reinforcement to greatly enhance pupil atten-tion and reading behavior. Pupils in the remedial reading class had not been attending well during periods of oral reading, and when they were called upon to read, they had often lost their places. She began continuous reinforcement (with candy) each time a pupil who was called upon to read knew the proper place. After a short period of reinforcement of this type, she switched to variable-ratio reinforcement and increased attending re-sponses to about a 100 percent accuracy. Certainly this is a much more effective way of getting desired behavior than scolding a child every time he loses his place.

The use of variable-ratio reinforcement has real virtue, because the behavior so established and maintained is quite resistant to extinction. When extinction procedures are implemented, rate of response is well maintained, punctuated by pauses. As extinction proceeds, pauses increase in length, and the overall rate is reduced (Lundin, 1961).

Interval Schedules When interval schedules are used, rate of response is much lower than with ratio schedules. Of course, the rate of responding varies according to the size of the interval. If the interval is long, the rate of response is low. Compared with ratio schedules, interval schedules tend to have an overall response rate that is low.

In the initial phases of conditioning with a *fixed-interval schedule,* there is rapid responding immediately following reinforcement, followed in turn by a general slowing down until the next reinforcement. As conditioning continues, and the organism begins to develop time discrimination, reinforcement is followed by minimal responding. Response rate rapidly increases as time for the next reinforcement comes near (Lundin, 1961).

Fixed-interval schedules are quite commonly found in human affairs. Perhaps the best illustration of fixed-interval schedules is the payment of wages or salary by intervals of time. Elementary teachers use a fixed-interval schedule when they use a reinforcing activity such as reading a favorite story to their class—at a specific time each day. It can be observed in such a situation that as the time approaches for the favored activity there is a general increase in appropriate pupil behavior. However, it should be noted that this type of schedule does not have much positive effect on the pupils' activities in the morning. If the interval is too long between reinforcements, desirable behavior is not readily maintained.

Extinction under fixed-interval schedules is characterized by more regular response than is true with continuous reinforcement. Behavior established with such a schedule tends to be quite resistant to extinction (Reese, 1966).

While conditioning with fixed-interval reinforcement schedules tends to be characterized by ultimate slowing down and pauses after reinforcement, *variable-interval schedules* are typified by a steady rate of responding, although the rate is dependent on the length of time intervals utilized. Activities that operate on this type of schedule are well illustrated by fishing and hunting; and bonuses in industry have the same effect (Lundin, 1961). Because reinforcement is a function of variable time intervals and appears to the recipient to occur at random, motivation would appear to be maintained by anticipation of a reinforcement at almost any time.

Teachers can use this type of schedule to great advantage for by intermittent reinforcing activities or bonuses throughout the day, pupil performance and interest in learning can be maintained at a steady rate for long periods of time. However, the reinforcing stimuli must be properly interspersed to prevent long periods of time without reinforcement.

As the reader may have already inferred, behavior maintained on a variable-interval schedule is very resistant to extinction, continuing for a long period of time before any noticeable decrement. As Lundin (1961) has suggested, variable-interval schedules probably explain why some people will continue to try in the face of failure. As a matter of fact, steady, even, predictable behavior may well be a function of this type of schedule.

Besides being extremely resistant to extinction, interval schedules have the added advantage of being much easier to administer. Ratio schedules require that response rate be counted or tallied. Interval schedules require timekeeping. Obviously, timekeeping is much easier to do than tallying response rates. Thus, interval schedules can be applied with much greater facility to groups than is true of ratio schedules. Consequently, interested teachers can make useful applications to their classrooms.

Negative Reinforcement

Even though we have talked at some length about positive control using reinforcement, we have not exhausted the uses of operant conditioning. Behavior which it is desirable to strengthen may be accomplished by negative reinforcement. This form of behavior control is not as widely used, however, because aversive stimuli are involved.

In our earlier discussion of positive and negative reinforcement, it was noted that when a response is performed that removes an aversive stimulus, that response or behavior is strengthened. That is, we perform a response (or a set of responses) that allows us to escape the aversive stimulus. Escape and avoidance behaviors are similar to one another in that we succeed in keeping the aversive effects of a stimulus away from us; they are different, however, in that with avoidance behavior a response is performed *to prevent the onset* of the aversive stimulus. With escape (or negative conditioning) a response is performed that *removes* an aversive stimulus.

Negative conditioning functions in many areas of everyday life experiences. Our behavior is greatly controlled in that we behave in ways that allow us to remove or escape the effects of aversive stimuli. For example, a child who has a very demanding mother will act to remove the aversive stimulus by leaving the house or ceasing to hear his mother when she makes one of her numerous demands; or during the winter we escape the cold by going inside.

When negative conditioning is used clinically to strengthen a response, obviously one must use some type of noxious or aversive stimulus. Typically, in experimental and clinical situations with people, electric shock and uncomfortable (but not injurious) noise have been used as aversive stimuli. These types of aversive stimuli are used because they are relatively easy to use and tend to induce a minimum of physical discomfort and few, if any, side effects. Other aversive stimuli that induce greater physical discomfort are undesirable to use because of the unwanted side effects they produce.

The experimental and or clinical use of negative reinforcement in behavior control is well illustrated by an experiment performed by Flanagan, Goldiamond, and Azrin (1958). In the first of a series of experiments, three stutterers were asked to read aloud while instances of blocking were carefully recorded. The reading continued for two ninety-minute sessions for each subject. Following this analysis, two different experimental conditions were implemented. In the first experimental treatment using aversive stimuli, each blockage immediately produced a one-second blast of 105-decibel white noise in the subject's earphones. After about thirty minutes of this treatment, the noise was terminated and the subject was encouraged to continue for another thirty minutes. In one of the subjects, stuttering was almost completely terminated near the end of the aversive period. Stuttering in the other two subjects was apparently reduced.

In the sessions using negative reinforcement, after thirty minutes of recording (reading aloud), a second thirty-minute period began in which blocking turned off an ongoing noise for an interval of five seconds. Stuttering rose under this experimental condition and decreased when negative reinforcement was no longer employed.

Modeling

The tendency to imitate, or perform responses similar to those of a model, plays an exceedingly important role in learning. Indeed, every parent is well aware of the extent to which a young child's behavior is a reflection of his own. If the imitations are reflections of the behavior we like in ourselves, we proudly applaud this acquisition. But we are occasionally chagrined when the child has imitated too well a behavior we have exhibited in an unguarded moment. It is also easy to observe the frequently uttered phrase, "Show me how, Daddy" as our young learners are busily engaged in the acquisition of new response patterns.

We have seen in our discussion of operant conditioning that before a response can be learned through such procedures, the behavior, or an approximation of it, must exist in the person's repertoire. A response that is not performed cannot be reinforced. If the behavior to be learned is complex and involves many elements, the probability that it will occur and thus can be reinforced may not be great. Thus, operant methods may be useful in controlling behavior that already exists, but inefficient in promoting new behavior.

Operant conditioning may not be as efficient as modeling in another respect. When it is desirable to teach behavior or to train people in skills that involve elements of danger, trial and error may be risky. Rather, appropriate models that exhibit the behavior may greatly reduce trial and error and provide real dividends in learning (Bandura, 1965).

A number of different terms have been used to describe observational learning. For example, the terms *modeling, imitation,* and *copying* are used interchangeably by some, while others use them in a more definitive way. But, as Bandura (1969) has suggested, the distinctions may not be of great importance, since a number of studies indicate that matching responses (responses made by the imitator that are the same as the model's) as well as more complete behavior repertoires appear to be determined by similar antecedent conditions. Perhaps it is unnecessary to make distinctions if we keep in mind that all three terms refer to learning acquired by an observer as a result of watching a model perform certain specific responses; the observer may perform the modeled activities during, immediately after, or some time after the model's performance. Also, depending on how the modeling activities are arranged and the learning situation constructed, observational learning may involve a live human model or a symbolic model (a picture or film-mediated version) with or without reinforcement for performance of specific responses by the observer.

Theories of Modeling

Several theories have been proposed to explain observational learning or modeling. An associative and classical conditioning conception was espoused by Holt (1931), the essence of which was that modeling occurs when modeling stimuli and matching responses by the imitator occur together in a short interval of time. Sometime later, Miller and Dollard (1941) proposed that modeling tends to result when an adequately motivated observer is positively reinforced for matching the appropriate responses of a model in a situation that is initially trial and error. Very recently, and on the basis of considerable evidence, Bandura (1969) has formulated a contiguity-mediational theory to explain model learning that occurs when no overt responses are exhibited by the observer of the modeled responses.

Bandura (1969) suggests that observational learning involves two processes and/or representational systems: imaginal and verbal. Images of the model's responses are formed as a result of sensory conditioning. That is, modeling stimuli induce perceptual responses in the observer that are sequentially associated and integrated as a result of temporal contiguity of the modeling stimuli. And even though perceptual processes induced by modeling stimuli are transitory, they tend to endure in the observer and can be retrieved at a later time. Subsequently, the recalled images of the modeled activities or responses function as mediators to direct the reproduction of the imitative, or matching, responses by the observer.

A second type of cognitive process is also involved in observational learning. As the modeled stimuli induce images in the observer, a type of verbal coding of the observed stimuli takes place. An example will illustrate what this process involves. Several years ago, a nine-year-old child of one of the authors had accompanied him to the university to pick up his mail that had accumulated during a holiday. His daughter observed as he opened his combination-lock mailbox. When he had completed the sequence, his daughter remarked, "That is an easy combination. All you need to remember is the first two letters of our last name (BL) and then add 3 to B and 5 to L." The combination was, in fact, 3 past B and around to 5 past L in a clockwise direction. Very quickly she had verbally coded the combination. The author was surprised by her incidental observation of the modeled activities. He asked her if she would like to open the mailbox. This she did, without error, to the delight of both parties.

This account also illustrates other elements that Bandura considers important in his formulation of observational learning. The child had made an appropriate attentional investment, discriminated the important modeled cues, and retrieved, as a result of symbolic representation (coding), the modeled events.

Regarding observational learning or modeling, one of the theoretical issues is whether reinforcement is a necessary condition for model learning. It appears that reinforcement *may be* an important condition for the *performance* of modeled responses but not for their *acquisition*. The evidence seems to suggest that the performance of observed or modeled responses is substantially influenced by appropriate reinforcement. The reinforcement may be vicariously experienced, self-administered, or applied externally. A failure of modeling to occur may result from any of several variables. That is, for modeling to take place, the learner must have sufficient attention investment, adequate sensory and retentional registration, appropriate symbolic representation of the modeled events, sufficient motor capacities, and favorable reinforcement conditions (Bandura, 1969).

The evidence also seems to suggest that the performance of matching responses by an observer may be facilitated by reinforcing the behavior in either the model or the observer. However, imitation of the modeled responses is decreased when either the model or the imitator is punished directly or vicariously (Bandura, 1969).

The Learning Effects of Modeling

Despite the fact that theoretical explanations have not been settled, that modeling does take place can hardly be contested. Studies tend to indicate that observational learning affects three general classes of response. First, modeling has demonstrated utility in the acquisition of new (*i.e.,* not previously in the repertoire) or novel (*i.e.,* unique or unusual) responses. Second, modeling may have an inhibiting or disinhibiting (liberating) effect on previously acquired responses, depending of course upon the behavior exhibited by the model. Third, observing a model may evoke or trigger in the learner a response that has assumed a somewhat neutral status in his repertoire. For example, a child who is not, say, particularly aggressive may upon observing an aggressive model become more aggressive.

The effects of modeling are not limited to motor response. Modeling activities of certain specific types may affect both cognitive competencies, interpersonal relationships, and coping behavior. Certain kinds of affective or emotional reactions can be modified. From a model who exhibits particular affective reactions, the observer may acquire the same or similar emotional responses. Avoidance or fearful reactions may be eliminated by observing the model's approach behavior toward fearful objects that do not result in negative consequences (Bandura and Walters, 1963; Bandura, 1969).

The use of modeling procedures to strengthen desirable behavior and to inhibit the undesirable has been clearly demonstrated by Bandura (1967). In one of his experiments, children with fear of dogs were placed in four experimental groups. Group I watched a child without fear of dogs interact, in a party setting, with a dog. Children in Group II watched a child without fear interact with a dog in a nonparty setting. Group III children watched a dog in a party setting without a child model interacting with the dog. Group IV children joined into party activities but were not exposed to a dog or child model. The results indicated that those children who had received modeling treatment (Groups I and II) lost their fear of dogs. At a later time, the experiment was duplicated in essential detail, with a film rather than a real-life version used, but with similar results.

It is apparent from this experiment that symbolic models as well as real-life models have considerable value in the acquisition of new responses. Symbolic models may be presented in other ways than on film: pictorially through a variety of media (television or audio-visuals) or by verbal or written instructions (Bandura and Walters, 1963).

Bandura (1965) has also demonstrated that physical and verbal aggression can be strengthened by using film-mediated models. In this type of experimental paradigm, one group of children viewed an aggressive model being punished, a second group watched the aggressive model rewarded, and a third group saw no consequences of the model's aggression. In post-test evaluations, subjects in the reward and no-consequence groups exhibited significantly greater numbers of imitative responses.

In order to determine the variables responsible for the learned imitative responses, Bandura followed the post-treatment evaluations by offering children in all groups incentives (rewards) for reproducing the model's responses. The use of incentives completely removed observed performance differences: Equal amounts of imitative learning appeared to have taken place in the group that saw the model rewarded, the model punished, and the model experience no consequence. Apparently, the imitative responses were learned as a result of modeling *and not as a consequence of reward*. Reinforcement seemed to provide the conditions by which the learning that had been acquired could be demonstrated.

It can be seen that film-mediated models may be as effective as real-life models for inducing the acquisition or change of certain behaviors. Nonhuman cartoon characters in films appear to have less dramatic modeling effects, although they are still useful (Bandura, 1965). Baer and Sherman (1964) have also shown that certain types of imitative behavior increased as a consequence of social reinforcement from a puppet.

The studies reviewed above demonstrate rather dramatically the potency of modeling (both real-life and symbolic types) in instigating desirable behavior as well as changing undesirable behavior. The capacity for inducing acquisition or change in a variety of response patterns is broad indeed. In human beings, modeling has been demonstrated to be effective in modifying specific types of aggressive behavior, play patterns, standards of self-evaluation and self-reinforcement, language learning, and in accomplishing modification and the postponement of gratifications (Bandura, 1969).

Using Modeling To Promote Behavior Change

If modeling has the potential for inducing significant learning in a wide range of response patterns, how can it be used most effectively in promoting learning considered important? Since the issues regarding this question have not been completely answered, it is difficult to be entirely precise. But as we have noted previously, effective model learning involves a number of variables; these variables relate to conditions operating in the learner as well as to the manner in which the modeled activities are presented. The observer must have adequate attentional, motor, and sensory processing and retentional abilities. And depending to some extent on the form of modeling used, the learner must have the representational abilities to covertly rehearse the modeling events as well as the capacity to retrieve the symbolic representations. If the learner has facility with language, so that coding of the modeled activities is enhanced, certain modeling activities are additionally applicable; that is, when such symbolic representation has been acquired, verbal modeling cues may prove highly effective. Without language facility, behavioral modeling cues may be absolutely essential (Bandura, 1969).

The characteristics of the model that most enhance modeling effects have not been entirely established. There are some data (Zinzer, 1966; Goldstein, Heller, and Sechrist, 1966) that suggest that modeling effects are enhanced when like-sex adult models are reinforced for performing behaviors to be induced in the observer. Moreover, subject-observers who exhibit low self-evaluations and highly dependent behavior are likely to demonstrate enhanced modeling effects.

It may well be, however, that the extent to which modeling effects are elicited is dependent on the type of reinforcement (positive or negative) that the model and/or observer receives and the degree to which the model and the observer have similar social roles and status.

If the observer who is learning effects is highly contingent on his stage of development and acquired characteristics, it is obviously important to know the present level or development of the learner as well as the behavior one wishes to enhance or modify. For example, with children who have very limited behavioral repertoires (because of limitations in age and experience or severe behavior deficits or disorders), it appears essential to carefully identify each element or response to be modeled, arrange them in a graduated hierarchy, and present the least difficult one first. Care must also be exercised to ensure learner attention and motivation as the modeling activities are performed. With children who are likely to experience most difficulty, selective reinforcement of each response that matches the model is highly effective. Such a procedure appears to elicit and maintain the response patterns (Bandura, 1969). The powerful effects of this type of procedure are dramatically illustrated by the work done by one of the authors with a child who would not talk at school (see Chapter 4).

Graduated enactments of desirable role behavior were used by Gittelman (1965). He employed role rehearsal to alter aggressive behavior in older children. To establish a hierarchy to be used in the behavioral rehearsals, he asked the children to identify and describe situations that tended to elicit hostile feelings and aggression. These aggression-arousing incidents were then arranged in an intensity hierarchy from the least to the most provocative. Subsequently, these situations were rehearsed sequentially to enable the children to learn to cope with them in a more acceptable and less belligerent manner.

Applications of this basic procedure are readily apparent. A child client may be asked to identify and describe the social situations and/or interpersonal relationships that create difficulty for him. When these situations have been defined, they may be arranged in a hierarchy from least to most difficult. A mini-situation is constructed for the rehearsal and enactment of each situation, starting with the least difficult. Reinforcement may be selectively administered at each stage. As the situations are being simulated, the enactments are video-taped. The video-tape is replayed and observed by child client and therapist to provide appropriate feedback for the client and to enhance his role enactments. If necessary, the situation may be reenacted until the appropriate social behaviors are skillfully performed.

Similar applications could be made with younger children in play therapy. Situations in which children experience conflict can be enacted (role-played) using anthropomorphic models for roles of people in real life. The child client may be asked to provide the dialogue for the anthropomorphic models (as well as himself), with the therapist serving as a facilitator of the drama. The simulated situation(s) may be video-taped for subsequent observation and review.

It is apparent that psychologists and counselors can effectively use modeling procedures with either direct or vicarious reinforcement, mediated through film (or with live models) with very potent results. Since films may be used to evoke imitative responses, these procedures are useful with individuals and groups of children. Conceivably, groups of children in whom it is desirable to strengthen certain types of behavior could be shown a film in which appropriate behavior is modeled and the desirable change is promoted.

Methods for Promoting Behavior Change: Weakening Undesirable Behavior

We have stated that behavior is maintained by both positive and negative reinforcement. Consequently, to change behavior, the reinforcing stimuli that maintain it must be withheld; that is, we must stop reinforcing it. When we do, the behavior tends to be extinguished. For example, if an indulged child makes unreasonable demands, the behavior will tend to decrease in strength when the parents stop conceding to (reinforcing) the demands (Lundin, 1961). However, it may take many nonreinforced trials before the demanding behavior is extinguished.

The Nature of Extinction

It was noted previously that the rate at which behavior is extinguished is a function of the schedule or reinforcement by which the behavior was learned and/or maintained. When behavior has been reinforced on a continuous schedule (100 percent reinforcement), extinction takes place rapidly. Responses learned with ratio schedules become extinguished less rapidly than is true with continuous reinforcement. Usually, responding continues at a high rate but rather dramatically drops off when the behavior is about to be extinguished. Extinction of behavior maintained with interval schedules is very difficult. After withdrawal of reinforcement responding continues at a low but somewhat persistent rate.

Obviously, if one wishes to change behavior that is considered undesirable, it is important to know something about the reinforcement history. The reinforcement history and schedule generally indicate how long the extinction procedures may take; the person implementing the extinction procedures will not be too inclined to terminate prematurely or give up in the belief that the procedures "will not work." Lack of consistency and persistence in withholding reinforcement may result in reinstating the behavior at full strength. And, for the disbeliever, this may amount to the actualization of a self-fulfilling prophecy. What the disbeliever wanted all along may take place because a reinforcement "just happened" to be given.

It should also be noted that there is an increase in responding after reinforcement has been removed. Consequently, the undesirable behavior one is attempting to remove may, for a while, become worse. However, if one persists in withholding the reinforcement, the behavior will eventually be extinguished (Sulzer, Mayer, and Cody, 1968).

The use of extinction procedures (nonreinforcement of the undesirable behavior) has been effectively demonstrated by Harris, Wolf, and Baer (1964). The objects of their experimentation were children three and four years of age who exhibited various types of undesirable behavior, such as excessive crying, passivity, isolated play, etc. Illustrative of the extinction procedures used are those employed with a four-year-old boy who tended to cry excessively from mild frustration. Observations of the behavior revealed that the boy averaged approximately eight "crying episodes" each morning at school. These episodes consistently obtained teacher attention, interest, and concern. The teacher was instructed to simply ignore the behavior; for ten days the child's crying was ignored while attention was given for self-help behavior. During the last five days of the ten-day period, crying was observed only once.

To ascertain whether reinforcement had previously maintained the crying behavior, crying was once again reinforced (by giving attention to it). The crying behavior quickly returned to a rate approximating the original baseline. However, with the implementation of the extinction (ignoring the crying) for another ten-day period, the behavior decreased to near zero.

The effectiveness of extinction in decreasing frequency of an undesirable behavior is clearly demonstrated by the Harris *et al.* study. It should be noted, however, that the procedures used involved both nonreinforcement of the undesirable behavior as well as the *reinforcement of the desirable behavior*. Such a procedure seems to be more efficient than simply withholding the reinforcement for the undesirable behavior.

The treatment of tantrum behavior in a twenty-one-month-old boy by the use of the withdrawal of reinforcement has been reported by Williams (1959). The boy, who had received much care during a rather severe illness during his first eighteen months, continued to make excessive demands for care upon his recovery. When these demands were not responded to, particularly at bedtime, he exhibited extreme temper tantrums.

When the child was put to bed, a routine performed alternately by the parents and an aunt, the child would have a tantrum unless they remained in his room until he had gone to sleep. The child, who obviously had considerable control over the parents, would protest loudly if the parents read while waiting for him to go to sleep.

In order to extinguish the behavior, the parents were instructed to put the boy to bed in a relaxed, unhurried way. Once the child was in bed, the parents left the room and closed the door. Initially, the exit of the parents from the bedroom was greeted with intense crying. The parents were instructed not to return, however. After ten such sessions, the child no longer cried or seemed upset.

Unfortunately, a week later, the boy began to exhibit his crying behavior, and the aunt reinforced the behavior by remaining in the room until he went to sleep. This necessitated the implementation of the extinction procedures again. After nine sessions, the crying behavior once again returned to zero. No undesirable side effects from the treatment were observed.

It would be fortunate if all behavior were susceptible to extinction as the two case reports indicate. Behaviors that can be extinguished usually are ones maintained by positive reinforcement, administered more or less continuously. There are, however, many responses or behaviors that have been induced by successful avoidance or aversive stimulation. That is, the behavior has been negatively reinforced. Such behavior is powerfully resistant to extinction. Obviously, when a response is performed that leads to the avoidance of or escape from an aversive or painful stimulus, it has important survival value. For example, Skinner (1953) cites the case of a salesman who rang a doorbell that caused the back end of a house to explode. Apparently, gas had escaped in the kitchen, and when the doorbell was rung sparks were generated to cause the explosion. Although Skinner does not comment on the behavior changes in the salesman, it no doubt changed his doorbell-ringing behavior.

Unusual resistance to extinction, as well as the potentially damaging effects that avoidance-learned responses have, is revealed in a well-known experiment with monkeys. Two monkeys were placed side by side in chairs that restrained them. The first, or executive monkey, was given an electric shock every twenty seconds, which he could delay by pressing a button. The second monkey was shocked in similar fashion, but button pressing did not delay the shock. Consequently, the executive monkey had the responsibility of postponing the aversive shock. The second monkey was not able to assume a similar managerial role, since his button pressing did not delay the shock. These procedures continued for many days and were alternated by six-hour periods of avoidance training and rest (Cohen, 1969).

After twenty-three days, the executive monkey died. Autopsy revealed perforations and lesions in the duodenum wall. The other monkey did not reveal similar physical or physiological damage. Subsequent experiments with other monkeys revealed similar devastating results in executive-type monkeys, although physical damage was even more severe. Apparently, the stress (fear) experienced by the executive monkey was the cause of his demise. This is a powerful demonstration indeed of the dangerous effects of constant stress on an organism (Cohen, 1969).

Once animals and humans have learned to perform responses to avoid aversive stimuli, these responses will be executed literally hundreds of times even though the aversive stimuli are no longer present. Apparently, intense aversive stimuli create automatic fear reactions that evoke instrumental responses to escape from or avoid the aversive stimuli. Such instrumental responses are so powerfully energized that one continues to perform them rather than take a chance of being reexposed to the physical or psychological pain. Subsequently, the fear reaction associated with the aversive stimulus maintains the avoidance behavior, because the fear is reduced when the avoidance response is performed. Consequently, one will not take the necessary steps to confront the feared situation, which may no longer be present or which can now be more readily coped with. Such is the case of people who exhibit various types of behavior disorders.

Satiation and Negative Practice

Most of us are acquainted with the well-known remedy of deterring a child's interest in and experimentation with smoking by buying him a box of cigars and encouraging him to smoke "to his heart's content." After he has smoked his way through a box of cigars, his appetite for smoking generally tends to decrease markedly. One way of explaining his decreased interest and experimentation with smoking is that the abundant provision of cigars leads to satiation. But another explanation is that after ten or fifteen cigars consecutively, smoking may have become an aversive stimulus.

The use of satiation and its opposite, deprivation, have demonstrated value in controlling and changing behavior. Satiation can be induced either by providing such an abundance of a stimulus that its reinforcement properties are lost (Ullmann and Krasner, 1965), or by continuously reinforcing a response until it is no longer performed (Reese, 1966). A close cousin to the stimulus satiation procedure is that of negative practice. When this method is used, the person who exhibits an undesirable behavior (nail biting, stammering, etc.) is encouraged to repeatedly perform the behavior. That is, the person is requested to perform, for example, the stammering response over and over. Eventually, the stammering stops for two basic reasons: (1) The response is extinguished because anxiety is no longer associated with it, and (2) the fatigue that accumulates by its repetition makes performance of the response painful and/or aversive (Ullmann and Krasner, 1965).

A simple illustration of the use of negative practice was reported by a school psychologist colleague of one of the writers. A teacher asked the psychologist what she might do to terminate the behavior of a third-grade boy who frequently performed imitations of various animal sounds. The psychologist instructed the teacher to place the child in an empty room adjacent to the classroom and direct him to make the imitations for ten minutes. If the child stopped the imitations, the teacher was instructed to have the child continue by the verbal direction, "Please continue." After a few series of ten-minute imitation periods, the teacher reported no more difficulty with animal imitations in the classroom.

Punishment

Of all the available methods of behavior control, punishment is probably second to none in frequency of use. Indeed, as lawlessness in our society has increased, the ordinary citizen has come to be preoccupied with punishment. Witness the often-expressed desire that more severe penalties be imposed on law breakers. While there should be effective action to control lawlessness, the specific effects of punishment are not always clear.

Before we are able to evaluate the effects of punishment, we must clearly define what is meant by it as well as analyze the variables operating when it is used. Skinner (1953, p. 185) has defined punishment as "the withdrawal of a positive reinforcer or presenting a negative one." Punishment aims to depress behavior, while positive and negative reinforcement aim to *strengthen* behavior. When the layman talks about punishment, he usually has in mind the presentation of some type of aversive stimulus (spanking, beating, slapping, torturing, ridiculing, disapproving, and threatening). The effects of punishment are dependent on how it is administered (its intensity, frequency, how it is scheduled, etc.) and the type of stimulation involved.

Whether punishment is effective also depends on the criteria applied or the objectives to be achieved. That is, before we can say it is useful we must ask whether we desire an immediate or a lasting effect, and at how high a price. There is some evidence to suggest that when punishment is administered in the form of aversive stimulation, it acts to suppress behavior temporarily. When it is withdrawn, the punished behavior rapidly gains strength. If the punishment is more severe and given consistently, it may act to suppress behavior for a longer period of time (Skinner, 1953).

A central concern about the usefulness and effectiveness of punishment is not only its utility in suppressing the punished responses but also the extent to which it produces side effects. That is, punishment may produce other undesirable behavior such as aggression or avoidance behavior. It can often be observed that the employment of aversive stimulation may act on behavior other than the punished response and strengthen behavior that is not desirable (*e.g.*, lying to avoid an aversive consequence). It may generate emotional reactions which could generalize and act to depress or inhibit many areas of behavior (Skinner, 1953; Lundin, 1961). Thus it may ultimately produce excessive inhibition and instigate various behaviors that are inefficient and self-defeating.

There are some instances in which punishment has been demonstrated to be effective. For example, Lovaas *et al.* (1965b) and Risley (1968) have used punishment in working with autistic children. They have reported success in using response-contingent shock in modifying deviant behavior in these children. Apparently, the use of shock as the aversive stimulus did not produce unwanted side effects.

Bandura (1969) cites the work of Feldman and MacCulloch, who have successfully used aversive stimulation in favorably altering sexual deviations. Homosexual clients are asked to rate the attractiveness or appeal of both clothed and nude males and females pictured on slides. If photographs of the client's male and female acquaintances are available, they are also used. The rating of the pictures of males and females results in a hierarchy of least to most appealing stimulus pictures.

In the process of conditioning, these stimulus pictures (starting with males) are projected on a screen in a darkened room. The client is told that he may leave the picture on the screen as long as it is sexually attractive to him, but he is informed that he may receive shocks while viewing them. However, he is able to operate a switch that removes the picture and the aversive shock. If he operates the switch within eight seconds, he is able to avoid the shock. If he does not, he will be shocked in the leg.

During treatment, one third of the avoidance responses that the client performs to pictures of males are reinforced at various, irregularly spaced times by the termination of the shock. Another one third of the training trials is given to irregular shock, administered whether or not the client acts to terminate the aversive stimulus. And for another third of the training trial time, the stimulus picture continues to be displayed (for varying intervals of time) even though the subject has executed the avoidance response. This procedure presumedly leads to avoidance conditioning regarding the sexual appeal of males.

To enhance the sexual attractiveness of females, slides of females are presented immediately after the male pictures are removed. This procedure tends to condition anxiety-relief responses to female stimuli. Approach responses to females are further increased by permitting the client to return the picture of the female and postpone the aversive stimulation associated with pictures of males. To avoid any undesirable reinforcement of avoidance behavior regarding females, the presentation of the female pictures is under the control of the therapist.

The presentation of the pictures is done so that the least attractive male is paired with the most appealing female. A particular male picture is repeatedly exposed until the client dislikes or is indifferent to it and removes the picture in a short time. Subsequently, the next female picture is presented if the client has repeatedly asked for a reexposure of the preceding female stimulus picture. This procedure is continued until the pairs of stimulus pictures are presented in hierarchial fashion. Approximately fifteen sessions are required with follow-up booster shots during the following year.

The results of these treatment procedures appear very encouraging. Most of the nineteen cases of chronic homosexuals reported appeared to change considerably in their sexual orientation. Homosexual practices were reduced or disappeared, and heterosexual interest was greatly increased.

Azrin and Holz (1966), in a rather comprehensive review of the use of punishment in behavior control, have suggested that the effects of punishment appear to be a function of the type of reinforcement schedule to which the previously punished behavior has been subjected and whether an alternate response is available and appropriately reinforced. If an alternate response is available, the punished response is rather quickly and completely suppressed. However, exercising caution, they suggest that punishment may have some unpredictable side effects.

It is apparent that the effects of punishment are not unequivocal. The reasons for this may be better understood when we analyze punishment (aversive stimulation) to determine how it produces its effects—apparently by inducing certain types of respondent behavior. This behavior is often referred to as anxiety or as some form of negative affect. Also, since neutral stimuli precede or are present at the time of a primary aversive stimulus, they may become conditioned aversive stimuli and subsequently act to trigger the emotional reactions and ultimately suppress the punished behavior (Lundin, 1961).

Suppose we have been given an insult (aversive stimulus) by one of our superiors. The insult activates respondent behavior (perspiration, flushed cheeks, increased heartbeat, anger, etc.). Moreover, stimuli present at the time (either environmental or stimulus characteristics of the person) become conditioned stimuli. The emotional reactions (respondent behavior) tend to inhibit the behavior to which the insult is directed. On future occasions, the conditioned aversive stimuli may act to inhibit certain responses around the superior, and it may generalize to others with similar stimulus characteristics. Indeed, the insulted person may act to avoid future situations of this variety. This reaction may be short-lived, however. As the emotional reaction diminishes in intensity, the punished behavior tends to regain its strength.

In the present state of our knowledge, it may be proper to say that certain forms of punishment may be useful under certain conditions. If used, it must be appropriately administered (and associated) with the behavior that is undesirable. The person with whom it is used must be certain what behavior is desired and must be able to perform it. Reinforcement of the desirable behavior is equally important. Moreover, long delays in punishment after the undesirable behavior is performed appear not to be effective. If or when it is used, care should be exercised to ensure that undesirable side effects do not occur.

Withdrawal of Reinforcement

The withdrawal of privileges (or reinforcement)—a form of punishment, according to Skinnner (1953)—is a well-known and frequently employed technique to depress undesirable behavior. It is to be distinguished from extinction in that withdrawal of reinforcement is contingent upon the performance of a response. In extinction, reinforcement is discontinued completely upon the initial occurrence of the response. That is, reinforcement is no longer presented upon the performance of the response. With response-contingent withdrawal of reinforcement, decrease in response strength is more rapidly achieved (Reese, 1966).

An illustration may help clarify the point. Consider a group of upper elementary grade children deeply engrossed and very much entertained by a game of Monopoly. As the trading and buying of property becomes more excited, one of the boys utters the words "damn it." The boy's mother hears him and immediately banishes him from the game. The reinforcement, the fun of playing the game, has been withdrawn. Presumably, the response-contingent withdrawal of reinforcement reduces the tendency to say "damn it."

An operating positive reinforcer is not the only reinforcement which may be withdrawn. Withdrawal of any other positive reinforcer that is contingent upon the performance of a response may produce the same effect. That is, withdrawal of some other privilege (going to the movie that night, playing in the Little League baseball game the following day, etc.) theoretically has the same effect. Obviously, the more powerful the reinforcer withdrawn, the more likely it is to produce the desired effects. It is possible, however, that if the magnitude of the withdrawn reinforcer is not commensurate with the act, the emotional reactions evoked (anger) may make the effects less predictable.

Barrett (1965) was interested in determining the relative utility of withdrawing reinforcement against that of aversive stimulation in eliminating a neuromuscular tic in a 38-year-old man. The experimental apparatus was so arranged that the subject's tic movements could be accurately recorded and aversive stimulation and withdrawal of reinforcement could be achieved by various presentations through the headphones worn by the subject. The positive reinforcement withdrawn was the termination of music selected by the subject. The aversive stimulus was "white noise" delivered through the ear phones. As appropriate to the two experimental treatments, the music was stopped or the white noise delivered upon the manifestation of the tic. Each experimental treatment was also performed so that withdrawal of reinforcement was not contingent on the tic, but operating continuously. The results demonstrated quite clearly that a more potent reduction in the tics was produced by withdrawal of reinforcement (music) contingent upon the performance of the tic than would have been achieved with aversive stimuli.

Time Out

A variant of withdrawal of reinforcement is a procedure descriptively labeled *time out*. Essentially, time out involves withdrawal from a situation in which reinforcement is operating. This method is well illustrated in a study reported by Tyler (1965). Tyler was interested in controlling the behavior of several delinquent adolescent boys interned in a treatment center. The undesirable behavior for which control was sought had been exhibited around a pool table (scuffling, throwing cue balls, bouncing balls on the floor, etc.).

The study had three phases. In phase one (seven weeks long), previously defined misbehavior resulted in immediate confinement to a time-out room for fifteen minutes. When specific misbehavior was manifest, without warning, discussion, or argument the boys were moved to the time-out room with the explanation, "You fouled up."

In phase two, a no-punishment (no removal to the time-out room for misbehavior) condition was instituted, lasting thirteen weeks. The purpose of this phase was to observe the effects of verbal reprimand on behavior. When the boys misbehaved they were given various warnings or threats, such as "I'm warning you," or "Now cut it out," or "Don't let it happen again." Misbehavior seemed to increase rapidly, and the punishment condition was resumed.

In phase three (twenty weeks), the time-out procedure was reinstated. With the resumption of time out, cumulative records of misbehavior decreased. It was concluded that swift, brief confinement was a useful method in controlling misbehavior.

There are two basic considerations that should be noted in the use of time out. First, when a child is removed to a time-out room, the reinforcement he would ordinarily obtain is terminated. Unless the child is receiving generous reinforcement for appropriate behavior when he is not in the time-out room, the potential effectiveness of the time-out procedure is greatly reduced. Second, when a child is placed in a time-out room (or some other time-out condition is invoked), his confinement there should be limited to a definite period of time. A period of ten or fifteen minutes is usually a maximum. Otherwise, extremely negative reactions to the whole procedure may develop in the child and markedly decrease any positive results that may accrue from the procedure.

Incompatible Behavior and Desensitization

For several years now, Wolpe and Lazarus (1966) have been using a method of producing behavior change called reciprocal inhibition. The procedure is based on the assumption that undesirable (neurotic) behavior can be unlearned or inhibited by the presentation of anxiety-eliciting events (or symbolic representations of them) in temporal contiguity to responses that are innately antagonistic to anxiety. That is, situations that elicit anxiety can be presented to a person so that responses other than anxiety occur. If one can get a person to make assertive or relaxed responses in the presence of anxiety-producing cues, anxiety is reduced. That is, assertive responses are incompatible with anxiety; if one can learn to be assertive in situations that have typically aroused anxiety, anxiety is decreased.

On this central principle, Wolpe and Lazarus (1966) and Wolpe (1969) have developed a procedure for relieving individuals of many anxiety-produced behaviors. It is called *systematic desensitization.* Three steps are typically involved. First, a list of phobic, or anxiety-producing stimuli are identified and arranged in an intensity hierarchy. Second, the person is trained to relax by methods originally developed by Jacobson. Third, the patient is encouraged to imagine or visualize the least disturbing item in the hierarchy until anxiety is no longer induced. Thus, step by step, the individual works through all items in the hierarchy and reconditioning is presumably complete.

Although this seems like a remarkably simple procedure, great care must be exercised in constructing the hierarchy as well as in working through it. Since complete relaxation must be maintained (to inhibit the arousal of anxiety) as each hierarchical item is presented, progression through each item must be slow. The patient must be carefully taught to report any anxiety, and the therapist must be alert to observe any manifestations not reported. Some items must be presented several times before the patient can visualize the scene without feeling anxiety.

Although systematic desensitization has been most frequently used with neurotic-type phobic reactions, Wolpe (1969) claims success with a number of other disorders. For example, he indicates success with sexual inadequacy, stuttering, certain types of psychosomatic illness, and character neurosis. He describes the case of a woman (with a diagnosis of character neurosis) who was sexually promiscuous, had difficulty holding jobs and adjusting to marital life, and had attempted suicide three times. Nine years of psychoanalysis had not succeeded in producing desirable change. Analysis revealed that her intense fear of criticism and rejection inhibited her assertiveness. She had difficulty tolerating the demands of others and was unable to project her own needs.

Wolpe urged her to express her own legitimate demands. When some success had been achieved, he requested that she construct a hierarchy of her fear of rejection and ridicule. After construction of the hierarchy, she was trained in deep muscle relaxation. The anxiety hierarchy of the themes of rejection and ridicule was then systematically worked through. After thirty-one sessions, she began to cope successfully in her relationships with others and appeared to deal effectively with indications of disapproval from others. Within a period of nine months, she was remarried and had maintained her social and emotional gains.

Wickramaserkera (1968) has reported the use of systematic desensitization with a twenty-five-year-old exhibitionist. The patient had been arrested for exposing himself in a public place. Just prior to the arrest, exhibitionism had begun to increase considerably, so that he was exposing himself as much as ten times a week.

The case history data revealed that the patient was fearful of any type of sexual contact with adult females. His preferred sexual objects were young females approximately eight to fourteen years of age. Although he had earlier achieved some relief from his exhibitionistic urge by masturbation, such behavior had become progressively less reinforcing.

The treatment plan had three basic features: (1) to transfer sexual approach responses from young females to female adults, (2) to increase reinforcement associated with actual physical contact and intercourse, and (3) to enhance a feeling of relaxation rather than agitation in the presence of sexual stimuli.

The patient was trained to relax with a tape recording in three one-hour sessions, combined with distributed practice of relaxation exercises for about an hour and a half each day between clinic sessions. The patient was also instructed to construct at home an anxiety hierarchy beginning with social contact involving himself and other adult females that terminated in sexual contact. In addition, he was asked to construct a similar anxiety hierarchy involving young females.

Systematic desensitization proceeded in the usual manner until the seventh session. At this point, it was considered desirable to shape responses incompatible with the anxiety precipitated by female adult sexual stimuli. Reading assignments were given that exposed the patient to progressively more erotic content involving adult females. This was done to direct the patient's thoughts and verbal behavior into areas of sexual stimuli with female adults. Reading sessions were approximately ten minutes in length, during which time the therapist administered continuous verbal reinforcement. By the twelfth session, the patient was reading highly erotic material without reinforcement from the therapist.

Starting with the twelfth session, the cooperation of the patient's fiancee was obtained in order to enhance appropriate approach responses regarding adult female sexual stimuli. The fiancee was encouraged to reinforce certain specified approach responses. However, beyond a predetermined point, certain sexual approach responses were strictly forbidden.

The results indicate that the patient did not expose himself after the fourth session, and his relationship with his fiancee improved. There appeared to be no symptom substitution or regression to earlier exhibitionism. A follow-up conducted at six and at ten months disclosed that the patient was married to his fiancee, and the relationship was described as "extremely satisfying."

An interesting application of systematic desensitization is reported by Lazarus and Abramovitz (1962). They treated nine phobic children by using emotive imagery rather than relaxation. That is, hierarchies of most-feared to least-feared situations were established. The child was then asked to imagine a sequence of anxiety-arousing events into which were woven a story of the child's favorite heroes. When imagination and emotion were appropriately aroused, the experimenters introduced, as part of a narrative, anxiety-arousing items in the hierarchy. Of the nine children treated between the ages of seven to fourteen, seven recovered in a mean of 3.3 sessions. Follow-up studies done twelve months later revealed no lapses or symptom substitution.

The reported studies give reason to be optimistic about the use of systematic desensitization in the treatment of various behavior disorders.

Wolpe (1969) conducted follow-up studies of 249 neurotic cases he treated. He has reported that "from two to fifteen years after treatment, only four of the 249 cases acquired new symptoms" (Wolpe, 1969, p. 37).

As we conclude our discussion of the application of learning principles to decreasing undesirable behavior, it should be apparent that there are a multitude of approaches that are useful. In subsequent sections, practical applications of these principles will be made in situations involving counseling as well as teaching.

The Observation and Recording of Behavior

We have alluded to the importance of observing and recording behavior in which change is desired. Observing and recording are necessary not only for specifying the exact behavior one desires to change, but also to establish an operant level before implementing treatment measures. During the course of treatment, it is also important to analyze treatment effects.

The significance of observation and measurement procedures is not always recognized, nor are these procedures consistently used. Some persons object to the use of systematic and objective observational procedures because they appear to be a laboratory frill; they are not considered a necessary part of the treatment process. But, as Bijou (1966) has suggested, accurate observation and recording of the behavior being modified indicates whether treatment procedures are effective and when they should be altered. If records of the behavior being treated are maintained, it is no longer necessary for the counselor or psychologist to make "testimonial" statements about the efficacy of his treatment procedures. Objective records clearly demonstrate the merits of the treatment. Small and continuous changes in the behavior of the client may be observed and serve to reinforce the counselor for his skill and effort.

Observation and Measurement of Behavior

There are many kinds of useful, objective methods for observing and measuring behavior. Some are more easily implemented in applied settings than others. Ruch (1963) identifies seven major behavioral criteria. They are briefly described below.

1. Accuracy of response—The number of correct or incorrect responses.
2. Speed of response—The amount of time required to make a correct response.
3. Strength of response—A quantitative measurement of a physiological response.
4. Resistance to extinction—The number of responses an organism will make without reinforcement of a previously learned behavior.
5. Resistance to interference—The degree to which a response is resistant when a conflicting behavior must be learned.
6. Probability of response—(This is a criterion generally used with a group.) The percentage of the group who make a correct response for each trial.
7. Effort of response—The increase or decrease in effort exhibited by the subject as learning progresses. The physiological measurement used is the amount of carbon dioxide exhaled or the muscular tension manifest.

It is obvious that just a few of these behavioral criteria can be used in schools or clinics, but others require the use of expensive equipment that is often not practical. Also, some of the described methods require the subject to learn a conflicting behavior; or a behavior he has recently been taught must be extinguished. Consequently, in most cases, many of these measurement methods are not entirely appropriate in an applied setting.

Defining Behavior to Observe

The first prerequisite in implementing behavior modification strategies is to identify and precisely define the behavior in which change is desired. Once it is carefully specified, baseline rates of the operant level are then recorded. Thus, when treatment is employed, its effects on the identified behavior may be observed.

An example of the care that should be exercised in defining behavior to be altered is stated by Hewett (1968). In this instance, he was interested in the extent to which attention is devoted to a task. Attention is defined as the amount of time a student maintains eye contact with a task. If the teacher is talking to the whole class, the student's eyes must be focused on the teacher. When the student is given an individual assignment, his eyes must maintain contact with the appropriate materials at his desk. If his eyes are focused on materials on his desk unrelated to the assigned task, he is described as inattentive. Hewett further specifies that a student be given thirty seconds to terminate an assignment (when requested to do so) before the behavior is labelled as inattentive.

Although criteria for specifying attention behavior seem quite rigorous, application of such criteria leaves little doubt about appropriate or inappropriate attention. By use of these rigorous criteria, students in Hewett's engineered classrooms are observed daily for five minutes. The number of seconds the student attends is carefully timed.

Another example of the care with which behavior must be defined and observed is reported by Werry and Quay (1969). Although they make reference to a number of behaviors they were observing, *out-of-seat* behavior is used here as an illustration. They define out-of-seat behavior

> as any situation in which the normal seating surface of neither buttock is applied to the child's seat or in which there is movement of his desk or chair so that its ultimate stationary position is altered (thus swinging a seat on its axis or tilting a chair on its leg is excluded) (p. 468).

The behavior of a child who is permitted to be out of his seat is not considered out-of-seat behavior unless he takes an unreasonable period of time, looks at other things, or interacts with others. Although the care with which out-of-seat behavior is defined may seem pedantic, it is necessary in order to avoid error. Obviously, it is not possible to observe behavior precisely until the behavior to be observed is carefully specified.

Methods of Recording Behavior

Behavior observation assumes a number of forms. Methods that are used vary with the specific behaviors that are being modified. Some systems that are reported in the literature are simple, while others are quite complex. The degree of detail in recording is dependent on the amount of help available to obtain the observations. Often, undergraduate students or even volunteer housewives can obtain the data if they are trained. When it is possible, the counselor or psychologist should make use of them. Occasionally, teachers may be able to observe while engaged in teaching. However, teacher observation of behavior should be confined to a single behavior-frequency count for a short period of time each day. Observational methods that may be used by teachers will be discussed in a subsequent section.

Recording Study Behaviors and Teacher-Pupil Interaction

A very complete method of observing and recording classroom behavior of elementary school children is reported by Werry and Quay (1969). They were concerned with three general categories of behavior: deviant behaviors, attending behaviors, and teacher-pupil interaction. Each of the three categories has various subcategories. Deviant behaviors include:

a. being out of one's seat (without permission or when the activity, though permitted, is prolonged),

b. physical contact or disturbing others,

c. making audible noise,

d. turning in one's seat (90 degrees or more),
e. vocalizations (answering without permission, swearing, etc.),
f. isolation (time-out), and
g. other behaviors not provided in these categories.

The second category of attending behaviors includes:

a. attending (the child must have eye contact with the task or teacher for not less than fifteen out of twenty seconds),
b. irrelevant activity (not the assigned task), and
c. daydreaming (more than five seconds out of twenty).

The third category is teacher contact. This category is subdivided into:

a. contacts the teacher initiates positively,
b. teacher-initiated negative contact,
c. pupil-initiated positive contact with teacher, and
d. pupil-initiated negative contact.

Behavior observations are recorded each twenty seconds for a fifteen-minute period of time. A ten-second rest period is also recommended after a twenty-second interval to insure proper recording of behavior. Behavior is recorded by its occurrence (rather than its duration). In other words, this type of behavior observation is a frequency count.

Werry and Quay (1969) recommend that as many samples as possible be taken on various occasions to insure a valid measure of the child's behavior, and that observers do not interact with the children. Interaction tends to make the observation less accurate, since children would not be responding in their typical manner and observers would be less able to concentrate.

Werry and Quay mention certain cautions that it is desirable to note. First, deviant behavior can only be defined in reference to a particular classroom. Classrooms vary in the amount of teacher permissiveness and control. Hence, certain types of behavior will be exhibited much more frequently in some classrooms than in others. Second, accurate observation requires that the observer be close enough to the child to see what he is doing and, if possible, hear what the child verbalizes. Third, observation should be done under "typical conditions" and not when a child may be receiving excessive individual attention. Fourth, though the amount of time a behavior is being observed is specified (twenty-second intervals for fifteen-minute total), it should not be considered as absolute. As previously stated, observational methods can be modified to fit each situation.

It is obvious from our rather brief synopsis of Werry and Quays' observational methods that the system has much to offer. Observational and/or behavioral categories are carefully defined, and the resulting observations should give an excellent picture of the identified pupil behaviors.

The following sections deal with more specific methods of recording behavior. The literature cited is taken from research studies, which include reference to the scoring system used, rather than from articles specifically dealing with observation and recording. The reason for this is to illustrate some less-detailed methods of scoring that have been used in specific settings.

Recording the Behavior of a Child with Peers and Adults

In order to determine objectively the effects of a reinforcement program of the isolate behavior of a child, Allen, Hart, Buell, Harris, and Wolf (1964) devised a behavior-recording system. They recorded both proximity and interaction of the child with adults or other children. Proximity was defined as being within three feet of another person. Interaction was defined as verbal or nonverbal behavior toward another person. Behavior was recorded every ten seconds by the observer.

The recording form had two rows for every ten-second interval. Behaviors were recorded only once for each interval. The first row was for proximity to and interaction with adults; the second row was for the same behavior toward peers. If the child was in proximity to another, the symbol / was placed in either of the two rows, depending on whether it was an adult or child or both. The symbol x was used to denote an interaction. The recording of the interaction was similar to that for proximity. If neither an interaction nor proximity occurred, the space was left blank for that interval. In this way, the record would demonstrate whether isolate behavior, proximity, or actual interaction occurred.

Recording the Influence of Teacher Attention on Study Behavior

In studying the effects of teacher attention on study behavior of children, Hall, Lund, and Jackson (1968) used a simple but efficient method of recording. They divided their record sheet into three rows. The first row was used to record either study or nonstudy behavior of the student. A child had to attend to his assigned task for at least five seconds of the ten-second interval in order for it to be called study behavior. The second row was used to record whether the teacher verbalized to the child. The third row was used to record when the teacher was within a three-foot distance of the child. All three of these behaviors were recorded each ten seconds for the individual child. In each of the three rows, either one of two behaviors was recorded. In the first row, study or nonstudy behavior was symbolized by S or N, respectively. In the second row, if the teacher verbalized to the child, a T was placed in the row, and if she did not, it was left blank. The third row indicated whether the teacher was within three feet of the child. This was symbolized by placing a / for proximity, or the space was left blank if she was further away.

Recording the Behavior of a Total Class

While studying the effects of group contingencies, Bushell, Wobel, and Michaelis (1968) used a method to record the behavior of an entire preschool class. At the beginning of each five-minute period, the observer looked at the first child on his list, noted the child's behavior and then observed the next child on his list. Each child was observed only long enough to record his behavior before the observer went on to the next child. Since the class had only twelve students, every observer was able to observe each child fourteen times daily.

Observers were told to record what the child was looking at, whom he was talking to and what he was doing with his hands. These behaviors were later classified as either study or nonstudy behavior. For each child, a score was determined for his study behavior. This was expressed as a ratio. The ratio was the amount of time observed each day, divided by the number of behaviors classified as involving study. The individual scores were summed up each day to obtain a total class score.

Another method used to record the behavior of a total class that was larger than the one in the study reported above was discussed by Thomas, Becker, and Armstrong (1968). They did a study of teacher behavior and disruptive classroom behavior. They randomly selected ten children to observe each day. These children were observed for two minutes each. Every minute was broken down into ten-second intervals. The observers recorded classes of behavior which occurred in an interval. In other words, a given class of behavior could be rated only once during a ten-second interval for a particular child.

Five types of disruptive behavior and one of appropriate behavior were listed. The first of the five disruptive behaviors concerned gross motor behavior, such as getting up out of the seat, rocking in the chair, etc. The second class of behavior was noise making. The third class focused on verbalizations, such as calling out or talking to others. The fourth disruptive classification was orienting behaviors, including turning one's head or body toward objects or another child for more than four seconds unless the turn was more than 90 degrees. The last disruptive behavior classification was termed aggression. This class included behavior such as hitting, shoving, poking others, destroying property, or annoying others.

Relevant behavior was defined as doing the assigned task, looking at the teacher when she was speaking, raising a hand, answering questions when called on, etc. For behavior to be considered relevant, it had to occur for the entire ten-second interval.

When a response occurred that was not in either of the two main categories, it was defined as *Other Task*. No class of behavior could be rated more than once during a ten-second interval. That is, if a child talked out twice during the interval, his behavior was recorded only once. However, a child could be rated in more than one class of disruptive behavior. An overall level of disruptive behavior was the percentage of intervals in which one or more disruptive behaviors occurred; if a child was observed for ten intervals and seven of them involved disruptive behavior, his disruptive behaviors occurred 70 percent of the time.

Recording Behavior in the Home

It is sometimes desirable to observe behavior at home. Trained observers have even been used in the home. For example, Zeilberger, Sampen, and Sloane (1968) trained observers to record instances of physical aggression, yelling, bossing, and any instructions that the child received from his mother. These were respectively coded A, Y, B, or I. If a child obeyed his mother, the I was circled; if he didn't comply, it was left uncircled. The observers recorded whether or not each of the behaviors occurred in a twenty-second interval.

Some of the mother's behavior was also recorded. Included were any verbal and physical contact with the child, physical closeness, and longer verbal contacts. A time-out procedure was employed in their study, so the number of time-outs and the minutes per time-out were also recorded. By observing both the mother and child, Zeilberger, *et al.* were able to study and manipulate how the mother's attention might affect the child's behavior. Also, the time-out technique could be studied to determine its effectiveness.

Wahler (1969) did a study similar to that of Zeilberger *et al.* (1968), but he added an interesting dimension to his observation. As in the study by Zeilberger *et al.*, Wahler observed oppositional children and their parents. Children were observed for either cooperative or oppositional reaction to a parental request. Social approach behavior, whether verbal or physical or toward one or both parents, was also observed, but only if it was child-initiated. Parental behavior was recorded when parents attended either verbally or physically to a behavior of the child.

Parental instruction, defined as any requests or commands made by either or both of the parents, was the second class of behavior recorded for parents. All behavior was recorded each ten seconds and every observation session lasted for forty minutes. Time-out procedures and the use of differential reinforcement were taught to parents, and observations were conducted during their training, which was concluded when parents properly administered time-outs (within ten seconds after the child exhibited oppositional behavior) and correctly used differential attention. Observations of both parent and child behavior were recorded throughout the study. However, Wahler (1969) was also interested in assessing the extent of parental reinforcement and determining whether these new techniques affected the parents' reinforcing value. He used a test by Gewirtz and Baer (1958), administered by having the child drop a marble in either of two holes. When the preferred and nonpreferred holes are determined for the child, parents are asked to reinforce, through approval, the dropping of marbles in the nonpreferred hole. This is done by the parents for ten minutes, and a score based on the percent of marbles dropped in the non-preferred hole by the child is computed. This test was administered four times—(a) during the initial baseline period, (b) during the use of time-out and differential attention, (c) during the second baseline period, and (d) during the reinstatement of time-out and differential attention—and seemed to be highly effective in demonstrating the effects of parental reinforcement during the use of time-out and differential reinforcement.

Recording the
Behavior of a Hyperactive Child

The use of operant conditioning with behaviors other than those described above is observed and recorded in various ways. Patterson (1965b) was concerned with the modification of hyperactive behavior—walking around the room, squirming, talking, and looking around the room or out a window. Responses were tabulated on the frequency of its occurrence; during each interval a mark would be recorded for every second a hyperactive behavior persisted: If a behavior persisted for the total thirty-second interval, the child received 30 marks for that interval.

Recording the Frequency
and Type of Verbalizations

Reynolds and Risley (1968) were concerned with, among other things, the type and frequency of verbalization by a disadvantaged preschool child. Observations of the child during free play were recorded by two different methods: (1) recording how often the child spoke and (2) recording exactly what she verbalized. In recording the frequency of verbalizations, each ten-second interval in which the child talked was recorded with a T. In other words, regardless of the number of times a child talked, only one T was recorded for that interval, unless, of course, the child did not verbalize. Content of verbalization was recorded by writing down everything the child said in a fifteen-minute period. Twenty-nine of these observations were used as a baseline and thirty were used during the experimental condition. These verbalizations were scored according to whom it was directed to (another child or a teacher) and according to part of speech (nouns and verbs) used. In addition, each time a noun or verb appeared for the first time, it was recorded as a different word. In this way, Reynolds and Risley were able to determine whether the treatment increased the child's verbal behavior. Also, when the increase occurred, the content of the verbalizations could be examined to see to whom it was directed and whether new words or repetitions were used.

Recording of Behavior Using Models

Observing the behavior of children in a modeling study appears to be slightly different from observations in an operant study. Bandura, Ross, and Ross (1963) had some children observe a model performing certain behaviors under various conditions. The children were then placed by themselves in a situation similar to the model's, with similar materials. Raters (observing through one-way mirrors) scored the behavior of each child by summing the frequency of occurrence of the specified behaviors. The behaviors listed were those previously exhibited by the models. Bandura *et al.* report 95 percent agreement among the raters scoring specific imitative responses in this particular study.

In a more recent study, O'Connor (1969) selected some children from a list of teacher nominations who were judged to be social isolates. These children were then observed in the classroom. In each fifteen-second interval, they were observed primarily to determine whether they were interacting with their peers. A social interaction was defined as any behavior toward another child which was responded to by the other child. Each child was observed for thirty-two intervals over an eight-day period. Children whose score was fewer than five interactions were used as subjects.

Immediately after treatment (a showing of the experimental or control movie), children were observed according to the pretesting criterion. The effects of treatment on improving social interaction was a comparison of the pretest and post-test of both the experimental and control groups.

In the two modeling studies, observations were not done on a continuous basis, as is frequently the case in operant conditioning. Rather, what appeared to be used were experimental designs of pretest–post-test control groups and the post-test only control group design. These are two of the three basic designs recommended in the literature (Campbell and Stanley, 1963).

Recording of Behavior Using Desensitization

The effects of desensitization are often reported in terms of the subject's ability to deal with the formerly feared object. Lazarus (1961) required some of his patients to undergo a test of their tolerance for their former phobia one month after therapy was terminated. Those who had acrophobia were asked to climb about fifty feet up a fire escape. In addition, they were asked to go by elevator to the roof of the building and count the cars in the street for a two-minute period. The claustrophobic subjects had to stay in a small room with the windows shut and a movable screen a few inches away. To be regarded as recovered, the subjects were expected to display no obvious distress for five minutes.

Ritter (1968) treated children for snake phobia. To determine if the children had a phobia to snakes, an avoidance test was used. The test generally requires increasing direct contact with a snake. Post-test results are determined by using the same avoidance test. Wolpe (1969) also uses avoidance tests or distance from the phobia object that the subject can tolerate as a measure of treatment success. However, sometimes Wolpe uses patient ratings of his freedom from fear of the phobic object or situation as the treatment criterion.

Less Complex Recording Methods

Less complex methods of recording behavior are often desirable for those who lack the background or the time or both, to do more complex recording. The same two basic methods that were reported in the research studies above can be modified for use in applied settings. It will be recalled that the first was the observation of the frequency of a response, the second was measurement of the duration of each response. Frequency of response can be counted simply by putting down a mark on a sheet of paper each time the behavior occurs. Also, a simple counter such as those used by some housewives to compute their bill when shopping can be used (they sell for less than a dollar). The duration of a response is usually measured with a stopwatch.

There are times when other types of objective methods of observing and recording behavior may be used. For example, one of the authors used the measurement of resistance to extinction to prove to a highly skeptical teacher that it was, in fact, the reinforcement that changed the child's behavior rather than just "maturation and luck." In this case, it was desirable to demonstrate that a withdrawal of reinforcement would extinguish a behavior while a reinstatement of it would rapidly promote the behavior to a high level. The behavior in question was to not yell out in class. Reinforcement for not yelling was withdrawn and the child's vocally disruptive behavior quickly returned. The demonstration had the desired effect. The teacher immediately returned to the author to learn more about that "reinforcement stuff."

Observing Specific Academic Responses

Haring (1968) mentions that, in addition to observing classroom behaviors, one can also measure academic responses as well. Correct or completed problems, words read or spelled correctly, or the number of comprehension questions understood are examples of academic responses.

Lovitt and Curtiss (1968) used answers to mathematical problems as their observational response. They counted the number of correct and incorrect responses and also recorded the amount of time taken to complete the problems. These figures were then converted to rates-per-minute. Using a similar method in a later study, Lovitt and Curtiss (1969) recorded the academic response rate of children in various subjects. All subject areas were figured together to obtain a daily response rate-per-minute.

As can be seen, academic responses can be figured separately for each subject area, or given one total score for all subjects. It appears to us, however, that much observational data are lost when each subject is not separately counted. This is because a marked improvement in one area will be buried in the average, which will change only slightly. The danger lies in that a method good for a specific subject area might be ignored when all subjects are averaged.

Simplified Methods of Recording Behavior

One of the keys to simplified recording is limiting the number of behaviors to be observed. Frequency of a specific behavior over a period of time can be counted by almost anyone with minimal training. For example, Patterson and Gullion (1968) give parents instructions for observing the behavior of their children; they request that the parents who use their program text count a particular behavior. Almost any behavior that is of concern to the parents can be used. This may range from the number of times a child fights with a sibling to the number of articles of clothing a child leaves around the house. Patterson and Gullion recommend that one part of the day be used in making the count. As in the example of sibling fighting, the parent may want to use the worst hour, such as after dinner or between three and four o'clock in the afternoon. The time of the day for any behavior usually does not matter as long as it is consistently used. Patterson and Gullion (1968) even recommend that, in some cases, a parent who has observed his child for a while might be able to train the child to count his own behavior.

Graphs To record the behavior of children, Patterson and Gullion (1968) recommend that parents plot the behavior daily on a graph. This method of recording gives a visual picture to the parent of his child's present behavior and also indicates how useful the new approaches are. Use of a graph may be illustrated by plotting the number of times a child gets out of bed at night (behavioral procedures for modifying this problem are discussed in a later chapter). Let us assume that the parent estimates (on a bad night) that the child gets up fifteen times before going to sleep. We would then plot our graph from zero to twenty (see Figure 4, page 67). This would allow for any extreme that might occur. The number of times the child got out of bed would be the vertical axis of the graph, the number of days the horizontal line. At first, there should be a baseline period (before treatment is begun) of a week to ten days. This will show the child's typical behavior. When treatment is started, a straight line can be drawn down the graph to indicate when the change in method takes place.

Let us assume that on the first night the child got out of bed ten times; the next night, nine times; and on the third night, only five times. However, on the fourth night, the child's behavior was extreme, and he was out of bed sixteen times. This was followed by 10, 12, 7, 9, 9, and 14 times for the succeeding nights. On the eleventh day, treatment was started, and the child got out of bed sixteen times (typical when a new rule is established). On the twelfth and thirteenth days, he got out of bed eight times. On the fourteenth day, the child got out of bed three times and on the fifteenth day, two times. The sixteenth day, the child attempted to get out of bed eleven times (this increase is typical and is usually followed by a sharp drop when an old behavior is being extinguished). The numbers of times reported for the remaining days were 2, 4, 1, 2, 0, 1, and 0. All of these figures are plotted in Figure 4.

Frequency Counts In the classroom, teachers can plot the behavior of any of their pupils in a manner similar to the example on page 67. Another form available is the use of a frequency-count report form (see Figure 5, page 68). Once again, a baseline record is kept for ten days before treatment. In this hypothetical example, the teacher is attempting to reduce the number of times a child calls out in class without permission.

On the first day of observation, the child called out ten times. During the next four days, the child called out 12, 10, 13, and 9 times respectively. The weekly total was 54, and the average was 10.8. For the second week of observation, the child obtained frequency counts of 8, 11, 14, 9, and 11. The weekly total was 53, and the average was 10.6. Treatment procedures were begun after two weeks of observation. The reported frequency counts were 14, 8, 5, 3, and 9 for the third week of observation and the first week of treatment. The weekly total was 39, and the average amount of talking out for the week was 7.8. The fourth week, the reported frequency counts were 4, 2, 0, 2, and 0. This was a weekly total of 8 times for the calling out behavior or a weekly average of 1.6.

Although the behavior in which we were interested was talking without permission, other behavior problems could have also been observed (some actual procedures for reducing this problem are discussed in a later chapter). The amount of time that the child is observed can vary from case to case, but time should be consistent for that particular case. In other words, a child in the example above could be observed for the total day, for the morning or afternoon, or just during a certain subject such as reading. Whatever the time to observe is, it should be decided before observations are done, and should be used throughout the entire observation and treatment program.

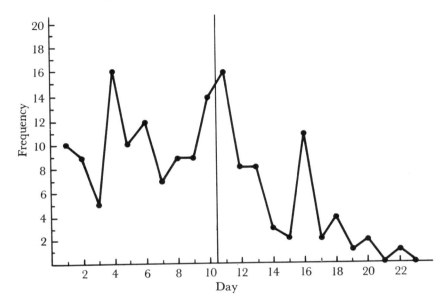

FIGURE 4.   *Graphic illustration of the number of times a child gets out of bed. (All data are hypothetical.)*

Time Observation Observation of certain behavior, such as inattention, can be more accurately reported by using a time observation rather than a frequency count. If a more elaborate system isn't used, such as the method mentioned earlier (recording whether inattention occurs each ten seconds), then simply clocking the behavior may be appropriate. As in frequency counts, a set amount of time has to be used. Usually fifteen minutes should be the minimum amount of time a child is observed each day. Once again, the time of day when the child is observed should be consistent. One subject, such as reading, might be observed for three five-minute segments or three subjects for five minutes each. Treatment, of course, should coincide with the time of observation.

Child's Name   <u>Robert T.   </u>

Behavior to Change   <u>Calling out without permission   </u>

Subject or Subjects Observed   <u>All subjects   </u>

Date of Baseline Recording   <u>November 20   </u>

Date of Treatment   <u>December 4   </u>

Amount of Time Each Day   <u>Total day   </u>

1111 1111	1111 1111 11	1111 1111	1111 1111 111	1111 1111	Weekly Total <u>54</u>
Total <u>10</u>	Total <u>12</u>	Total <u>10</u>	Total <u>13</u>	Total <u>9</u>	Average <u>10.8</u>
1111 111	1111 1111 1	1111 1111 1111	1111 1111	1111 1111 1	Weekly Total <u>53</u>
Total <u>8</u>	Total <u>11</u>	Total <u>14</u>	Total <u>9</u>	Total <u>11</u>	Average <u>10.6</u>
1111 1111 1111	1111 111	1111	111	1111 1111	Weekly Total <u>39</u>
Total <u>14</u>	Total <u>8</u>	Total <u>5</u>	Total <u>3</u>	Total <u>9</u>	Average <u>7.8</u>
1111	11		11		Weekly Total <u>8</u>
Total <u>4</u>	Total <u>2</u>	Total <u>0</u>	Total <u>2</u>	Total <u>0</u>	Average <u>1.6</u>

FIGURE 5.   *Illustration of a form of recording the frequency of the number of times a child calls out in class. (All data are hypothetical.)*

An example (also hypothetical) of the use of time counts is recorded in Figure 6. In this illustration, a teacher was observing the amount of attention a certain child would pay to his reading assignment. Each five minutes, the amount of attention was recorded. During the first five minutes, the child attented one minute and twenty seconds. The second five minutes resulted in attention to task of one minute and ten seconds. The third five minutes, twenty seconds of attention was observed. This was a total of two minutes and fifty seconds for the fifteen minutes of observation. The total time for each of the next four days was two minutes and fifteen seconds, one minute and 46 seconds, two minutes and fifteen seconds, and three minutes and 25 seconds. The total weekly time of attention was twelve minutes and 31 seconds for the five days of observation. This was an average of two minutes and 46 seconds of attention for a fifteen-minute period of observation. Also, some notes were kept on the types of behavior occurring during inattention. Some of these behaviors were daydreaming, playing with a pencil, looking at others, and doing an unassigned task.

Daily totals for the second week were two minutes and 48 seconds, two minutes and seven seconds, two minutes and 24 seconds, two minutes and fifteen seconds, and three minutes and 56 seconds. The weekly total was thirteen minutes and thirty seconds, and the weekly average was three minutes and six seconds. Notes on behaviors exhibited were also made.

At the beginning of the third week of observation, procedures were introduced to increase the child's attention to the task. The weekly average for the third week was ten minutes and 55 seconds and for the fourth week, twelve minutes and nineteen seconds. The behavioral notes seemed to show that daydreaming had been reduced, but doing an unassigned task still remained as one of the behaviors incompatible with attention to task.

Total Class Observation

When a total class is being observed, either a frequency count or a time count can be used, depending on the behavior observed. If a teacher wanted to change behaviors, such as by reducing the amount of time it takes the class to quiet down after recess, how long it takes children to terminate their work when she tells them to stop, how long it takes them to line up and be quiet before going to lunch, or any behaviors involving a time element, then of course the observational method used should be timed. A stopwatch is needed to observe this type of behavior. Timing should begin when the instructions by the teacher are completed and should cease when the last student no longer engages in the observed behavior.

If, on the other hand, the frequency of occurrence of a behavior needs to be increased or reduced, a frequency count is used. Examples might be the number of students who shout out in class, the number of students who talk when they are told not to, the number of children who fight, etc. For this type of observational method, all that is needed is a class list. A mark is placed by the name of each student who exhibits the behavior being observed. No more than one mark per student needs to be placed during each period of observation. This means that even if a certain student performs the observed behavior a few times during the observational period, he is only given one mark. This is done because the concern is the behavior of the total class rather than the behavior of the individual.

Still another method that the classroom teacher can use when observing the total class is termed the "freeze" approach. Though only applicable in certain situations, sometimes this observational method will help to change behavior. Essentially, the approach requires the students in the classroom to stop and stay still when the teacher yells "Freeze." To illustrate the method, let us suppose that a teacher is bothered by the fact that students do not come right into the room and sit down at their desks. She notices that many walk around the room for quite a while before being seated. The teacher then instructs her students that when she yells "Freeze," they are to stop and maintain a statuelike position. Once the students are still, the teacher then places a mark by the name of each student seated.

Child's Name   Billy S.

Behavior to Change   Poor attention

Subject or Subjects Observed   Reading, Math, Science

Date of Baseline Recording   October 4

Date of Treatment   October 18

Amount of Time Each Day   3 five-minute intervals

Time	Time	Time	Time	Time	Behaviors Noted	
1'20″	17″	1'03″	18″	24″	Daydreaming.	
1'10″	1'23″	27″	1'02″	1'50″	Playing with pencil.	
20″	35″	16″	55″	1'11″	Looking at others.	
Total	Total	Total	Total	Total	Weekly Total	Average
2'50″	2'15″	1'46″	2'15″	3'25″	12'31″	2'46″

Time	Time	Time	Time	Time	Behaviors Noted	
1'13″	1'06″	1'05″	39″	1'03″	Daydreaming.	
1'08″	49″	37″	1'23″	52″	Coloring.	
27″	12″	42″	13″	2'01″	Looking out window.	
Total	Total	Total	Total	Total	Weekly Total	Average
2'48″	2'07″	2'24″	2'15″	3'56″	13'30″	3'06″

Time	Time	Time	Time	Time	Behaviors Noted	
3'12″	3'46″	3'16″	2'53″	3'43″	Doing unassigned	
3'36″	4'18″	4'10″	3'43″	3'24″	tasks.	
4'19″	2'14″	4'08″	3'34″	4'17″	Playing with pencil.	
Total	Total	Total	Total	Total	Weekly Total	Average
11'07″	10'18″	11'34″	10'10″	11'24″	54'33″	10'55″

Time	Time	Time	Time	Time	Behaviors Noted	
3'13″	4'23″	4'41″	4'12″	4'21″	Looking at book when	
2'41″	3'55″	3'25″	4'47″	3'52″	teacher is talking.	
4'03″	4'16″	4'40″	4'14″	4'42″	Doing unassigned task.	
Total	Total	Total	Total	Total	Weekly Total	Average
9'57″	12'34″	12'50″	13'13″	12'55″	61'29″	12'19″

FIGURE 6.   *Illustration of a form for recording the amount of time a child attends to his task. (All data are hypothetical.)*

This observational method can be used in the recording of other types of behavior, such as not doing assignments, talking to one's peers without permission, not being in line, etc. Behavioral methods of changing such behaviors are discussed in a later chapter.

This concludes our discussion of observation and recording. It is hoped that the reader is now aware of the need to obtain data when attempting to change behavior, as well as of the methods of doing so. Ways of analyzing child problems and formulating change strategies are discussed in Chapter 5.

The Process of Behavior Change: Formulation and Implementation of Strategies

Our discussion of the methods by which behavior may be observed, recorded, and measured has underlined the central importance of these activities to definition of the behavior to be changed and determination of treatment effects. There are, however, several other elements that must be considered in formulating behavior-change strategies. Corrective measures must be launched that are pertinent to solution of the problems or to enhancement or change of behavior.

As we noted in Chapter 1, care must be exercised to clearly define the behavior to which treatment is directed. The particular problem for which a child is referred may not be the problem that has the highest treatment priority. While a particular problem behavior may be the central focus of concern for a parent or teacher, it rarely exists in isolation. Problem behavior seems to have a ripple effect that generates new complications and consequences in the broader social environment. Ultimately, a child may manifest a singular behavior that captures adult concern and exclude from their attention other problem behavior that it would be desirable to change.

One way to determine the relative significance of a problem behavior is to raise the simple but pertinent question: "To whom is the child's behavior considered a problem?" How this question is answered will suggest whether the child's behavior is in fact a problem or whether the personal idiosyncrasies and expectations of the adults involved are unrealistic. If the problem behavior appears isolated and is exhibited with little intensity or frequency, the real problem may exist in the adult who considers it such and not in the child. Hence, the adult is the "real client" and not the child.

It is apparent that one of the more significant elements in formulating change strategies is to determine how desirable behavior change can be promoted in an efficient and effective manner. Obviously, one must determine who the "real" or significant clients are and formulate a plan accordingly. It is neither efficient nor desirable to focus treatment exclusively on a child when the significant people in his life continue to reinforce the problem behavior. And since a child's behavior is largely influenced by the significant adults, they must be actively involved in the treatment process. We are not suggesting that an all-out search for the "causes" of the child's behavior be undertaken, but it is necessary to identify the *variables* that appear to *maintain* it.

Four basic steps are usually involved in formulating change strategies, as well as in attending to the kinds of questions we have raised. First, the present manifest problem behavior is defined and analyzed. Second, a developmental and social history is secured to further delineate the dimensions of the problem and its present adaptation. Third, behavior-change goals are clearly specified. Fourth, methods of enhancing or modifying behavior are identified and implemented. Each of these steps will be briefly discussed in the following sections. In Chapter 8, "Counseling with Parents," we will consider other factors in working with parents, or parents and child, in the remediation of problem behavior.

Analysis of Problem Dimensions

Analysis of a child's problems begins with the stated complaint or difficulty identified by the referral agent: A parent or teacher may indicate that a child is excessively aggressive; another child is described as very withdrawn; still other children are referred for assistance because they exhibit deficiencies in reading or arithmetic. Occasionally, a parent seeks help for a child because "he does not appear to be happy." The problems are varied and each appears in a matrix of circumstances that is unique to it.

Once the problem behavior has been specified by the referral agent, it is desirable to expand the analysis. That is, *when, where,* and *with whom* is the problem behavior exhibited? First, if the central problem is excessive defiance or aggression, is it exhibited in the classroom, with one or both parents, or with peers? Second, in exactly what circumstances or situations does the aggression appear? Does the child become aggressive only when he loses in competitive situations, or is it a more pervasive coping style? What appears to incite his aggression in each situation in which it is manifest, and what seems to maintain or reinforce it?

By making this type of systematic analysis of the problem behavior or set of behaviors, we are able to make a determination of the stimuli or events that may be evoking it as well as to analyze the extent to which past and present expectations made of the child are realistic. Also, once the problem parameters have been established by systematic interview, careful observation of the child's problem behavior in the appropriate circumstances helps us to determine the reinforcing contingencies. If the frequency and intensity of the problem behavior are noted, we have some idea of its severity.

Systematic delineation, by interview and observation, of the situations in which the problem behavior is expressed, and with whom, tends to indicate *what* and *who* are maintaining the behavior. Once we have made these determinations, we are able to decide who the most significant client is. Obviously, if the child's problem behavior is exhibited in a variety of situations, a number of people may be considered as significant clients.

Presumably, if a child exhibits identical or similar behavior in a variety of situations, the behavior is being reinforced by people in those situations. That is, the assumption is made that if a child's behavior is learned (or maintained by constant reinforcement), then under appropriate learning conditions it may be unlearned. This appears to be true in the great majority of cases. However, there are some children whose problem behavior has physical or organic determinants. It may not be exclusively the result of the reinforcing conditions existing in a particular situation. These conditions must be identified and considered in behavior analysis and behavior change. For example, a chronically ill child may not be a productive learner regardless of the reinforcing contingencies. Similarly, a child who has a physically caused hearing deficiency tends to have difficulty making adequate progress in learning activities that require adequate auditory reception. The presence and extent to which these deficiencies affect the problematic behavior must be evaluated before change or corrective measures can be arranged. For these as well as other reasons, a developmental and social history may be very helpful in problem analysis.

The Function of the Developmental and Social History

A developmental and social history is useful for identifying health status, physical deficiencies, and problems (chronic disease and sensory deficiencies), as well as for obtaining a picture of a child's developmental pattern. A comprehensive history should reveal areas of arrested development and the extent to which cognition (intellectual development) and social and emotional behavior are appropriate and/or adaptive. Since most behavioral disturbances are manifest in three general areas of functioning—cognition, social behavior, and affects or feelings—systematic inquiry into these areas provides an overall assessment of the adequacy of a child's coping efforts. Consequently, it is possible to spot developmental deficiencies before they become problematic and to formulate preventive as well as corrective strategies.

A developmental history also reveals the reinforcement history of the problem behavior, the extent to which the problem behavior may be resistant to change, and the parents' reinforcement style. We are immediately alerted to the disciplinary practices of the parents—the extent to which positive and negative reinforcement are used—and the relative success of these practices. The relative reinforcement properties of significant adults in the child's life may be determined and utilized in formulating change tactics.

There are other elements of the child's development that it is important to consider in securing a history. It is important to identify the child's strengths (abilities, special talents, and achievements) as well as situations that are excessively frustrating to him. When a child's strengths are known, they may be used to increase the extent to which he is positively reinforced and the amount of positive feedback he receives. Knowledge of the situations that are frustrating to the child makes it possible to program the child's activities so that the undesirable behavior is reduced in frequency. For example, if a child is readily provoked to temper tantrums by competitive situations, it may be desirable to decrease the number in which he participates until more systematic change strategies can be used to alter the temper tantrums.

For very practical reasons, it is useful to discover the people to whom a child appears to have quite aversive reactions. For instance, if a child has a high-conflict relationship with his mother (or other significant females in the immediate family), he is likely to generalize these reactions to certain females at school, and there may be open warfare with his women teachers. In this case, a highly effective emergency intervention strategy may be to move the child to a male teacher's room. Ultimately, of course, his problems with females will have to be altered, but until time and personnel permit, this is a useful emergency measure.

A good developmental and social history also should reveal stimuli, events, and conditions that may serve as potential reinforcers. We say *potential* reinforcers because, as we noted in Chapter 2, a reinforcer is a stimulus that increases the probability of a response. It is not possible to determine whether or not a stimulus is reinforcing until it is operative. Stimuli or events that are likely to have such potential may be revealed by inquiring about the activities or things a child selects when free choice is possible. The child's verbalizations about the things he likes, as well as the kinds of things that he does in his free time, provide additional clues. It is also possible to determine stimuli that may be reinforcing by directly administering to the child the questionnaire in the Appendix, "A Method for Identifying Potential Reinforcers."

Although stimuli (tangible objects, candy, etc.) may have potential reinforcement property, *events* also do. It is important to determine them. That is, does the child like going to the store, circus, zoo, or movies, taking a note to the office, talking to the coach, or sitting in the front seat with Dad on a trip to the store? Potential reinforcing events are endless in number. Once they have been discovered, they have considerable capacity to promote the behavior considered desirable. If parents (and other significant adults) are not aware of them, it may be suggested to them that they keep a list of events that they personally observe the child pursuing freely and enthusiastically.

Finally, the developmental and social history is useful in establishing change or treatment priorities. If the history-taking has been comprehensive, it is obvious that a complete picture of the child should naturally emerge. His areas of successes and failures, competencies and deficiencies, relationships and coping styles, and areas of conflict are revealed. If the additional step of observing the child in the critical areas is also taken, we are ready to formulate the treatment priorities.

Specifying
Behavior-Change Goals

A careful analysis of the developmental and social history should readily reveal the high-conflict areas or problem behaviors that appear intense and occur frequently. If some of these behaviors are extremely disruptive or injurious, these problem areas are usually the ones that have the highest priorities; intervention strategies are immediately launched to promote desirable change in them. If a child is about to be expelled from school because of his excessive aggression and defiance of authority, it is important to deal effectively with those behaviors immediately.

As we have indicated previously, an exception occurs when the child's behavior appears to result from unusual pressure or unnatural demands made by the significant adults. For example, we have occasionally observed youngsters whose treatment from parents has been so abusive and provocative that the child's aggressive or escape behavior appeared quite natural under the circumstances. In such cases, the highest priority is doing something with the pressures and demands made by the adults. After such changes have been achieved, it may then be desirable to work with the child.

A comprehensive history usually reveals a number of behaviors in which change may be desirable. Some of these behaviors may be identified as immediate and short-term goals, while others are long-term goals. The intense, frequently expressed, and highly distressing behaviors are usually worked with first. But some of these behaviors may be imbedded in a larger behavior complex that may be the focus of concern later.

Suppose a parent is very upset by an eight-year-old child's thumbsucking. Because it is distressing to the parents and the object of considerable ridicule by the child's peers, it is desirable to change it. It is an immediate-treatment or change goal. However, thumbsucking is often only one of several dependent behaviors that may be exhibited by a child. The thumbsucking may be the goal that has the first priority, but change of the other dependent behaviors may be desirable long-term goals. Once the thumbsucking has been terminated, the other dependent behaviors may subsequently—and sometimes concurrently—become the appropriate treatment targets.

The behavior-change goals that have the highest priorities must be based on the unique variables operating in each case that careful analysis usually reveals. Moreover, the behaviors in which change is desired must be clearly specified. It is not particularly helpful to state as a goal "to help a child feel better about himself" or "to develop a more positive self-image." When a goal is stated in these terms, one must still answer the question, "Exactly how, and in what ways, do you wish the child to feel better or change his self-image?" It is relatively rare to find a child who feels *totally* bad about himself. Rather, his "bad" feeling is anchored to specific referents. Similarly, a person's self-image has both positive and negative aspects. He may have a positive self-image of his capacity to play baseball and a much lower evaluation of his capacity to perform successfully in arithmetic or reading. If remedial procedures are implemented to help him with his mathematical and reading ability, it is likely that his self-image in each of these areas will be considerably enhanced. When the specific behaviors in which change is desired are clearly defined, the goals as well as the change procedures are much simpler to identify. The goals must be stated operationally (in observable behavior terms) to have much relevance to the promotion of behavior change.

In addition to the clearly problem behaviors that capture our immediate concern, there are others in which a child experiences difficulty that have not achieved "problem status." In a sense, they are like sores or boils that begin to fester but do not cause great discomfort or alarm. However, these problem behaviors may become alarming if they are allowed to continue their somewhat unhappy and unproductive course. Consequently, a comprehensive treatment plan brings them under appropriate review and modification.

The areas to which we refer are social or emotional behaviors or behaviors relating to academic performance at school. Teachers or parents can often identify them and some tests (such as those devised by Valett, 1969) can be useful. Once these trouble spots have been identified, strategies can be formulated to direct them on their proper course. What we are suggesting is that prevention is as important as therapy or remediation.

Formulation and Implementation of Change Strategies

When short- and long-term behavior-change goals have been properly identified, change strategies must be formulated. This not only involves the determination of methods by which change may be promoted but also *how* and *with whom* they will be implemented. That is, will the child, parent, or parents and/or teacher be involved individually or jointly? These decisions are generally made during the problem-analysis stage, but they are further refined at this time. We will consider problems of implementation first and conclude with a discussion of stratagems for change.

That one has identified the person or persons who are most significant in maintaining the problem behavior does not necessarily mean that they will be enthusiastic participants in the change process. The relevant question is "To what extent are parents, teachers, and other significant people willing to become involved?"

Significant people might be reluctant to get involved for a number of reasons. Some parents may attribute the child's problem behavior to sources other than themselves and thereby disclaim any responsibility. That is, the child's behavior may be laid at the doorstep of rather vague hereditary causes which are presumed unchangeable. Or the parent may be convinced that the child is simply not exerting enough "will power." If he did, he would not have the problem. Teachers may be reluctant to involve themselves because of inadequate time, too many demands, or an objection to the use of "bribes" or extrinsic incentives to promote the desirable behavior.

These types of objections and/or attitudes must be carefully assessed and, if possible, appropriately worked through with the individuals involved. There is no single procedure that is always successful. The authors have found two approaches, used individually or in combination, that are helpful. First, when therapeutic and/or change procedures are initiated with the child, the significantly involved adults are given the role of observers of the child's behavior. Frequent conferences are held with the significant adults to discuss their observations of the child's behavior. If conferences with these adults are scheduled frequently enough and the counselor or psychologist handles them skillfully, communication barriers are broken down, trust begins to develop, and the adults begin to take a more active role. Since the involved adults are not "blamed" for the child's problems and are in an advantageous position to observe changes beginning to take place in the child, additional cooperation becomes likely.

A second procedure that has proven useful is to simply invite the significantly involved adults to agree to a moratorium of the typical methods or ways of relating to the child that have been used in the past. They are asked to cease using the practices and imposing the expectations that they characteristically do for a specified period of time (usually a week or two weeks). They are told that such a practice has been found effective in helping many children. If their acceptance can be secured, the counselor or psychologist specifies exactly how the child's behavior will be handled in each of the high-conflict areas. The involved adults are asked to keep a record of the child's behavior (particularly in the problem areas), and the behavior is discussed with the psychologist in the conferences. Having the adults keep records of the child's behavior (and their reaction to it) is useful for determining whether or not they are performing their roles adequately and for helping the psychologist to make needed adjustments. Also, the adults may discover how their behavior is ineffective and maintains the child's behavior. By the time the moratorium has ended, the significant people are usually positively involved. If the procedures have proved effective, the child's behavior may have begun to change. The behavior changes may provide additional incentive or reinforcement for the adults' efforts. Thus, it is possible to consider a more comprehensive treatment plan.

As we have noted before, the type of total treatment plan that is implemented is dependent on the problem analysis, on who the significant clients are, and on the extent to which they can be involved as the *object* of change or the *agent* of change. At this point, it is desirable to consider change methods (or therapy) with the significant clients who can be appropriately engaged. The problem dimensions are clearly discussed, the form of intervention is specified and the roles of each person are clearly delineated. For example, the type of therapy (individual or group) and the kind of therapy (play, family, or behavior) is discussed with the client or clients. If the client is a child, this may simply involve discussing generally his feelings about coming for assistance, appointment arrangements, and the type of things in which he will be involved. When parents or teachers are involved, roles, responsibilities, and appointments are carefully discussed. It is particularly important to provide adequate opportunity for the clients to raise questions and to express their attitudes and feelings regarding the procedures and treatment process. The clients' doubts, as well as any unrealistic expectations they may have of "cure," must be recognized and properly clarified. It is also critical during the initial stages (and throughout the entire treatment process) to keep records of the child's behavior. With this information, adjustments in procedures can be made and proper assistance can be provided to the adult clients to help them perform their roles effectively.

Strategies for Promoting Behavior Change

The previous discussion and analysis has identified some of the major steps that must be taken before change strategies can be implemented. The task of formulating specific strategies to change problem behavior is the final and most crucial step. Of course, strategies or therapeutic interventions are always based on the analysis of the client's problems, the variables operating to maintain problem behavior, and the use of principles that will promote the desired behavior. It is not possible to provide a procedure or strategy that exactly fits every client. It is possible, however, to provide in general outline paradigms or stratagems that illustrate how principles and procedures may be applied to a variety of nonadaptive behavior.

The stratagems that we will give represent learning or behavior-change principles in combinations that are in some ways unique. Because they illustrate how stratagems can be formulated and applied in clinical situations, the thoughtful practitioner may find them useful as models which may be adapted to a variety of school and clinical uses.

The parameters of each stratagem are briefly described and are summarized in chart form. Each stratagem has three essential components: (a) basic steps, (b) procedures for implementing, and (c) special considerations and cautions. Studying the chart and following the steps more readily utilizes the stratagem. The basic information is contained in each chart and the written commentary for each stratagem is limited to the essential theoretical elements and the facets of its application. Each chart is read by starting with the first basic step at the left, and moving to the right; procedures for implementing and special cautions are noted at each step. When each of the elements in the first step is appropriately conceptualized and carried out, the steps are followed in order.

Stratagem 1: Extinction and Positive Reinforcement

The process of favorably altering nonadaptive behavior essentially involves two basic elements: (a) unlearning (or reducing in strength) the nonadaptive behavior and (b) learning adaptive behavior. Although these two may not be entirely separate or occur independently, both must be achieved.

For a great number of problem behaviors, the basic operant procedures (see Chapter 1) are useful. That is, by systematic reinforcement of the desirable behavior, changes are often achieved. Similarly, the use of extinction (termination of all reinforcement for the nonadaptive behavior) may effectively eliminate some undesirable behavior. However, when these two procedures are used separately, more time may be required to achieve the desired result. Also, when extinction procedures are used in isolation, the nonadaptive behavior may increase in strength for a short time. Consequently, the change agent may become frustrated or disappointed and may give up or "just happen" to reinforce the nonadaptive behavior. For these reasons, it is desirable to use procedures that effectively combine useful change principles.

In Figure 7 extinction and positive reinforcement are combined so that nonadaptive behavior may be eliminated and desirable behavior promoted simultaneously. Since each of the basic steps, procedures for implementation, and special considerations are specified, extensive comment is unnecessary. If the basic steps and procedures are followed, the strategies can usually be carried out effectively. Problems that typically arise are identified in the third column and should be carefully considered.

Basic Steps	Procedures for Implementing	Specific Considerations and Cautions
1a. Obtain baseline rate of behavior to be eliminated and/or changed.	1a. Observe child in appropriate situations.	
1b. Identify exactly the behavior to be eliminated and/or changed.	1b. Write down the exact behavior it is desirable to eliminate and/or change.	1. State the *overt* behavior desirable to eliminate and/or change.
2. Terminate all reinforcement for undesirable behavior.	2. Withdraw all positive and negative reinforcement coming from all sources (parents, teachers and peers). a. Use time out when necessary. *Example:* "You are having difficulty with (behavior) today. Please go to the time-out room."	2. Do not unintentionally reward the behavior (ignore undesirable behavior and do not criticize). a. Use time out in a matter-of-fact, nonhostile way. Use it as soon as undesirable behavior is exhibited.
3. Modify the environment to decrease the possibility that undesirable behavior will be evoked.	3. Avoid placing the child in a situation in which undesirable behavior is a natural response. *Example:* If you are extinguishing aggression, do not place child in competitive situations.	3. Remember that undesirable behavior may increase in strength for a while.
4. Reinforce the opposite and desirable behavior with a continuous schedule. a. Reinforce approximations of desired behavior if not present in behavior repertoire.	4. Set up situations when desirable behavior is likely to occur. *Example:* Have aggressive child sit with teacher during reading (assembly) and reinforce for non-aggression.	4. Be certain that rewards used are reinforcing. If in doubt, begin with primary reinforcement.
5. Change reinforcement schedule when undesirable behavior decreases in strength and desirable behavior increases in frequency.	5. Reinforce every fourth, ninth, fourteenth, etc., desirable response. a. Provide bonus reinforcements occasionally.	5. Do not change to a variable ratio or interval schedule until appropriate behavior has the desired frequency.

FIGURE 7. Stratagem 1: Extinction and positive reinforcement.

Attention may be profitably directed to a few of the elements that are crucial in its application. In using the stratagem, it is important to identify initially the *behavior to be eliminated* and *the desirable behavior to be promoted.* Specification of these behaviors is followed by systematic observation and recording of the behavior to obtain a baseline rate. Behavior observation and recording is continued throughout the treatment period to determine the extent to which procedures are effective as well as to make necessary adjustments. Once the behaviors to be eliminated and changed have been specified, extinction and positive reinforcement are used simultaneously. The novice may experience difficulty at this stage because *all* reinforcement of the undesirable behavior is not terminated, reinforcers of the desirable behavior are not in fact reinforcing, or an inappropriate schedule of reinforcement is used. If the problem or undesirable behavior is well entrenched, use of time out may be needed for a period of time, whenever the problem behavior occurs. If used properly, time out effectively terminates all reinforcement that may be operating in the situation to sustain the problem behavior. When the desirable behavior has attained sufficient strength, a change to a variable schedule is advisable in order to make the adaptive behavior resistant to extinction.

The length of time the procedures are used is, of course, dependent on the variables operating in each case, their effects on the child, and the extent of their success. Behavior changes are typically noted within a period of two weeks. As the child's behavior begins to change, the significant adults begin to respond more positively to the child and the new behavior begins to be self-reinforcing. That is, the child obtains satisfaction—reinforcement—for exhibiting the desirable rather than the undesirable behavior.

Though the stratagem is not appropriate to behavior that is not under voluntary control or cannot be performed by the child, the use of extinction and reinforcement simultaneously is, as subsequent chapters will show, applicable to a wide range of behavior that *is* under voluntary control.

Stratagem 2: Modeling and Positive Reinforcement

The theoretical discussion of modeling (Chapter 2) suggested that observational learning might effectively promote behavior not already in a person's behavior repertoire, as well as change nonadaptive behavior. If reinforcement is given to the model for performing certain behaviors, or the learner is reinforced for imitative or matching responses, learning is even more efficiently promoted. Learning can be further enhanced if these two procedures are combined with successive approximations to promote the desired behavior. The modeling and positive reinforcement stratagem combines these three important ingredients. Although this stratagem is more complex and difficult to use than Stratagem 1, it is a powerful behavior-change method.

FIGURE 8. Stratagem 2: Modeling and positive reinforcement.

Basic Steps	Procedures for Implementing	Specific Considerations and Cautions
1a. Obtain baseline rate of behavior to be changed.	1a. Observe and record behavior to be changed.	1. Behavior must be stated in operational terms.
1b. Identify the exact behavior to be changed.	1b. Write down the behavior that it is desirable to promote.	
2. Identify the successive approximations of the behavior to be modeled beginning with the least difficult or anxiety provoking.	2. Model (demonstrate) to child the first behavior approximation in the hierarchy.	2. Be certain that child can perform the behavior at each step. a. If anxiety associated with the behavior is too great, you must start with an approximation that can be performed.
3. Use continuous reinforcement for each execution of the modeled response(s).	3. Identify a variety of reinforcers, beginning with a primary reinforcer. a. Reinforce the first and each successively modeled response.	3. Avoid satiation by overuse of specific reinforcer.
4. Sequential modeling of each response in the hierarchy.	4. Model or demonstrate each response in the hierarchy. a. Reinforce the successful performance of each approximation.	4. Limit the number of modeled approximations to a few each session. a. Increase each modeled approximation to appropriate strength before proceeding to new approximations.

Basic Steps	Procedures for Implementing	Specific Considerations and Cautions
5. Change schedule of reinforcement to variable ratio.	5. If approximations have increased to appropriate strength, reinforce every third, seventh, etc. modeled approximation. a. Utilize tokens or points as reinforcers and set exact time to be exchanged for toys, etc. b. Provide a bonus reinforcement occasionally.	5. Allow child to exchange tokens or points immediately in early sessions. a. Not more than 2 sessions should pass without exchange being made.
6. Structure situation so that behavior generalizes to appropriate situations outside of treatment.	6. Reinforce child in the presence of those to whom the behavior is to generalize (parents, teachers, and peers).	6-7. Make certain that behavior has acquired sufficient strength before beginning the generalization process and using other reinforcing agents. a. Reinforce the new contingency managers.
7. Switch reinforcement to people in the situations in which child's behavior will be performed.	7. Instruct people in natural situation how to reinforce and have them reinforce child in the presence of therapist.	
8. Maintain records of behavior in which change is desired.	8. Carefully evaluate the effects on behavior change.	8. If change is not taking place at any point, analyze difficulties, return to an earlier step, and increase the strength of that approximation before moving on.

This stratagem is especially useful when a response (or behavior) does not exist in the client's repertoire, fear or anxiety inhibits the desirable behavior, or it is difficult to promote the desirable behavior because the problem behavior is extremely resistant to extinction. It is also effective in promoting a wide range of new behavior.

The essential elements of the modeling and reinforcement stratagem are presented in Figure 8. It is important to note that the behavior to be promoted—or changed—must be operationally stated, and the successive approximations to the terminal behavior must be clearly specified before the procedures are initiated. Once this has been done, the procedures are initiated by modeling or demonstrating the first approximation that can and will be performed by the child. Each successive response approximation is modeled by the child and immediately reinforced with stimuli of known reinforcement property. In any one session, a single approximation and matching response may be performed several times with appropriate reinforcement (see Chapter 6, Children Who Will Not Talk). Each response approximation is increased to sufficient strength. However, care must be exercised to make certain that the beginning approximations are not excessively reinforced. As the child makes progress in imitating (matching) the successive approximations, the earlier responses need not be modeled, and the child may not be required to perform them. At the beginning of each session, new approximations are introduced as the child demonstrates his capacity to perform those at earlier points in the hierarchy. However, if at the beginning of any session the child is unable to readily perform previous approximations in the response hierarchy, it may be necessary to backtrack to earlier approximations.

As the child performs those responses that approximate the desired behavior, a change from a continuous- to a variable-reinforcement schedule is introduced. Also, if a primary reinforcer has been used previously, it may be desirable to change to tokens or points that can be exchanged for toys or reinforcing events. If the sessions have been conducted in the psychologist's or counselor's office, it is necessary to instigate procedures that will help the child generalize the terminal behavior to situations in which he must ultimately perform them. Consequently, the modeling and reinforcement procedures are performed in the presence of the people who compose the natural environment to which the behavior should generalize. When this procedure has been carried out for a period of time, a new reinforcing agent (teacher or parent) may become the contingency manager. Finally the new contingency manager reinforces the desirable behavior in the natural setting until it is well entrenched in the child's behavior repertoire.

Stratagem 3: Role Shift and Positive Reinforcement

The psychological practitioner is often asked to deal with child problems that adults find so persistently frustrating they are unable to take effective action. The significant adults may feel that in spite of their repeated attempts to change the child's behavior, the conflict continues unabated. The child's behavior may not be seriously disruptive or injurious, but it is continually distressing to the adults around him. The child may be stubborn, passively resistant, or extremely dependent, or may exhibit a variety of other behaviors that create conflict in home and school. When faced with a problem of this type, the role-shift and positive-reinforcement strategy may produce the desired effects.

The theoretical rationale for this strategy is based on role theory. According to the theory, each of us enacts in everyday life a number of different roles consistent with our position and status in groups to which we belong. In enacting these roles, we assume behaviors and attitudes that are consistent with them. As we perform these roles, other people with whom we interact perform reciprocal or complementary roles. For instance, if you thank someone for something he has done for you, his reply (behavior) to your expression of appreciation is likely to be "You are welcome." His reply complements your role behavior.

If others do not perform roles that are complementary to or consistent with the ones we enact, we experience role conflict and/or disturbed interpersonal relations. Similarly, if our attitudes and actions are not consistent with role expectations, we experience anxiety, and role conflict ensues. Consequently, there is some pressure to change our behavior (role enactments) in ways consistent with the social role expectations and demands (Sarbin, 1964; Blackham, 1969).

When a person assumes a new or different role—that is, when a role shift is introduced—the behavior and expectations of others change, and the person tends to alter his behavior to meet the new role demands. Hence, the introduction of a role shift modifies the type of interaction that takes place between the person assuming the new role and others responding to it. For example, consider the situation of a teen-age girl who is excessively critical in most of the interactions she has with her mother. And the more critical the teen-ager is of her mother, the more hostile and restrictive the mother is with her daughter. Now, suppose you have persuaded your teen-age client to make a role shift from being mother-critical to compliment-giver for a weekend trial. If the teen-ager performs her compliment-giver role adequately, there is likely to be a dramatic change in the conflict. Once the mother begins to reciprocally adapt to the teen-ager's new role behavior, additional shifts are promoted in the teen-ager, and conflict tends to decrease markedly (Keirsey, 1965).

It can be seen, then, that the introduction of a role shift by one person necessitates an adjustment in the behavior of the other. The old ways of behaving are simply no longer effective. When a mother changes her role behavior in conflict situations with her child, a new response is elicited from the child. As he begins to perform a new and more desirable response, reinforcement of the new behavior tends to increase in frequency. If the mother continues to perform the new role prescription and also reinforces the desired child behavior, she promotes behavior change.

The essentials of the role-shift and positive-reinforcement stratagem are presented in Figure 9. Before its procedures can be initiated, the conflict situations and the roles (behaviors) that the significant adults perform in those situations must be identified. Their actions and verbalizations are carefully identified, for each of these elements has significant reinforcement value, either positive or negative. Once such identification of behavior has been made, the adult is instructed to perform specific role prescriptions in the conflict situations.

Let us illustrate by another example. Suppose a mother has the habit of constantly nagging her son each morning to get ready for school. The more mother nags, the more Johnny resists. To help deal with this situation, she is instructed to perform a different role. She is told to make the request only once that he get ready for school. She is instructed not to nag, criticize, or punish. If Johnny does not carry out the demand within ten minutes, she quietly goes to his room and indicates that she will help him get dressed. Johnny is allowed to assume as much of the responsibility as he wishes, and mother begins to reinforce these efforts. On each successive morning, the same procedure is followed, with reinforcement being given for each preparatory gesture. When Johnny has gotten dressed by himself, a bonus reinforcement (or reinforcing event) is given. When independent getting-dressed behavior has increased to reasonable frequency, tokens or points may be given, and the reinforcement schedule may be changed.

It is apparent from the example that several things may be operative when role shift and positive reinforcement are used. The mother's behavior becomes more predictable, the child's old resistance and delay tactics are inappropriate, and he gets reinforced for behaving differently. Since the mother's verbal behavior is no longer likely to evoke negative counter-reactions, Johnny's mini-rebellion is brought to a halt.

There are a few other elements that are crucial to the success of this stratagem. Obviously, parents must be cooperative and willing to follow the specifications of the role prescriptions. Consequently, it is often helpful to encourage parents to "give it a try" for a specified but limited period of time. Most parents who are distressed by a child's behavior will try almost anything for a *limited* period of time at least. One can even appeal to their willingness to try "an experiment," since their previous methods of handling the situation have proved unsuccessful.

Once the trial period has been agreed to, the role behaviors, as we noted previously, are carefully specified in each high-conflict situation. The role prescriptions are carefully discussed until the adult (which word can be understood to mean, whenever fitting, more than one adult) feels that he is able to carry out the role. The child behaviors that successively approximate the desired terminal behavior are identified and the adult is instructed in appropriate reinforcement procedures. During the trial period, the involved adult is requested to maintain records of both his behavior and the child's behavior in each of the conflict situations. In each of the sessions with the psychologist or counselor (which are initially very frequent), the records, interactions, and feelings of all parties in the con-

Basic Steps	Procedures for Implementing	Specific Consideration and Cautions
1. Identify specific role conflict situations.	1. Ask parent (teacher) to describe high conflict situations and identify the role each person assumes in the conflict.	1. Identify the exact behavior and verbalization expressed by each party in the conflict.
2. Select the most highly conflicted situations and introduce role shifts for the significant adults.	2. Prescribe role shifts parent or teacher will perform where conflict is most intense (where parent or teacher is most upset and child is receiving most punishment or negative reinforcement). *Example:* If mother is a nagger, prescribe role in which mother gives one command and then acts to get child to complete desired behavior.	2. By concentrating on areas of high conflict and prescribing appropriate role shifts, much of the negative reinforcement the child is receiving is terminated.

3. Instruct significant adult(s) on new roles to be performed.	3. Specify actions and type of verbalizations in the role prescriptions parent or teacher will perform in conflict situations.
	  a. Indicate to parent or teacher that you wish to try this "new procedure" for two weeks.
	  b. Have significant adult make anecdotal record of all conflict situations involving child and himself during trial period.
		3. For successful results, all actions and typical verbalizations in the new role must be specified for the involved adults.
		
		  a. Anecdotal records of adult actions and verbalizations helps involved adults and therapist determine to what extent role behavior is appropriate.

4. Specify with significant adult(s) the desirable child behavior in the conflict situations and set up reinforcement system.	4. Have parents state the exact behavior desired in each conflict situation.
	  a. Identify potential reinforcers.
	  b. Instruct parent (teacher) how they are to be administered in each situation.
		4. Supervise the administration of reinforcement.

5. Evaluate effectiveness of role enactments and use of reinforcement.	5. Have significant adult(s) review their own and the child's behavior in each conflict situation in weekly sessions with therapist.
	  a. Make necessary adjustments in adult role behavior as need arises.
		5. Make certain that the involved adult(s) keep records of their own and child's behavior in the conflict situation.
		  a. This procedure helps the adults become aware of the effects of their behavior on the child.

FIGURE 9. Stratagem 3: Role shift and positive reinforcement.

flict situations are reviewed in detail. Such a procedure helps the parents to adequately maintain the role prescriptions and reinforcements. In each session, adjustments in role and reinforcement are made as needed. If the involved adults are given adequate assistance in performing their role prescriptions and properly reinforcing the child, dramatic changes in child behavior can be achieved. One of the authors, for example, was able to dramatically reverse in two weeks the behavior of a child who was about to be withdrawn from the second of two schools, each of which he had attended for less than six months.

Stratagem 4: Behavior Contract, Positive Reinforcement, and Withdrawal of Reinforcement

A behavior contract is an agreement between two or more parties to behave in certain prescribed ways in situations denoted by the terms. As such, it defines expectations, demands, and responsibilities that must be carried out and the consequences of infractions. The role of each person is clearly specified, so that there is no question about whom any default should be attributed to. Because the behavior contract, as outlined in Figure 10, is definitive, interaction among the parties is highly predictable, and each person is therefore encouraged to assume his responsibilities. The specificity of the terms makes people face up to "the games they play" and prevents the conscious use of defensive posturing, such as readily invoked excuses. Since the interaction among parties is clearly structured, a sense of security and safety appears to be an important by-product of the stratagem.

The addition of positive reinforcement and withdrawal of reinforcement to a behavior contract further specifies the rewards and their withdrawal that depend upon the behavior of the child client. Consequently, as Keirsey (1965 and 1969) has indicated, clients who tend to be impulsive, excessively manipulative, or lacking in adequate behavioral controls may be helped considerably.

Prerequisite to the implementation of this stratagem is a careful definition of the child's problem behaviors, the situations in which they are expressed, and the willingness of the involved adults to try the procedure. The adults' motivation is usually enhanced when they recognize and accept the fact that other methods have not been successful in helping the child and that more effective intervention strategies are now necessary. Each involved adult (teacher, principal, parent, etc.) is interviewed individually, the dimensions of the child's problems are discussed, and the probabilities for success of the procedures are carefully explained. If there is some initial resistance to the procedure, it is usually helpful to persuade the adults to try it for a limited period of time (one to two weeks). With adult concurrence, the child client is interviewed, and his difficulties are discussed honestly without criticism or disapproval. It is suggested to him that a method can be devised that will "get adults off his back" and give him more opportunity to assume responsibility for his own behavior. After his acceptance, a group staging conference is held among all involved, to describe, explain, and discuss the terms of the contract previously drawn up by the psychologist or counselor.

As is true of any situation in which reinforcement is being used, the reinforcing stimuli or events must be carefully selected and varied to avoid satiation. In the initial stages, reinforcement is liberally administered (continuous ratio) until the desirable behavior is being performed frequently. Also, care must be exercised to insure that positive reinforcement surpasses the reinforcement that is withdrawn for undesirable behavior. To enhance the ease with which reinforcement is administered, tokens or points can be given for the performance of the desirable behavior and removed for the undesirable behavior as specified in the contract. However, if tokens or points are used, the opportunities to exchange them for reinforcing stimuli or events must be frequent. At the appropriate stage and in consultation with all parties—especially the child—a change is made to a variable schedule to increase the durability of the desirable behavior.

Throughout the period of the contract, the procedures must be adhered to rigidly. Each of the major people involved must be carefully supervised to insure that the terms are carried out. And even though the child may exhibit undesirable behavior not specified in the contract, such behavior has no influence on the terms of the contract. That is, reinforcement cannot be withdrawn that is specified in the contract. Such behavior is separate from the contract and must be handled independently and judiciously. Of course, the contract can be changed if adjustments need to be made to effectively promote the desirable behavior. However, these modifications must be jointly agreed upon by all parties, written into the old or new contract, and signed by all parties.

The stratagems that we have described in this section are only a few illustrative ones. The thoughtful practitioner can use his ingenuity to formulate others that meet the requirements of each case or problem situation. Indeed, the literature and research that are reviewed in the next chapter clearly demonstrate a variety of individual-intervention or change strategies that may be used to promote desirable behavior change.

FIGURE 10. Stratagem 4: *Behavior contract, positive reinforcement, and withdrawal of reinforcement.*

Basic Steps	Procedures for Implementing	Specific Considerations and Cautions
1. Identify exactly the behavior to be eliminated and the behavior to be promoted.	1. Write down the behavior to be changed.	1. Specify each behavior in terms of its overt expression.

2. Hold initial conference with those involved in child's problems.
  a. Discuss problem with child.
	2. Introduce contract idea to involved adults, indicating it will help child learn control.
	  a. Indicate to child that you wish to help him control his behavior. Suggest that a method can be devised to help him get things he wants and to get people off his back.
		2. Emphasize to each involved person that other approaches have not yielded success. Now it is time to take dramatic intervention procedures.

3. Devise behavior contract for presentation to all involved people.
  a. Contract specifies behavior to be eliminated and desirable behavior to be reinforced.
  b. Begin with the reinforcement of successive approximations of desired behavior if problem behavior is highly resistant to extinction.
	3. Hold group staging conference with involved people (child, parent, teacher, etc.) indicating exact contract terms.
	  a. Contract specifies consequence when child exhibits desirable and undesirable behavior.
	  b. Reinforcements (which are varied) and withdrawal of reinforcement are clearly specified for all behavior.
	  c. Points may be used for reinforcement and withdrawal of reinforcement. Child is able to exchange points for free time, toys, etc., any time he has sufficient number.
	  d. Make certain all involved people understand and accept contract.
	  e. All involved people sign and receive copy of contract.
		3. Specify clearly the role of each person and how all phases of contract will be handled.
		  a. Contract cannot be withdrawn for behavior the child exhibits that is not identified in contract.
		    1. i.e., reinforcement cannot be withdrawn for misbehavior not specified in contract.
		  b. Reinforcers for which points are exchanged *must be reinforcing.*

Basic Steps	Procedures for Implementing	Specific Considerations and Cautions
4. Supervise roles and administration of procedures.	4. Program is initiated the day following the staging conference. a. Check frequently with involved people to insure that terms are carried out.	4. Do not change schedule until behavior desired is being performed with high frequency.
5. Modify reinforcement schedule as appropriate.	5. When behavior has increased in strength change reinforcement schedule so that desirable behavior will not extinguish. a. Increase number of points required to get toy or reinforcing events.	5. Check to make certain that reinforcement and withdrawal of reinforcement are properly administered.

Therapeutic Intervention with Child-Behavior Problems

In this chapter we wish to devote attention to therapeutic methods that have utility in the treatment of a variety of behavior problems in children. Since our chief interest is in translating learning theory into therapeutic strategies, the applications presented here are based on learning principles.

We do not want to create the impression that the methods that will be presented are the only ones or the most effective ones, but the evidence of our own experience as well as the evidence found in the literature indicate that they do work. Moreover, we want to underline the idea that the employment of a method must always be considered in conjunction with the welfare of the child. The child's health, development, and adjustment should never be subordinated to the application or the use of a method. If it does not enhance his well-being or if it is injurious, it should not be used. Constant vigilance must be exercised to insure a positive result. Counselors and psychologists should treat children and not problems.

Most of the methods reported are based on scholarly literature or actual experience of the present authors in their work with children. The therapeutic interventions will be presented according to specific behavior-category problem areas, many of which counselors and psychologists are requested to work with. There are other categories of behavior problems that do not occur frequently in children; yet when they do, immediate attention is required (*e.g.,* fire-setting). No attempt has been made to cover the entire range of possible behavior or adjustment difficulties exhibited by children. Rather, a sufficient variety of problems and methods is discussed to enable the thoughtful counselor or psychologist to apply them to a wide range of problem areas.

Phobic Reactions

Since many adults and children have some type of phobia, an explanation of phobic reactions would be a proper beginning for our study of therapeutic intervention. It is only when a phobia interferes with a person's everyday functioning that it becomes a matter for concern. The deconditioning of neurotic phobias was attempted by Jones (1924) many years ago. The child she worked with had a phobia of furry animals. Counterconditioning was accomplished by feeding the child in the neighborhood of a rabbit in a cage—at first placed a considerable distance away from the child, but gradually brought nearer to the child's table. Toward the end of the treatment, the rabbit was placed on the table and even on the child's lap. Extinction of the child's phobia extended to other furry objects besides the rabbit.

Lazarus (1960) used a method not greatly different from that of Jones. He treated an eight-year-old child who had a fear of moving vehicles. The fear, which persisted for two years, was apparently related to a car accident in which the child was involved. Therapy was initiated by talking to the child about motor vehicles other than cars. When the child volunteered any type of positive statement about other vehicles, he was casually offered a piece of chocolate. Lazarus then set up a series of "accidents" with toy cars. After each of the play accidents, the child was given a piece of chocolate. This type of activity continued for some time until Lazarus was able to encourage the child to sit with him in a stationary automobile. At this time, the accident in which the child had been involved was discussed. The child was once again provided with chocolates as the discussion continued. Soon afterward, the child was taken for short rides in the car. On the seventeenth therapy session, the child willingly went for a ride with a stranger and traveled approximately a mile-and-a-half to a store at which the child bought chocolate. According to Lazarus, the child soon began to enjoy car rides without the inducement of chocolate.

It is, of course, not always possible to use the phobic object in a therapy session. If the phobic object is so aversive that the child will not go near it, or if it is highly impractical to deal with the actual phobic object, other methods have to be used.

Lazarus and Abramovitz (1962) attempted to eliminate children's phobias through the use of "emotive imagery." Although this method is similar to that used by Wolpe, his relaxation methods were not used. Their technique involved determining the nature and magnitude of the child's fears and arranging these in a hierarchy. The hierarchy ranged from each child's most to the least feared situations. The clinician then determined who the child's favorite television, movie, and fiction hero images were. When this had been done, the child was asked to close his eyes and to imagine some events which involved his favorite hero. Gradually, the clinician introduced into the story phobic items low in the hierarchy. As each item in the hierarchy was introduced, the child was instructed to raise his finger if he felt any discomfort. At this sign of discomfort, the phobic stimulus was withdrawn temporarily from the story, but later on, of course, was reintroduced. The method was continued until the most feared situation in the hierarchy was tolerated without stress.

Lazarus and Abramovitz (1962) used this method with nine phobic children ranging in age from seven to fourteen years. Seven children were considered improved in an average of only 3.3 sessions. Follow-up results indicated that there were no symptom substitutions.

Ritter (1968) used a method of vicarious and contact desensitization in treating snake phobias. In this study, the actual phobic object was present during treatment. Both boys and girls, their ages ranging from five to eleven years, were used as subjects. To determine which children had snake phobias, a snake-avoidance test was used. There were two experimental conditions; in both, the children had two 35-minute treatment sessions. In the *vicarious* desensitization condition, the children who had snake phobias watched their peers and the experimenter pet and play with the snake. The *contact* desensitization treatment was similar to the above condition but also involved having the examiner move around the room making an effort to have children participate with him. The results showed that the contact group had significantly greater reductions in avoidance behavior than did the desensitization group. Both groups showed a significantly larger decrease in avoidance responses than did the control group. Ritter concluded that group-contact desensitization is a very useful and inexpensive therapeutic method for eliminating children's phobias of animals.

The severity of the children's phobias in Ritter's study is questionable. The children obviously had some avoidance reactions to the snake. However, it was reported that only one child was afraid to enter the room when the snake was present. Children were also included in the study who were not afraid to briefly touch the snake but were fearful of holding it for five seconds. This leads to the conclusion that the intensity of the phobias was not too great. Perhaps this is why results were obtained in a total of 140 minutes, or two therapy sessions.

Bandura (1967) used a method similar to Ritter's vicarious desensitization, in which modeling behavior was compared with other approaches. This study was cited earlier, and it will be recalled that he worked with four groups of children who were afraid of dogs. The first group watched a child without fear of dogs interact with a dog in a party setting. This group had eight sessions in which the model interacted progressively more closely with the dog. The second group observed the same activity in a nonparty setting. The third group observed the dog at a party setting without the child model. The fourth group joined in the party activities without exposure to the model or the dog. There were eight experimental sessions.

A test for avoidance behavior was readministered and demonstrated that most of the children who had received the modeling treatment (the first three groups) lost their fear of dogs. A later study found similar results when the modeled behavior was presented in filmed performances.

All of these methods for reducing neurotic phobias employ a common principle: successive approximation. It will be recalled from the studies presented above that in no case were the subjects in the initial phases of treatment required to be in direct contact with the phobic object—even when the actual phobic object was used. When subjects observed a model, the behavior of the model was to successively approximate direct contact with the particular phobic object. Over a period of time the children with various phobic categories engaged in "braver" behavior toward their phobic object.

School Phobia

Though school phobias have many of the characteristics of other phobias, it was decided, because children with school phobias will be of special interest to many of our readers, to give the school phobia separate consideration.

The "emotive imagery" method of Lazarus and Abramovitz (1962) has also been used in treating a case of school phobia in an eight-year-old girl. Their method required the child to think of school situations involving a fictional character afraid of school. The child then had to give the fictitious character verbal reassurance about going to school. In four sessions, the school phobia was eliminated.

Patterson (1965a) has also discussed a method for working with school phobia in a first-grade child. The child with whom he worked did not want to stay in school unless one of his parents was present. The child was also unable to play outside without checking to see if his mother was still in the house.

During the first session, a reinforcing contingency was set up. A chocolate drop was given for each 30-second interval that the child did not look to see if his mother was still there. Use of this reinforcement procedure enabled the mother to leave the room and sit outside the closed door after five minutes. The child and the experimenter engaged in doll play. The play was structured so that when the child replied that the boy doll was not afraid of being alone, he was praised and received a chocolate drop. The themes of the feared situations varied from the experimenter's office, going to school, physical injury, peer aggression, playing with other children, and so on, until all important situations were dealt with and appropriate behavior was reinforced. These procedures proved effective and the child returned to school. The results were achieved in twenty-three twenty-minute sessions with the child, followed by highly structured ten-minute interviews with the parents. It required ten hours of staff time and twenty bags of chocolate drops.

Kennedy (1965) has suggested that school phobia occurs every year in about seventeen cases per thousand of school-age youngsters. He cited the work of Coolidge and the Judge Baker group who found two types of school phobia. The first type was a neurotic crisis, while the second type appeared to be chronic, occurring in families in which one or both parents had serious emotional problems.

Kennedy included in his study only type-one school phobias, involving fifty cases over an eight-year period. The treatment comprised several steps. First, as soon as the problem was identified, parents were encouraged to refer the phobic child on the second or third day after the problem occurred. Second, the parents were requested to handle the child's somatic complaint in a casual manner. Third, the child was forced to attend school and to stay in the classroom. The father was asked to take the child to school; the mother could visit the school if she wished, but could not stay. A structured interview with the parents was the fourth step; the parents were given instructions to follow, and received support from the staff. The formula stressed to the parents was that they were not to discuss school attendance with the child, were to be firm, and were to compliment him when he stayed in school. The fifth step was brief counseling with the child after he was in school for a few hours. Interviews with the child used stories that had as their basis the need to go on in the face of fear. Last, a follow-up phone interview with the parents served as both a source for data gathering and prevention of further school phobias. The phone calls were scheduled two weeks after treatment, six weeks later, and then once a year. The results (based on self-report data and follow-up with the school principal) showed that there was no evidence of any recurrence of the phobia or of substitute symptoms in any of the fifty cases.

Kennedy's method basically required parents to ignore all somatic complaints relating to school avoidance and to reinforce through praise the child's staying in school. Kennedy's approach is also interesting in that behavior incompatible with attending school was not allowed to continue and therefore was not able to be reinforced.

Though both studies reported in this section obtained positive results, their differences should be noted by the reader. The child in Patterson's (1965a) study had a more intense school phobic reaction than seemed to be true of the children in Kennedy's (1965) study. It will be recalled that the child Patterson dealt with was fearful of being without his parents even at home. In severe cases Patterson's elaborate procedures may be necessary, while for less involved cases Kennedy's methods may work more efficiently.

Children Who Will Not Talk

There are children who do not stay away from school as the school-phobic child does, but will not verbally communicate with others at school. The child with this problem will talk at home, but will not talk with peers or adults at school. Such a child is often found in kindergarten, but many times this problem behavior seems to remediate itself before first grade. Some children maintain their refusal to talk for many years. Despite this, however, they do appear to learn. Teachers report that they will respond to printed material and will occasionally answer "yes" or "no" by shaking their heads or pointing.

Though it is not known why children display this behavior, it is plausible that initially not talking is used either as a defensive mechanism or for manipulation. These children see school as aversive and frightening. By not communicating, they are able to reduce some of their anxiety in the school situation. However, although the anxiety tends to decrease after several months in school, the behavior still persists. It is possible that the behavior persists because both teachers and students tend to reinforce this not talking by giving attention to the child. Also, not talking activates many people to see if the child can be induced to talk, producing more attention for the child.

Two children who had a history of not talking at school were seen by one of the authors. As is typically true, teachers had tried a variety of approaches to stimulate talking. One teacher offered the child five dollars if he would talk to her; another offered the same child a big "all-day sucker"; still another placed the child in a room with his brother and friends, left the room and hoped that he would talk, but monitoring by intercom revealed that this procedure did not produce talking. None of these efforts worked; nor did the parents' threats of punishment.

By the use of appropriate learning-theory principles, both of these children were persuaded to talk with one of the authors during the first session. Since one of the children had not spoken at school for three-and-a-half years, this was notable progress. By the end of the fifth session, both children were talking occasionally to their teachers (who were present from the fourth session on). As a matter of fact, the method ultimately proved so effective that one of the teachers jokingly asked the author if he might reverse the procedures to "shut the child up."

Briefly, the procedures used were as follows. In the first session, both modeling and successive-approximation principles were used. As the child entered the toom, an empty cup was placed by him and a cup full of candies was placed by the clinician. First telling the child, "Watch me," the clinician moved his mouth in a specific way and asked the child to do the same thing. When the child complied, a candy was placed in his cup. The clinician then opened his mouth wide, and asked the child to do the same. Each time the child complied, he was given a piece of candy. Always modeling the response that the child was asked to imitate, the clinician also asked the child to pretend to blow out a match and to imitate various sounds. Eventually, the various sounds composing the child's name were sounded out. When this was accomplished, the child's first name was enunciated. As soon as the child had successfully spoken his first name, the same procedures were used to get the child to speak his last name.

In the second session, the same principles used in the first session (modeling and successive approximation) were again employed. The empty cup was once again placed in front of the child, and he was requested to perform the same responses. This required only one-fourth the time it had taken in the first session. The remaining time was spent encouraging the child to imitate one-word responses such as "good," "yes," and "no," and then to repeat three-word sentences. Finally, he was encouraged to speak longer sentences. Although a fixed-ratio reinforcement schedule was used during these two sessions, praise was regularly paired with a candy reinforcer.

In the third session, successive approximation, secondary reinforcers, and variable-interval schedules were employed. When the child entered the room he was told, "Today we are going to do something a little different from what we have done before. I am going to let you earn check marks as well as candy. The check marks can be traded in later for a small toy. You will not always know anymore when you are going to receive the candy and check marks, but every time you receive a piece of candy, it will also count as one check mark. When this card [containing about eighty squares] gets filled, you can trade it in for one of these five trinkets that you see." The child was given his choice of the toy for which he wanted to work.

He was no longer asked only to imitate the word spoken by the clinician. He was first asked his name, then asked to tell his grade level, the name of his school, etc. Each response had to be spontaneous and not motivated by desire to be eligible for the reinforcement. In the beginning, reinforcement was continuous, being given for every alternate appropriate response. Ultimately, he was changed to a variable schedule. When approximately fifty check marks were earned, the session was terminated and the child was told that next time he would be able to complete the card.

In the fourth session, the child's teacher was present, sitting in the corner of the room. The clinician informed the child that he had only thirty spaces left to fill his card in order to get the toy. Since the teacher was present, it was considered advisable to start with the same procedures that were used in the first session. A continuous-reinforcement schedule was used. That is, the child was reinforced for every response. After ten check marks and candies were earned, the teacher was requested to move to the table where the child and clinician were working. The clinician then told the child that now only the child's teacher would be able to record the check marks he earned. Many of the procedures employed in the second session were repeated. Just before the child approached his last ten check marks, he was told that the teacher would continue to give him the last ten check marks required to get his toy. In addition, he was asked to do things for her. The teacher, who had been instructed by the clinician before the session began, asked the child to do the things that were requested of him in the first session. As soon as the child acquired his last check mark, he was promptly given the toy he had chosen. A new card was taken out and the child was told that he could continue to earn check marks on the card. At this time, the child was told that the clinician was running out of candy. Consequently, the candy would be discontinued and only check marks would be given. The teacher continued to ask questions and reward the child by a continuous-reinforcement schedule.

The fifth session took place after school in the child's classroom. It was hoped that the previous sessions' effects would generalize to the classroom, the teacher, and the child's peers. At the beginning of this session, the child was told how many check marks he had earned previously and was allowed to choose one of five toys. The teacher continued with the same procedures that she had used previously with the child. She attempted to get the child to respond to her without imitation. At this point, a variable-interval schedule was employed. The session was terminated before the child completed his card, the child being informed by the clinician that he would begin to earn check marks in the classroom from his teacher—he would be able to earn up to five in the morning and another five in the afternoon. In order to earn check marks in the classroom, he had to go to the teacher's desk and respond appropriately to her. When the teacher implemented these procedures in the classroom, she was advised not to require the child to respond when his classmates were observing him. However, it was essential to have his classmates present.

When the child had earned ten check marks, the clinician drew up a contract with the child at the end of the day. (The contract method was discussed in an earlier chapter and will be mentioned again in a later section of this chapter.) Basically, the approach required the child to sign his name to the following statement:

> I,   , will earn check marks when I act as a student. A student is one who answers questions when his teachers ask him and one who talks to the other students when they talk to him.

The teacher was advised that if the child responded only to her and not to his classmates, she was to keep him after school with one of his friends. She was to take out her check-mark card without telling the child what she was doing, but making it obvious enough for him to understand. The child received check marks for appropriate responses to questions asked in the presence of his friend. When this was achieved, the teacher had the child's friend ask him questions. As the nontalking child responded, check marks were given. The teacher was told that if difficulties still persisted in the classroom, a few children should be asked to stay after school, and the same procedure should be employed. The use of these procedures in the classroom, in the presence of the teacher and classmates, insures that the greatest generalization effects will be achieved.

Another type of communication difficulty may be encountered: the child who is very resistant to making appropriate verbal responses. He responds to questions with a "yes" or "no," shrugs his shoulders, or says, "I don't know." A method that creates mild deprivation is applicable to a child like this.

One of the authors employed such a method with a child who resisted talking. During the initial session, the child was given salty peanuts and encouraged to eat them. He was told that he could have as many as he wanted. When the child became satiated with peanuts, he was told that he could earn some soda pop. He was instructed that he could earn twenty checks which could be exchanged for a soda pop. Essentially, to earn a soda pop the child was required to respond to questions to which a short answer was not acceptable. That is, a response of "yes" or "no" did not receive a check mark. However, questions were asked that did not create anxiety. For example, he was asked questions like, "What kinds of things do you like to do?" or "What do you do in your spare time?" Gradually, questions were asked that were more personal and relevant to the verbalizations being sought. He was reinforced for appropriate responses by receiving a check mark and praise. When twenty check marks had been earned, he immediately received a soda pop.

Since this method utilizes the creation of mild deprivation (salty peanuts make one thirsty), there may be some objection to its use. If this approach is not considered desirable, the check marks might be used to earn a small toy. At any rate, in the second session it is advisable to use check marks that can be exchanged for a toy. In later sessions, the reinforcement can be discontinued. We have discussed ways of changing behavior of children who refuse to talk; we turn now to children who have trouble speaking correctly.

Stuttering

It might seem to some that speech problems should be the concern of only the speech therapist. However, there are certain types of speech difficulties whose causes appear to be psychological. For our purposes, speech problems may be classified in two. ways: (1) those in which there is an apparent learning deficit and (2) those that are attributable to emotional difficulties. Stuttering is typically classified as an emotional difficulty.

Stuttering appears to be reinforced by the anxiety reduction that occurs when verbalizations are completed. One of the objectives of speech therapy would be to make anxiety reduction contingent upon nonstuttering rather than stuttering (Browning, 1967). Flanagan, Goldiamond, and Azrin (1958) have demonstrated that the degree of stuttering can be increased or decreased. Using a noxious stimulus, they attempted two different experimental conditions. In the first, a noxious stimulus was presented and could only be terminated when stuttering occurred. In this experimental condition, the stuttering increased. In the second condition, the noxious stimulus was presented only when stuttering occurred; stuttering decreased.

The study suggests that certain elements in a child's environment can affect his speech difficulties. For example, Flanagan *et al.* indicate that the child's mother may become attentive when he is stuttering and thereby reinforce it. If the mother at first decides to ignore the child when he stutters, but later on, when the usual burst of stuttering occurs, she observes that the child's stuttering is increasing (this frequently happens during the onset of extinction), her anxiety tends to increase, which may cause her to again pay attention to the child. When she behaves in this way, she is reinforcing the child on a variable-interval schedule. Extinction is difficult to achieve.

Browning (1967) treated stuttering in a very practical way. Although the child with whom he worked was schizophrenic, his methods can easily be applied to "normal" children. Browning first had an assistant obtain a baseline rate of the percentage of words emitted that contained speech errors. After this baseline rate was obtained, he trained the child to relax with procedures similar to Wolpe's. The child was subsequently brought to his office for ten-minute daily sessions for a total of eight days. While the child was in his office, he was not permitted to speak; if he wanted to talk to the therapist, he was told that he would have to go into the hall. This prevented the development of an association between stuttering and the therapist's office. Relaxation training was used to instigate a counter-response that could be used to reduce the anxiety that was associated with stuttering.

At this point, procedures were employed to help the child successively approximate normal speech. This phase lasted 35 days. At first, the child silently rehearsed each word before saying it aloud. Gradually, as the sessions progressed, the number of words used in a sentence was increased; then the number of sentences was increased. Up to this point, all words or sentences were preceded by a silent rehearsal. Eventually, spontaneous conversation was attempted. Correct speech was rewarded with marbles that could be traded in for toys; praise was paired with the marbles.

During each of the sessions, relaxation periods were followed by correct speech in order to associate anxiety reduction with errorless performance. At first, the therapist directed the child to engage in relaxation, but eventually the child himself initiated the relaxation response. To develop self-control of speech errors, the child was taught to stop speaking when speech errors might come about, relax, and then to successfully complete what he was about to say. Once the child was able to speak without errors, the training sessions were conducted in various settings so that the treatment effects would generalize.

Later stages involved the staff of the treatment center in which the child resided. The staff members were instructed not to respond to the child if he made a speech error, but as soon as the child repeated his statement correctly without stuttering, they were to praise him. However, at times it was also necessary for the staff to help the child discriminate when he was stuttering by turning their heads slightly. Sometimes they told him that he should try again to say what he was going to say. Because the staff acted as' social reinforcers for the correct speech of the child, it was eventually no longer necessary for the child to see the therapist.

Browning (1967) indicates that his procedures can be used in a clinical setting or by parents to help the child extinguish his stuttering responses. What Browning claims to do is first to make the response of correct speech available to the child. He then creates greater conflict in the child for stuttering by not responding to him when he stutters and giving an appropriate response when he speaks correctly. This procedure changes the speaking contingencies. That is, stuttering, which was earlier reinforced because anxiety was reduced when the child was finished speaking, now can only be reduced when correct verbalization is completed. Browning wisely cautions that the approach can only be used if the child is able to speak correctly. If the child were not to have correct speech available to him, this would of course result in increased anxiety and the method would be ineffective.

As Browning (1967) used positive reinforcement to reduce speech difficulties, so did Russell, Clark, and Sommers (1968), who were treating adult stammerers. When the subject responded to a visual stimulus—words and phrases on a screen—by reciting it correctly, he was reinforced. Administered on an intermittent schedule, the reinforcement consisted of viewing a new word or phrase, hearing a buzzer, seeing a flashing green light, and seeing a counter move back toward zero.

The results showed a decrease in the percentage of errors made on an oral reading task. There was some indication from self-report data that treatment effects were generalized to settings outside the laboratory.

From their work, Russell *et al.* (1968) concluded that the tendency among psychologists to use punishment or negative reinforcement—as has been done in many speech-difficulty treatment studies—rather than positive reinforcement to change behavior is an unfortunate tendency. However, as Russell *et al.* (1968) warn, subjects may resent aversive treatment; when positive methods seem to work as well as aversive methods in promoting specific behavior, why continue to use aversive methods?

Excessive Fantasy and Bizarre Talking

Everyone engages in daydreaming and fantasy. It is typically employed to gain momentary refuge from the demands of reality or to mobilize one's resources to solve problems. As such, fantasy is normal and may even help the person to better cope with day-to-day demands. However, when daydreaming or fantasy is excessive or is substituted for reality, it is nonproductive (Coleman, 1956), and there is need of therapeutic assistance.

Bijou (1966) has discussed the case of a four-year-old boy who exhibited excessive fantasy behavior. The procedures used to change the behavior were rather simple, but highly effective. First, a baseline record was kept on the child's fantasy for a nineteen-day period. During this time, the child was responded to in nursery school in the usual manner. That is, teachers participated in the child's fantasy play and restrained him only if it appeared that he might hurt other children; he received attention and understanding when it appeared desirable. The experimental period was begun on the twentieth day. The teachers were then instructed to attend to the child only when he engaged in appropriate play and not when he exhibited fantasy behavior. The result was a gradual decrease in the amount of fantasy behavior and an increase in appropriate play.

This same procedure can be used when a child is exhibiting bizarre talking. Applying Bijou's methods with the child to psychotic adults in a hospital, Ayllon and Michael (1959) demonstrated how psychotic talk that had persisted for years could be greatly reduced in about a two-month period of time. To decrease bizarre talking, response was made to the patient only when she exhibited appropriate talk; she was ignored when she exhibited psychotic talk. A method that combines both secondary reinforcement and modeling was used by one of the authors to treat a kindergarten child who expressed a good deal of bizarre talk—nonsense words, repetitious phrases, inappropriate singing, and verbalized sexual thoughts. After the third week of individual-play therapy sessions, another child, a few years older, was introduced. Prior to entering the sessions she was instructed to ignore all "silly" talk of the younger child and to listen when she was not talking "silly." The psychologist and the older child role-played some typical verbalizations that the younger child might express in order to train and desensitize her to the comments that the younger child might make. In the subsequent play therapy sessions, the psychologist attended to the model for appropriate talk and would make comments like, "Caryn talks so nicely, I like to listen to Caryn talk, I can always understand what Caryn is talking about," etc. When the younger child talked appropriately, both the model and the psychologist would pay attention.

The procedure resulted in a decrease in inappropriate talking and an increase in cooperative play during the therapy sessions. At home, the mother stated, the child was now able to play with other children rather than by herself.

The same type of procedure can also be useful with children who lie. Many people unknowingly reinforce children for lying. This is done by attending to the comments that the child makes and by attempting to "catch him in the lie." Focusing on the lying behavior, as was demonstrated for fantasy and bizarre talking, tends to increase this type of behavior. Ignoring a child when he lies and attending to him for truthful talk will often result in a decrease in lying.

The ability to control the ways in which clients respond has been discussed by Krasner (1962). He has indicated how client talk can be controlled through appropriate reinforcement. With children, especially those with more severe problems, the therapist may have to use both primary and secondary reinforcement to control either the type of behavior exhibited by the child or the type of talk.

Urination and Defecation Difficulties

Children who exhibit excessive fantasy or bizarre talk will usually not receive as immediate attention as those children who experience difficulty in urination and defecation. When the classroom teachers become aware of a child with toilet difficulties, they want immediate help. These children have often been successfully toilet trained at a much younger age, but many years later either one or both of these problems (urination or defecation) appear.

Various types of apparatus have been used in the treatment of enuresis (Lovibond, 1963) and defecation problems (Quarti and Renaud, 1964). Although these procedures have been successful, they have not been adopted by many professionals. One of the reasons for this is that the use of equipment can be costly to the average person (Wickes, 1958). Consequently, our discussion of the treatment of these problems does not involve methods which require equipment. If the reader is interested in approaches requiring an apparatus, the references above should be consulted.

Madsen (1965) has discussed the use of positive reinforcement in toilet training. Though the procedures he used were employed with a nineteen-month-old child, they can readily be used with older children experiencing elimination difficulties at school. Madsen's method required that a child be given a candy reward whenever successful elimination occurred. No pressure was placed on the child and she was permitted to leave the toilet when she desired. The child was told that she would be given candy when she eliminated in the toilet. Candy and praise were given for either urination or defecation. Once the child had eliminated in the toilet several days, she was encouraged to tell her parents when she had to eliminate. Eventually the child was reinforced only if she requested to be placed on the toilet.

This method can be adapted with children at school. However, as Madsen (1965) has pointed out, there must be a physiological readiness as a necessary condition for training. If this method is used at school, the child with the difficulty should be sent frequently to the nurse's office. Upon urination or defecation in the toilet, the child should be rewarded with candy. Since it is impractical in a school situation to entertain the child while he is sitting on the toilet, the child may be permitted to read comic books. Gradually, the frequency with which the child is requested to use the toilet is decreased. That is, at first he may be requested to go every half hour, then every forty-five minutes, etc., until the interval is appropriate. When these results have been achieved, the child can be told that he can decide when he wishes to go to the toilet. He should be rewarded every time he eliminates successfully in a toilet.

For working with more severe cases, Neale (1963) has suggested a similar procedure. He worked with children exhibiting encopresis, or involuntary defecation. In all of the cases children were previously trained but, as Neale postulates, anxiety had become associated for various reasons with the child's inability to defecate in a toilet. (Neale emphasizes the need for an accurate medical diagnosis to determine the presence of physiological causes before any techniques are applied. This practice is also very desirable in cases of enuresis.)

Since the children treated were in a residential treatment center, it was possible to take the children to the toilet after each meal and at bedtime. Some of the children were provided with candy and comic books to read while sitting on the toilet. These measures were used to inhibit anxiety reactions that had become associated with the toilet. To assist in the treatment of two cases, certain foods were given that provided additional bulk for the colon to work and to insure that the stools would not be painful to pass. When each of the children successfully eliminated in the toilet, he was rewarded. Rewards consisted of either candy, stars in a book, pennies, etc. Reinforcements were changed when it was felt that the child was getting bored or satiated. Neale believed that the most powerful rewards the child obtained were approval from the nurse and the child's own knowledge of his improvement.

Once the child was no longer soiling, the four-times-a-day routine was abandoned and the child was instructed to eliminate whenever he felt the sensation of need to. When the child reported a successful result, he was reinforced. If the child soiled his pants, clean ones were provided without any comment. This was desirable because often the child who soils has received much punishment.

Sometimes medical treatment along with behavioral methods might be employed. Lal and Lindsley (1968) cite an example where both were used. They were concerned with reducing constipation in a three-year-old boy who as an infant had had severe diarrhea. After the diarrhea had been treated for about three months, the child became afflicted with constipation and was able to defecate only if a drug was administered. Under Lal and Lindsley's treatment, in order to elicit a bowel movement, a suppository prescribed by the child's physician was used, but was needed only once during the treatment. Once the child defecated, the behavioral procedures were employed by the child's mother; playing in the bathtub and parental praise were used as reinforcers. The mother was instructed to hug or praise the child if he defecated in the toilet and to leave the bathroom immediately if he did not defecate while sitting on the toilet. She reported that soon after the reward system was begun, the child would ask to be placed on the toilet. In the beginning the child spent about two hours on the toilet, but this was slowly reduced to fifteen minutes. Also, the use of the bath as an immediate reinforcer was phased out. The results, confirmed by a follow-up eight months later, showed that once the behavioral methods were begun, the child did not have constipation difficulties.

Still another treatment approach in dealing with a child's elimination difficulties was described by Peterson and London (1965). At the time the child, three years four months old, was referred, he had not defecated in a toilet for more than three months, and while he was defecating he would hide. Since the child experienced pain when defecating, not eliminating was negatively reinforced.

The treatment was conducted over an eight-day period. Two types of reinforcers were used. Popsicles were used as primary reinforcers and parent praise as secondary reinforcers.

During the first session, the therapist attempted to hypnotize the child but was unsuccessful. However, the therapist continued in a somewhat hypnotic fashion to deal with the child's problem. Lying the child on a couch and beginning to stroke his forehead, the therapist told the child that he knew he did not like to go to the "potty," but that his parents very much desired him to. The child was told that he would subsequently do it and feel good when he eliminated. Arriving home after the first session, the child went with his mother to the toilet and eliminated. Both the praise and the popsicles were given. In the second session, similar somewhat hypnotic suggestions were used. The parents were instructed not to make any comments about the sessions. For the next four days, the child successfully defecated in the toilet. In the final session, five days later, when the therapist congratulated the child on his success and asked him if it felt good when he went to the bathroom, the child answered affirmatively. Asked if he intended to go regularly and not have any more trouble, he again answered positively. These suggestions were repeated several times in a hypnotic fashion. In addition, the therapist lavished praise on the child for his good behavior and emphasized the happiness that characterized the child's home. One year after the treatment was terminated, follow-up revealed complete remission of symptoms.

All of these procedures for treatment of elimination problems focus on the positive rather than the negative behaviors. This focus is especially desirable with defecation and urination difficulties, because the child may have previously associated anxiety with the toilet. In most of the studies reported above, candy, stars in a book, popsicles, taking a bath, etc., were paired with praise. In severe cases, some physiological methods were employed (*e.g.,* limiting the diet or the use of suppositories). Parents who were requested to implement the behavioral methods were able to do so. These methods seem to further show that elaborate equipment does not have to be used to obtain results. With parental cooperation and the skillful application of learning-theory principles, success can be achieved in many cases.

Timid and Unassertive Behavior

Unlike a child with any of the behaviors mentioned above, the shy, withdrawn child has been viewed by educators as having few serious difficulties. This was originally shown by Wickman (1928) when he reported a negative statistical correlation between the respective judgments of teachers and clinicians toward behavior problems. Since that time, however, educators have become more aware that withdrawn behavior can be a real handicap to a child (Schrupp and Gjerde, 1953). Consequently, when it appears in a classroom or in clinic situations, it is usually desirable to encourage more spontaneous, outgoing behavior.

The enhancement of more assertive behavior has been discussed by Wolpe and Lazarus (1966). Although their methods are specifically for use with adults, they can readily be applied to children. Wolpe and Lazarus believe that teaching clients to express their feelings decreases the client's anxiety level. That is, the expression of assertiveness results in a reciprocal inhibition of anxiety. However, care must be exercised in helping a person to become assertive, for assertiveness that invites retaliation will diminish attempts to be assertive. In the case of a child, this may be avoided by using successive approximation. For example, a nonassertive child may be given an assignment in which he is asked to assert himself in a mild way. Gradually, as he comes to feel comfortable with this form of assertion, more vigorous types of assertive behavior may be introduced.

In the initial work with a nonassertive child, the counselor may first point out why inhibited behavior is undesirable. Also, it may be beneficial to help the child analyze how a lack of assertiveness handicaps him in his daily life. While assertive training is being undertaken, children should be asked to observe carefully their relationships with both their peers and adults and to discuss them with the clinician. This will enable the counselor or psychologist to understand the child's feelings and also to gain insight into how he reacts in a situation when he is inhibited. Wolpe and Lazarus (1966) recommend playacting in training clients to be more assertive. During this time, children can be asked to reenact incidents that have occurred. At first, the clinician plays the role of the other person, later the roles are reversed. During the process of role-playing, periodically the clinician might wish to overdramatize his assertive actions so that the child will learn some new behavior through imitation.

A modified form of the use of role-playing for encouraging the expression of assertive behavior is presented by Wagner (1968). Although he used female, adult psychiatric patients, his method can easily be applied with children. Wagner had his patients role-play ten situations in which they were encouraged to express anger. Another person who was previously trained would accept the patient's anger and become apologetic for having gotten him angry. In another group, the patient's anger was negatively reinforced. The results demonstrated that positively reinforcing anger seemed to increase the expression of anger when compared to those negatively reinforced and those in a control group.

Just teaching a timid child how to express assertiveness through role-playing or giving him assignments will not be sufficient. Timid children not only need to learn how to be more assertive; they also need to discriminate when assertive behavior is appropriate. One way of doing this is drawing upon the experiences of the child and discussing the consequences and implications for being assertive in specific circumstances. The use of tape recorders, as well as videotapes, is beneficial in showing the child how he sounds and looks when he encounters someone who is being assertive toward him. Whenever possible, the counselor or psychologist should attempt to modify the child's environment so that he can obtain reinforcement for exhibiting assertive behavior. Too often, nonassertive children have not had the opportunity to learn assertiveness.

Bandura and Walters (1963) cite an earlier study of Bandura's where he compared child-rearing practices used with aggressive and inhibited boys. The results indicated that the children who were inhibited had parents who were basically nonpermissive and nonpunitive in their attitude toward aggression. This means that inhibited children have little opportunity to imitate aggressive behavior of their parents or obtain reinforcement for their aggressive behavior. Boys who displayed a good deal of aggression had parents who tended to permit aggression toward other children, but not toward the parents themselves.

Modeling is also useful in encouraging assertive behavior. Bandura, Ross, and Ross (1961) demonstrated the effect of modeling on aggressive behavior. In their study, they had a group of children observe adult models who were behaving aggressively; a second group observed nonaggressive models; and a third group was given no exposure to a model. After all of the children were mildly frustrated, they were tested for imitative behavior. Those children who viewed the aggressive model displayed more aggressive behavior than did the children in the other two groups. A similar study was later performed (Bandura, Ross, and Ross, 1963). The experimenters had one group of children observe real-life aggressive models. The children in the second group observed the same models on film. In the third group, the children observed an aggressive cartoon character. The results showed that all children experiencing the experimental conditions demonstrated significantly more aggression when mildly frustrated than the control group who viewed nonaggressive models.

As was cited earlier, when a subject exhibits low self-esteem and highly dependent behavior, modeling is more effective (Zinzer, 1966; Goldstein, Heller, and Sechrist, 1966). This evidence seems to indicate that the use of modeling procedures can be especially valuable for teaching assertive behavior in the inhibited child.

It appears from the studies in this section that aggressive behavior can be encouraged with appropriate reinforcement. Perhaps a combination of all of the suggested methods might be most effective. Approaches that include giving a child specific assignments in expressing mild assertive behavior that are followed by reinforcement combined with role playing of the new behavior may be highly effective. These methods may also be combined with modeling to encourage assertive behavior in a timid child. That is, if a child observes (and identifies with) an adult who is assertive, he tends to model that behavior.

Inappropriate Crying

In some cases, timid children cry easily. Often there are no real physical or emotional factors involved. When crying gets to be excessive, it requires modification. But excessive or inappropriate crying cannot generally be considered a serious behavior problem. Crying appears to occur for a number of reasons, some of which seem quite appropriate when the circumstances are considered. There are, however, some children (and an occasional adult) who cry excessively to manipulate others in nonconstructive ways. Crying may be used excessively to gain the attention of others or it may be a manifestation of excessive dependency. Under these circumstances, the behavior does not appear to be constructive and it may be desirable to change it.

Hart, Allen, Buell, Harris, and Wolf (1964) studied two boys in a preschool setting who cried excessively. Since they considered the crying to be operant in type, they used operant conditioning techniques (reinforcement and extinction) to reduce inappropriate crying. Teachers were instructed to ignore the child when inappropriate crying occurred and to utilize reinforcement each time he responded appropriately to a painful situation. Teacher attention and approval (secondary reinforcers) were employed. The results indicated that within five days after the treatment procedures were introduced, both children had a maximum of two crying incidents each day. Since the baseline rate (pretreatment crying) was approximately five to ten episodes per day, treatment appeared to be effective.

As is typical in many studies, the procedures were reversed. When they were reinstated, successive approximation was also employed. Teachers were told to gradually reinforce only verbal responses to painful situations rather than crying. Eventually, even verbal responses were differentially reinforced. That is, only certain types of verbal responses (those more socially acceptable) were reinforced. Only when the child responded in this predetermined appropriate verbal manner did the teacher use reinforcement. In both cases, crying was almost eliminated. However, in one of the cases, the teacher unknowingly reinforced the child on an intermittent basis for crying behavior when she thought it was eliminated. This resulted in the crying behavior being resistant to extinction, but it was eventually modified.

When inappropriate crying occurs in therapeutic situations, procedures similar to those of Hart *et al.* may be employed. Inappropriate crying can be extinguished by inattention, and reinforcement may be utilized to promote noncrying behavior. Secondary reinforcement (attention) is often sufficient to maintain noncrying behavior. Occasionally, primary reinforcement (candy) may be necessary if the therapist's attention and approval do not have sufficient reinforcement value.

As we noted earlier, inappropriate crying is primarily restricted to children and adolescents. It occasionally appears as inappropriate (attention-getting behavior) in adult clients. If such behavior is nonadaptive, similar procedures may be used to promote desirable behavior in adults.

Effeminate Behavior

Crying of the type discussed in the last section may often be a sign of timidity or weakness. Though this type of behavior is often annoying to those around the child, it usually does not receive the concern that effeminate behavior in young males obtains. This concern is a natural one, since harmonious interpersonal relationships require that each sex perform the roles that the broader society specifies. When a child (especially a boy) does not exhibit appropriate sex-role behavior, he is often the object of ridicule and may have difficulty adapting to the demands of the social environment. Consequently, appropriate therapeutic intervention is often desirable.

Kagan (1964) points out that in later years the boy who possesses feminine traits may become anxious that he has homosexual tendencies. Whether or not he does is unimportant, for his feelings and the anxiety it may cause him point to the need for behavior change. Kagan goes on to mention that during a child's early school years his sex-role behavior can be modified, but later in life one's standard of behavior is much more resistant to change.

Burns (1970) attempted to change the behavior of an effeminate third-grade boy. Observations on the playground and in the classroom revealed that the boy made three times as many contacts with girls as with boys and twice as many contacts with a female teacher as with boys. During recess, the child was seen with a small group of girls who often played with dolls.

The treatment plan that was implemented to assist the boy had several elements. The counselor recommended that the teacher positively reinforce the desirable behavior and extinguish the undesirable behavior. The teacher was encouraged to smile and verbally reinforce the child when he played with male peers and to ignore him when he played with girls. The child's parents were encouraged to purchase boy's toys rather than play materials used by girls. The father was urged to spend more time with the boy to enhance the boy's imitative or modeling behavior of the male role.

In addition to parental and teacher involvement, a male counselor saw the child three times a week for half-hour sessions. The individual sessions continued for four weeks. When the child talked about masculine activities, the counselor would display interest, but he would ignore the boy when he expressed feminine interests.

The results showed that after treatment the child spent twice as much time playing with boys as with girls. The time spent with the girls was only in talking rather than playing with them for the entire recess period. Very little time was spent with the teacher. A report from the child's teacher revealed that he engaged in many more masculine activities such as playing ball and playing with trucks and cars. Parent's reports also indicated less effeminate behavior at home. A follow-up conducted a year later indicated that play activities involved boys completely, but he still talked to the girls for a while in line and when going in or out of the classroom.

In dealing with effeminate behavior in a fourth-grade boy, Myrick (1970) had a physical education teacher instruct the child twice a week in developing skills in sports. The teacher would praise the child for all of the effort he made and occasionally let him demonstrate to the class a skill he had mastered.

The classroom teacher of this child was instructed to get him to interact with a popular male child. This was done by seating the effeminate boy with a class leader and having them work together on classroom problems. The purpose of the change in seating was to provide the child with a model. The classroom teacher also held two discussions that dealt with personal feelings and fears about new situations (such as making new friends). When the physical education teacher was not instructing the class, the child's regular classroom teacher used the same approach the physical education teacher used.

Five different measures were used to evaluate the results of the treatment. First, the amount of time spent with girls or boys on the playground was recorded. Fifty-seven percent of the child's time was spent with girls on the playground prior to treatment. After treatment, a major portion of his time was spent with boys. The second measure of change was lunchroom behavior. Prior to treatment, the child spent a good deal of time with girls in the lunchroom. Post-treatment behavior revealed a marked change to an almost exclusive association with boys. The third measurement was types of physical education activities in which the boy participated. These activities switched from passive activities (four squares, jump rope, etc.) to more aggressive activities (touch football, soccer, etc.). On the fourth measure, the child's sociometric standing changed from twenty-fourth to eighth in a class of thirty-three students. His scores on the fifth criterion measure (semantic differential) indicated changes in attitude toward school, boys, girls, and self. These changes were in the expected direction.

Both Burns' (1970) and Myrick's (1970) studies indicate that learning principles may be effective in changing effeminate behavior in boys. Each study used a male model (father or peer) and positive verbal reinforcement (praise) to enhance appropriate masculine role behavior. Although the boy client in Myrick's study was taught specific masculine (athletic) behaviors and nonmasculine behavior was ignored in the other, both elements appeared to contribute to the desired behavior change.

Aggressive Behavior

The section above dealt with effeminate behavior sometimes found among certain young boys. It will be recalled that their behavior was basically passive and nonaggressive. However, when behavior is aggressive, whether exhibited by a boy or a girl, it probably causes more concern to parents and teachers than any other type of behavior. In the classroom, on the playground, and in social groups, aggressive behavior disrupts ongoing activities and generally evokes counteraggression in others. Consequently, aggressive children are frequently referred to counselors and psychologists.

Those working with aggressive children have often assumed that the desirable therapeutic method is to encourage catharsis. That is, if a child releases some of his anger, he will have less need to be aggressive. There are some, however, who are beginning to question this view. For example, Nighswander and Mayer (1969) question the validity of catharsis in reducing aggressive behavior in elementary-school age children and maintain that catharsis may increase aggressive behavior.

It is possible that if aggression increases when catharsis is permitted, it results from the fact that children have not been taught to discriminate when it is an appropriate response. Some children need help in being able to understand events that elicit anger. When they do, there tends to be a decrease in aggressive behavior (Mallick and McCandles, 1966).

Obviously, children need to learn when aggression is adaptive and when it leads to punishment or negative consequences. Bandura (1967) cited the work of Chittenden, who attempted to teach domineering and hyperaggressive preschool children alternative solutions to conflicts that they might encounter. The children observed various scenes in which dolls reacted to a frustrating situation. The dolls first expressed aggressive reactions and then they expressed cooperative reactions. The results of the aggressive actions which the dolls exhibited were unpleasant, while the cooperative reactions were shown to be rewarding. The children who observed the actions of the dolls showed a decrease in aggressive and domineering behavior as compared with a similar group of children who received no treatment.

Gittelman (1965) has used procedures with older children that produced results similar to those achieved by Chittenden with preschoolers. Gittelman asked the children he worked with to note situations in which aggressive behavior resulted in negative consequences. Situations invoking aggressive behavior were listed in an intensity hierarchy from mild to severe. Groups of children were formed, and each member acted out these situations beginning with the least severe and moving toward those which provoked more intense anger. As each situation was role-played, more effective ways of dealing with anger were learned.

In more severe cases of aggressive behavior, where self-control is minimal, various approaches have been attempted. Graziano and Kean (1968) taught psychotic children muscular relaxation with a resulting decrease in aggressive outbursts. When aggressive behavior is self-directed, positive reinforcement (Peterson and Peterson, 1968), time out (Wolf, Risley, and Mees, 1964), and electric shock (Tate and Baroff, 1966; Lovaas, Freitag, Gold, and Kassorla, 1965) have been used to control the behavior.

The authors have successfully used a method to deal with aggressive behavior typically found in the schools. The approach is in part based upon the work of Keirsey (1965).[1] The persons most involved with the child (parents, teacher, and counselor) identify one or two of the most severe behaviors that the child exhibits (*i.e.,* hitting other children, throwing things, making loud noises, etc.). A frequency count is kept to determine the frequency of the behavior. A contract with the child regarding that behavior is drawn up. In it, the most reasonable time period that the child can control his behavior is stated. The behavior and time interval is listed on a written contract in the following manner:

> I, Tommy Adams, agree that I will try not to get into fights or hit. When I do not hit or fight with other children for a half hour, I will receive one check mark. If I should happen to lose control and hit or fight, a check mark will be taken away. When I have received twelve check marks, I may choose a candy bar or small toy. However, if four or more check marks are taken away, I will give up watching television for that day.

The contract is signed by all parties involved (teacher, parents, child, and counselor). Note that the withdrawn privilege must be something that the child likes doing, and it should be withdrawn for a maximum time of one day. Both parents and the teacher must agree to give check marks according to the terms of the contract. All other behavior should be handled in the usual way. It should not interfere with the behavior or behaviors specified in the contract. That is, if the child receives points or checks for not hitting, they should not be removed because he was verbally·aggressive, rude, uncooperative, etc. As the child is able to control his behavior for the stated period of time, the length of the interval should be increased.

One of the important values of this approach is that children receive recognition for desirable behavior. As soon as the child's behavior begins to improve, adults working with the child should use secondary reinforcement (praise) to further enhance the child's satisfaction in controlling himself. As a matter of fact, the authors occasionally find children who will indicate that they no longer need the check marks. They are able to control the behavior by themselves.

There are two other procedures that deal effectively with aggressive behavior. We wish only to note them here and refer the reader to the next chapter for a complete discussion. These methods are time out and systematic exclusion. It will be recalled that the time-out technique was discussed in an earlier chapter, but its application will be presented in the following chapter on classroom-management problems. It will suffice, at this point, to indicate their utility with aggressive behavior and also to note that their use is not confined to a school situation. They are equally effective at home, on the school bus, at Boy Scout meetings, and in other social situations.

[1]Since Keirsey's contract approach is discussed in the next chapter, it is not discussed here.

Truancy and
Excessive Absences

Truancy is one of the specific forms that aggressive behavior can take. It need hardly be said that truancy is damaging to both the student and the school system; the absent student has sacrificed the continuity essential to the learning process, and his absence, affecting the "average daily attendance" by which school funds are allotted, costs the district operating monies. In some districts, absenteeism is so high that it is profitable to employ a full-time attendance officer to keep children in school.

It is important to differentiate between the school-phobic child and the child who is excessively absent. In our discussion of the school-phobic child, we indicated that he experiences intense anxiety when he thinks about or tries to go to school. The child who is truant usually does not experience great anxiety, but he does not receive sufficient reinforcement to continue school attendance. Truancy appears to have a number of causes. Some children are truant simply to demonstrate their independence of, or resistance to, adult authority. Other children, typically culturally disadvantaged, receive very little encouragement from their parents to stay in school; home duties may have a higher priority than school attendance. There are still other children excessively absent from school because parents do not assume responsibility for the child or his wholesome development.

Michael and Meyerson (1965) have discussed ways of thinking about and promoting the school attendance of "drop outs." Their comments also seem applicable to children who are excessively absent or truant. Essentially, they suggest the desirability of making an analysis of the type of reinforcers available to the child in school and how often they are given. Also, they believe that it is desirable to identify the conditions which induce the child to avoid school or even serve to punish him. When reinforcement or the lack of it has been determined, a school program should be developed so that desirable learning activity is reinforced. If a token reinforcement system is skillfully used in the classroom, attendance and interest are increased, and learning is enhanced. The desire to learn will eventually be stimulated by the natural reinforcers operating in the environment.[2]

Another method, used on a small scale by the authors with children who are excessively absent, is the "triangle method." First, it is found out with what group of children each child comes to school. Each child who is frequently absent is placed with two other children with whom he is friends but who attend school regularly. The three children are told that they will work as a group and have a chance to earn toys, candy, and special privileges. It is explained that when all three of them

---

[2]Token system approaches are discussed in detail in the next chapter.

are in school on any particular day, their group will earn three points. This means simply that the earning of points is dependent upon the absentee child's being in school. The behavior of the other members cannot earn points. Hence, the absentee is motivated to maintain his friendships by coming to school. Also, because he can earn points that can be exchanged for toys, his status is enhanced in the eyes of his peers. Of course, the absentee's school-attending behavior is further encouraged by the fact that the two other group members tend to use some persuasion in increasing his school attendance.

Modifying behavior by the use of peers has been done by Wolf and Risley (1967). They worked with a child under two conditions. In the first experimental condition, the child earned five points for decreasing her disruptive behavior. Under the second condition, the child earned only one point (one-fifth of the previous amount needed to obtain the reinforcement), and each of her peers also received a point for her improved social behavior.

The results showed that when peers are reinforced for improved behavior in another child, the child's behavior is more easily modified. Using peers in this manner puts pressure on the child when negative behavior occurs, but it results in secondary reinforcement when the desired behavior is exhibited.

With children who frequently miss school on specific days of the week, it may be desirable to add an innovation to this procedure. When these days are identified, the children are told that on those days a "bonus" may be earned. The bonus they will receive is a "free-time ticket." The free-time ticket will allow them to see cartoons or a humorous movie in the cafeteria or counselor's office. Additional bonus activities may be added as reinforcements. The children can be allowed to earn thirty minutes free time on the playground or to visit with the counselor. Opportunities to choose from many activities are most effective. This type of "reinforcing-events menu" can greatly enhance the desired behavior.

Fire-Setting

Still another form of aggressive behavior is fire-setting, which does not very often reach problem proportions in children. Many normal children are of course fascinated with fire and enjoy bonfires, fireplaces, and lighting matches, but few carry this fascination to the point of lighting fires indiscriminately. When it does appear in problem proportions, it is important to treat it immediately.

Holland (1969) has reported highly successful results in treating a seven-year-old boy. His treatment, interestingly enough, was performed by working with the parents. The first step was to suppress fire-setting behavior through punishment so that new behavior could be learned. An object (a baseball glove) was used that was prized by the child. The child was told by the father that if he set another fire, the glove would be permanently taken away from him. At the same time, procedures were implemented so that adaptive behavior might occur. The father told the child that if any matches or match covers were found, they were to be brought to him immediately. During that evening, the father deliberately placed an empty match packet on a table. Since the packet was empty, it was assumed that the child would comply with his father's request. When the child brought the packet to his father, he immediately received five cents and was told that he would be taken to a store and he could spend the money as he wished. It was hoped that because the child was given the freedom to spend the money in any way he wished, the value of money as a reinforcer would be increased. During that same evening and on subsequent evenings the father placed packets containing matches around the house. The child promptly returned these to his father. The boy was reinforced each time that they were returned for a total of eight times. The value of the reinforcers varied from one cent to ten cents. It is interesting to note that during this time the father was instructed to tell the child that he should not expect money all of the time. This was done, of course, in order to place the child on a variable-ratio schedule. Match-finding occurred with such frequency, it was clear that even matches and match covers found outside of the house were saved and given to the father during the evening.

Holland (1969) recognized that the child might, if he found matches outside of the home when neither parent was there, have the opportunity to set fires. Therefore, a procedure was used to strengthen match non-striking behavior. About one week after the program was started, the child's father told him that if he wanted, he could strike a pack of matches while the father supervised. During this time, the father placed twenty pennies by the pack of matches. The child was told that for every match he did not strike he would receive one penny. Every time the child struck a match, a penny was removed. During the first trial, the child struck ten matches. During the second evening, the child earned seventeen pennies, and during the third trial, twenty pennies were received by the child, and thereafter the child would not strike matches. The father told the child that he would not know how much money he would receive or even if he would obtain any money if he did not strike a match. The reward varied from no money to ten cents. Secondary reinforcement (praise) was also paired with the monetary rewards.

The results showed that at the end of the fifth week, the child's fire-setting behavior was eliminated. Upon follow-up eight months later, the child's fire-setting behavior had not recurred. However, it should be noted that during this eight-month period, the father continued to use ratio reinforcement. ·

Holland's method combined both punishment (threat of taking away a highly valued object) and positive reinforcement (money and praise). We noted in Chapter 3 that a combination of these two approaches (punishment and reinforcement) might be useful under certain conditions. Holland's study demonstrated the utility of this combination. In addition, the use of continuous reinforcement with a change to an intermittent schedule at a later time also helped to maintain the desirable behavior. Holland (1969) did not assume that teaching the child to return the matches he found would generalize to a decrease in his striking of matches. Consequently, the match-striking behavior was dealt with separately.

The methods we have presented in this chapter are only a few that can be successfully employed individually with child behavior problems. In the next chapter, we will discuss other applications of learning-theory principles to problem behavior occurring in group situations. We hope that the counselor can thereby provide valuable assistance to teachers in managing distressing situations in the classroom.

Chapter 7

Classroom Management

Most elementary school children spend approximately twenty-two percent of their waking life at school. A major portion of that time is spent with one teacher or relatively few in some type of instruction in the classroom. We cannot, therefore, underestimate the importance of these experiences in influencing what the child learns or what he may become. If the experiences, learning activities, and relationships he encounters are positive, they may be of inestimable value. If they are not positive, his learning may falter and his assessment of himself and his capacities may be greatly devalued.

Skinner (1968) has noted that the use of aversive control in the classroom is much too frequent and rarely very helpful. Methods of aversive control often make children want to escape either physically or psychologically. Negative attitudes toward school, truancy, tardiness, vandalism, and indifference to learning may often be traced to the use of such methods. Therefore, it is not unnatural and is highly desirable that counselors and psychologists assist teachers in making the classroom a more productive learning environment.

Counselors and psychologists have not always been cognizant of the possibilities for useful consultative assistance that the classroom affords. Nor have other psychological services been well received by school people. As a matter of fact, as Barclay (1967) has suggested, counselors and psychologists have often been viewed as "visiting dignitaries" who mysteriously appear and withdraw children from the classroom. Frequently, counseling has been regarded as a mysterious "happening" that takes place behind closed doors. What occurs there appears to have little relevance to the goals the teacher has in helping children learn. When teachers seek help with classroom behavior problems, the advice given has little relevance to the realities of life in the classroom. The counselor's or psychologist's dictums to "give more warmth" or to "be more empathetic" tend to increase the teacher's frustration and despair. Such suggestions rarely have much functional value.

Because teachers are, like parents, significant adults in the life of a child, attempts to enhance development or to modify child behavior must include them as essential elements in the process of change. A teacher performs the function of a significant model upon which children pattern their behavior. The attitudes he assumes, the behaviors he exhibits, and the manner in which he administers reinforcement are significant variables that shape pupil learning and behavior styles.

Although teachers may not view themselves as powerful agents of reinforcement, the effects of the teachers' reinforcement properties are readily observed in every classroom. Indeed, every action, sanction, prohibition, reward, or punishment has some potential reinforcement effect. But these actions may not always promote the behavior that is desired.

Teachers are not always willing to conceptualize their classroom behavior in these terms. Extrinsic incentives may be viewed as undesirable or as elements that stifle the operation of intrinsic ones. Consequently, the attempts of a consultant to systematize or to more productively order the use of reinforcement may not be greeted with enthusiasm.

Some of these teacher objections may be overcome, however, if the consultant helps the teacher analyze the reinforcement that is presently employed in the classroom and the degree to which desirable learning and behavior are being promoted. Relatively brief observations and analysis typically reveal that a disproportionate amount of time is spent in disciplining children. Moreover, analysis of the effects of the common disciplinary measures is often persuasive and may enhance the teacher's motivation to implement procedures that are more efficient as well as effective.

Objections and Difficulties with Classroom-Management Techniques

Two major obstacles typically arise when learning-based classroom-management techniques are implemented in the classroom. First, as we have noted above, some teachers may have philosophic objections to their use. Second, some teachers may have great difficulty following the specific steps recommended by the counselor or psychologist.

Some teachers feel that the use of artificial or extrinsic incentives in facilitating learning is undesirable. Yet, as we have indicated and as Shostrom (1968) confirmed, many teachers use these as well as other more negative forms of behavior control. He noted that teachers often speak to a child in sharp tones, isolate the child, and use sarcasm or methods that create guilt.

Reinforcement is often equated with bribery, even though they are, in fact quite different. Bribery is typically used to stop something or have it occur because it benefits the person giving the bribe. Reinforcement, on the other hand, is used to benefit the person receiving it (no doubt it will sometimes benefit both parties). The intent of reinforcement, unlike bribery, is to teach the person a new behavior, while bribery is to temporarily alter the behavior. When reinforcement is used correctly, tangible reinforcers like candy, trinkets, money, etc., are phased out and the person's behavior will be maintained by social approval and so-called "intrinsic motives." Reinforcement is, of course, based upon scientific principles and can be used to greatly benefit those individuals who have deficits in their learning or behaviors that limit their effectiveness. Of course, reinforcement in the wrong hands, like other principles discovered in science, can be used toward destructive ends.

The second major area that appears to pose problems for teachers is the appropriate application of reinforcement. Teachers may not administer reinforcement immediately after the desirable behavior is performed, which may make it impossible to instigate the behavior. If teachers use a point or check-mark system, it is desirable to have a definite period each day when points can be exchanged for known reinforcers.

Teachers are often disappointed because the use of reinforcement does not dramatically change the specified behavior. Instant results (by the end of the day or two days) are expected, yet they are inclined to forget that deviant behavior has a long history and requires time to change. Teachers need to be reminded that systematic reinforcement of successive approximations may be necessary before the terminal behavior can be established. Thus, it is often helpful to maintain records to note changes in the behavior that is being reinforced. Changes in behavior can then be more easily seen, and teacher persistence may be greatly encouraged.

A teacher may prematurely terminate a reinforcement procedure because he feels it is doing more harm than good. Typically, this occurs when a child's behavior is being extinguished by its being ignored. During the extinction process some old behaviors may increase in intensity before they extinguish. When this happens, teachers may feel that the method is making the child worse. Such problems can be avoided by informing the teacher before the methodology is begun that an increase in the deviant behavior can be expected for a short period of time. Also, from time to time, there will be a spontaneous recovery of the old behaviors.

Another problem that arises with a fair degree of frequency is that of withholding reinforcement for the desired behavior because the child has misbehaved in some other way. That is, a teacher refuses to provide reinforcement that a child has earned because of another act that he has committed. For example, a teacher may refuse to reinforce a child for sitting quietly in his seat, because he has hit a child on the playground. The psychologist must emphasize to the teacher that when this occurs individual behaviors must be dealt with separately and when they arise. It must be explained to the teacher that if the child does not receive reinforcement when he has earned it, the desirable behaviors will be extinguished. The teacher may be instructed to tell the child: "This is what you have earned for completing your check-mark card, but you must stay after school [or whatever punitive methods he wants to use] for hitting someone on the playground."

The teacher must understand that one behavior does not affect another behavior. In other words, a child is not totally "bad," as many teachers will agree, for performing one particular act. Nor can a child be considered a "good" student because of one performance. Thus, when a child receives punishment, it should be for a specific act that has occurred; it should not be for all of his behavior.

Classroom Designs for Helping the Educationally Handicapped

Before specific classroom learning or behavior problems are considered, it seems desirable to describe briefly two classroom designs that have been formulated to help small groups of children. Our purpose is to illustrate that educationally and emotionally handicapped children may be effectively taught in small groups using behavior-modification principles. Hence, by understanding the basic design features of each of the two models we will describe, the teacher can more readily make applications to the regular classroom.

One of the more widely used and better-known classroom designs is Hewett's (1967, 1968) engineered classroom. It is designed to assist a class of nine children who have educational or emotional difficulties. Hewett believes that significant learning or behavior change may be achieved when three basic ingredients are designed into a classroom: (1) appropriate educational tasks, (2) rewards that are meaningful to the learner, and (3) appropriate teacher control.

Hewett (1968) believes that emotionally handicapped children have not acquired the necessary behaviors needed to learn. The goal of his classroom design is to teach behaviors that are required if successful learning is to occur. Hewett (1968) lists seven behaviors in a graduated hierarchy of seven levels: attention, response, order, exploration, social approval, mastery, and achievement.

The most basic skill to learning, according to Hewett, is the capacity to direct attention to a task. As almost any teacher can verify, most children with learning problems have difficulty paying attention. Daydreaming, talking to others, looking around the room, and getting up out of one's seat are all examples of inattention. In addition to appropriate attention, other behaviors must be learned. Once a child can attend to a task, making an appropriate response to an assignment is the next crucial ability. This means that the child must participate in the learning tasks. He must attempt to do his assigned work and respond appropriately to teachers and peers when called upon. The next skill required to be mastered if learning is to take place is being able to order one's behavior. This means following directions, obeying rules, completing assignments, etc. As Hewett points out, teachers are often more concerned with order problems in children than with any other behavior in the hierarchy. This seems to be because children with order problems are often disruptive.

When a child is able to attend, make appropriate responses, and be systematic, he is then able to learn exploratory behavior. This category of behavior requires the child to care about exploring his environment, acquiring accurate knowledge about the world around him, making independent choices, etc. The fifth behavior needed in order for learning to occur is responsiveness to social approval. This means caring about and obtaining the approval of others and attempting to avoid disapproval. However, it also means not being overly dependent on others for attention and praise. Mastery is the sixth prerequisite behavior for successful learning. It is the ability to utilize one's intellectual capacities. A difference between the child's ability and his performance is a lack of mastery of the subject matter. The last and highest level of behavior needed to learn is achievement. This is explained by Hewett as the pursuit of learning for intrinsic reasons.

To help each pupil acquire the basic skills or abilities considered desirable, the classroom is arranged into centers. There are order, mastery, and exploratory centers. The order center, consisting of such activities as copying designs, puzzles, blocks, etc., is designed to help the child to attend, respond, and appropriately order his behavior. The exploratory center includes activities relating to science, art, and communication, and is intended to encourage intellectual exploration and enhance social behavior. The third and main area of activity is the mastery center, where both pupil and teacher desks are located, and is where academic assignments are undertaken. Two isolated study booths are in this area for use when a child needs less distraction.

The centers are not only used as part of the classroom day, but they also serve as interventions when a child is having trouble with a mastery assignment. In this way, Hewett (1968) utilizes some respondent-conditioning methods. He believes that many children who are having emotional difficulties have negative attitudes toward learning. If a child can be desensitized and reconditioned to finding school pleasurable, learning will take place.

Before a teacher sends a child who is having trouble with his assignment to another center, she may try three different interventions. First, she may send him to the study booth; second, she may change the child's mastery assignment; and third, she may use social approval or disapproval in dealing with the child's difficulty with his assignment. If none of these methods works, the fourth step would be to give an exploratory task to the child. An order task, the fifth step, is believed to involve less stimulation and is sometimes more appropriate. The sixth intervention involves taking the student outside of class and giving him a task so that negative reactions toward the classroom and learning do not occur. The seventh step is for the teacher or aide to give full attention to the student. Two additional interventions, sometimes employed, involve placing the child in a time-out room for brief periods of time, or when all else fails, excluding him from school for the day.

Operant techniques are also used, because pupils have a work card on which they can earn check marks. These marks are given on a fixed-interval basis every fifteen minutes. A maximum of ten marks are given each fifteen-minute period. When cards are completed, they can be exchanged for candy, small toys, or trinkets. Check marks are given for all activities. Even when an intervention is used with a child, he obtains check marks—except for being placed in a time-out room, or, of course, when he is excluded for the day.

For a complete treatment of Hewett's approach (1968), the reader is referred to his excellent book, *The Emotionally Disturbed Child in the Classroom*. Hewett's model seems to have considerable potential for working with elementary school children with learning or behavioral difficulties, but he is cautious about recommending it for older children, because it is not as readily adaptable.

The second approach or model to be presented was formulated and reported by McKenzie, Clark, Wolf, Kothera, and Benson (1968). They designed a token-reinforcement system (using money as reinforcement for grades) to increase the academic performance of ten children (ages ten to thirteen) in five academic areas: reading, arithmetic, spelling, penmanship, and English composition. The children were given weekly assignments in each of the five areas, and the teacher aide recorded the number of responses completed and done correctly and the child's grade.

The teacher used various incentives (reinforcements) to encourage academic performance. The incentives used were the earning of recess if assignments were completed for the prior week, a free-time activity if work was completed before the period ended, classroom-helper jobs for pupils who were working or had made recent improvements, eating lunch with other children if classwork was completed before lunchtime, teacher attention for appropriate work behavior, and weekly grade cards that parents were asked to sign. The weekly grades were A, B, C, or Incomplete if assigned work was not complete. Parents were of course encouraged to praise A and B grades.

A unique feature of the motivational system was that of having the parents pay their children for the grades they obtained. The payment each child received was based on his weekly allowance as well as his academic performance. The total amount of money that could be received by each child varied from 70¢ to $3.50. The suggested method was to divide the total possible allowance by seven (music, physical education, and five academic subjects) and give the child this amount for every A. Half of the amount given for an A was given for a B and one-tenth the amount for a C (for example: A=50¢, B=25¢, and C=5¢). When an incomplete appeared on the child's report card, the amount that could be received for an A was subtracted. If, however, a debt was incurred because of the incompletes, he was permitted to do household chores to pay off the debt.

Parents were encouraged to allow their children to spend as much of the money they earned as possible. The children, who were expected to purchase items and activities they valued without parental assistance, were not permitted to earn money other than that received for their academic performance. These measures were employed to insure the reinforcing value of the money to the children.

The children were eventually returned to the regular classroom. However, the system was altered by including penalties for grades of D and F. The results showed that performance increased from 68 percent during the baseline period to 86 percent. Both reading and arithmetic attending behavior increased significantly and all pupils except one enhanced their academic performance. It is apparent from these results that the described system may have considerable utility in a public school setting. The token-reinforcement system can be administered with sufficient ease by the teacher, and the system is not costly, since parents provide the money reinforcement. In addition, it has the advantage of enhancing home-school relations.

Managing Classroom Problems

The following techniques are offered as illustrations of learning-theory applications to specific classroom and instructional problems, but are not meant to be a complete list of ways in which teachers can improve all phases of instruction. Since each classroom situation is unique, the methods may have to be altered to meet particular teacher needs. However, the specific learning principles must be carefully adhered to.

Inattention

In the preceding section we presented two designs (Hewett, 1968; and McKenzie *et al.,* 1968) that have been used in classes for the educationally handicapped child. As criteria, both studies cite increases in attention to appropriate tasks. Hewett (1968), it will be recalled, believes that attention to task is the basic skill needed before the child is able to learn. In the regular classroom setting, helping children to develop greater increases in attention is also a common problem. The methods described by Hewett cannot be used directly in a regular class. Modifications are necessary since Hewett's classrooms have only nine children, a teacher, and a teacher aide. The present authors have observed this method used in regular class settings with a fair amount of success, considering the number of pupils involved.

In a regular class, pupils should also be given a work-record card. At the end of each subject (not to exceed forty-five minutes in length) the teacher administers the check marks, though younger children should be reinforced after less time. The same number of marks (ten) as in Hewett's design can be used. In addition, the teacher may give additional points for numbers of problems, pages, etc., completed accurately.

The fixed-interval reinforcement schedule used by Hewett is easier to manage than a variable-reinforcement schedule; this is especially true in a regular class setting. However, check marks can be given to a few of the problem children on a variable basis as a further reward for new behavior. If this type of reinforcement is used, it is important that the teacher state the reason for the child's earning or not earning his check marks. However, it is not wise to allow the child to argue about check marks that are earned.

When a card is completed, the child should be able to exchange it for a reinforcer. Various types might be provided, such as candy, trinkets, a twenty-minute time privilege of doing whatever the child wants to do, a daily leadership role as projectionist, etc. (a method for discerning potential reinforcers will be discussed at the end of this chapter).

At the end of each day, the teacher should set aside a small period of time for children who have completed their card to select a reward. If the child does not complete his card that day, the next day he continues where he left off. With younger children in particular, check marks should not be taken away. When inappropriate behavior is exhibited, some check marks should not be given to the child, and the reason should be stated to him. If the system is to work, teachers should be generous, especially in the method's initial stages. This generosity with check marks should be directed to the children who are having the most trouble paying attention. Earning check marks will encourage them to want to earn more.

To ensure that this method will work correctly, teachers should give children assignments with which they will have success without difficulty, although they should be cautioned not to give children tasks so easy that they become bored and inattentive. If a child is having great difficulty paying attention during that day, the teacher should attempt to give the child an assignment that will focus his interest. She may ask the child to go to the back of the room and work on a puzzle or science experiment. When attention has been increased, the academic materials can be slowly reintroduced. Gradually, the level of difficulty can be increased. The number of check marks a child receives should be based on his capability and not on what others in the class can do.

Hewett's method is, of course, not the only token system that has brought about changes in attention or academic growth.

Wolf, Giles, and Hall (1968) used a token reinforcement system for low-achieving fifth and sixth grade children in a poverty area. The reinforcement system used was similar to saving stamps given in stores. Every child was given a folder that had different colored pages, each color representing a different reward. For example, one of the pages was for a weekly field trip, another was for money and items available in the "store," another was for long-range goals that might take several weeks, and another page was for daily snacks. When the child completed an assignment, he was given points by the teacher, who marked the squares. The teacher determined the number of points obtained for completing an assignment. In addition, bonus points were given for grades. Using these procedures, Wolf, Giles, and Hall (1968) were able to attain significant changes in pupil achievement. Though the classroom they dealt with had a small number of students with aides, the method might be adapted to a regular class setting. Also, in many communities part-time volunteer aides from various women's social clubs can be used.

O'Leary and Becker (1967) worked with seventeen nine-year-old children described as emotionally disturbed. They used a token-reinforcement system. The tokens were ratings placed in a small booklet on each child's desk. The children were told that they could receive from one to ten tokens, depending upon the extent to which they followed directions. The points or ratings they obtained could be exchanged for reinforcers that were available in the back of the room. The reinforcers were small prizes such as candy, comics, etc. Using these procedures, the teachers were able to significantly decrease the amount of deviant behavior in the classroom.

Token-reinforcement systems do not, of course, have to be limited to just elementary-school aged children (Broden, Hall, Dunlap, and Clark, 1970; and Nolen, Kunzelman, and Hering, 1967). The system does, however, have to be modified. What the points earn is one of the crucial factors for success in the junior high or high school program. Elementary-school aged children generally respond more favorably to trinkets, while older children usually choose an activity or special privileges. We will discuss choosing potential reinforcers later in the chapter.

Token systems are not the only way to help a child increase in his attention to task. Hall, Lund, and Jackson (1968) demonstrated how teacher behavior could affect a child's attention. They had an observer sit in the classroom and hold up a small piece of colored paper when a particular child was attending to his task. This was done to help teachers discern when study behavior was occurring. The signal was presented in such a manner that the pupil was unaware of it. Upon this signal, the teacher would verbally reinforce the child's attention, or ignore the child when he was not attending.

Hall, Lund, and Jackson (1968) state that the teachers did not have to pay more attention to the pupils than before the study started. It was the type of attention that the pupils received that made the change. The teachers who were involved in their study were initially unfamiliar with reinforcement principles. Yet, through in-class supervision, they were able to learn and carry out an effective procedure to increase attention to a task.

In the regular classroom, secondary reinforcement (praise) might be used most effectively with pupils who have milder difficulties in paying attention. It is the opinion of the present writers, however, that students with severe problems need tangible reinforcers such as toys, candy, or time-activity privileges paired with secondary reinforcers. Both methods should be discussed with teachers, and they should be helped to decide whether check marks or social reinforcement (social approval) are most useful in their situations. If the teacher wishes, he can experiment with one of these first and later shift to the other.

Refusal to Complete Assigned Work

Another problem similar to inattention is refusal to complete assignments—often one of the most difficult and perplexing problems that teachers face. With relatively high frequency, teachers report minimum success in getting all children to complete assigned work. Indeed, on any particular day, ten to twenty percent of the children may not have done so. Obviously, teachers can use help in dealing more effectively with this problem.

And for this, Addison and Homme (1966) have developed an ingenious technique, described as a reinforcement menu. When this procedure is used, children are asked to do a specific assignment. Upon the completion of the assignment, they are given the opportunity to choose one of several activities from the reinforcement menu. The reinforcement menu consists of stick figures engaging in various activities. For girls, these activities may include playing with Barbie dolls, playing with puzzles, coloring, or playing in a doll house. A similar procedure is used with boys. As soon as the assignment is completed, the child is permitted to select one of these activities and work on it for a predetermined period of time—usually limited to fifteen minutes.

This procedure was originally formulated by Premack (1959). Simply stated, the principle is that any response of high probability can reinforce any other response of lower probability. The method pairs a low-probability behavior that children dislike, such as completing arithmetic, with a high-probability behavior, such as playing with one of the toys. When a low-probability behavior follows and is paired with a high-probability behavior, the low-probability behavior often seems to increase in value to the child. When used in school situations, however, the procedure has one inherent problem. No time limits are set for when the child must complete his work. In other words, even though the child takes a long time to do his arithmetic, once it is completed, he is still allowed to perform one of the desired activities. Consequently, the teacher will have to be very flexible in the scheduling of his class activities.

Too often, in a regular classroom, teachers only permit the more successful child to engage in desired activities when school work is completed. By the time the slower child finishes his work, the period or day is ended. However, when this method is used, he is still able to select a desired activity. The teacher will find that the child will attempt to complete his work rapidly in order to participate in the chosen activity. It should be noted, of course, that care must be exercised in selecting work of appropriate difficulty for a child. Otherwise, assignments will not be completed and reinforcing activities cannot be used.

Daley, Holt, and Vajanasoontorn (1966) found the reinforcement menu to be highly effective with mentally retarded girls. When arithmetic was paired with one of the choices on the reinforcement menu, they found a great increase in the number of arithmetic assignments that were completed. Also, because it was paired with a reinforcement event, arithmetic came to be a pleasurable activity for many children. Daley *et al.* discovered that the girls began to select arithmetic as one of their choices on the reinforcement menu for completing a reading assignment.

Addison and Homme (1966) have indicated that this method can be effectively used with many age ranges, and that it has been used successfully with high-school drop-outs as well as grade-school children with academic problems. It has also been used in psychiatric wards and with Anglo and Indian preschool children.

The menu approach, they indicated, tends to create some pleasant conflicts for the child, since he may desire to do more than one of the activities. There is a way to reduce this conflict of choice. When the child chooses one activity, he can be told that he may choose another activity next time. Addison and Homme (1966) also recommended that for variations in the reinforcement menu approach, a special activity can be employed. Viewing cartoons, field trips, messy but fun activities, or even a party might be used. Since it is a "special" that is presented infrequently, it is easier to manage and has the motivational appeal of a rare event.

The effect of this procedure is an increase of motivation to complete school assignments. The effects may generalize even further. That is, there may be an increase in school attendance and a decrease in classroom-management problems. This procedure also has the added advantage of giving the child a chance to choose among a few events that he enjoys and therefore decreases the chances of satiation: the loss of desire for an object or stimulus. For example, when candy has been eaten in excess by a child, it is not desired and loses its reinforcement properties.

Addison and Homme (1966) have pointed out that this approach tends to eliminate much of the guesswork involved in choosing reinforcing events or objects. Also, when a child scans a menu, he may see something that he has not thought about, and these activities become highly desirable to him. By actually seeing it, the child is reminded of what is available to him. Novel events can be added to the reinforcement menu, as for example, one mentioned in the study. A child was given the opportunity to push the contingency manager or teacher in an office chair around the room. This particular event, Addison and Homme noted, was a powerful reinforcer for urban middle-class children as well as Indian children who had never left the reservation.

The reinforcing-events method is an inexpensive use of reinforcement with children. There are no tangible objects that must be purchased, and, as we mentioned previously, it allows each child to work at the speed at which he is capable. But even though the method is simple, practice is required to use it successfully in the classroom.

Increasing the
Accuracy of Academic Responses

Some children may complete assigned work but do it inaccurately. Obviously, inaccurate work makes it difficult to know whether the child is learning. Zimmerman and Zimmerman (1962) have reported how a child in a class for emotionally disturbed children continually exhibited very poor spelling, even though he received considerable teacher help and encouragement. Apparently, the help the teacher was giving was reinforcing the inaccurate spelling.

To enhance spelling accuracy, Zimmerman and Zimmerman employed behavioral methods. The child was first given a ten-word spelling quiz. When the teacher had scored the' test, she asked the child to go to the blackboard and spell particular words correctly. Each time the child misspelled a word, she did not respond. When this happened, the child often commented that he was a poor speller. These comments were ignored by the teacher. When a word was spelled correctly, the teacher complimented the child for his spelling. Each of the ten words were given to the child by this procedure.

When the child had spelled all ten words correctly, the teacher praised him, gave him an A and asked him to help her color some Easter baskets. As a result of this procedure, there was a decrease in the comments the child made about his poor spelling, and there was a decrease in the amount of time required to spell each subsequent word correctly. On subsequent occasions, this method was continued by the teacher with a great improvement in the child's academic performance.

Similar methods can be used with an entire class to improve accuracy of response. Lovitt, Guppy, and Blattner (1969) used a contingencies-reinforcement system to increase spelling accuracy with thirty-two pupils in a fourth-grade class. Before their experimental procedures, spelling lessons were assigned each Monday, and the words were presented each day of the week in some form for study. Each Friday, the class was given a spelling test on the assigned words.

During the experimental period, pupils were given a test on Tuesday, Wednesday, Thursday, and Friday of each week. If a pupil obtained a 100-percent score on any test (Tuesday through Thursday), he was not required to take the test on the remaining days of the week. During the time that other pupils were taking the spelling test, the successful pupil could participate in any other school-related activity at his desk that he wished. After ten weeks of this procedure, another was added. In addition to the free-time activity that was earned for a 100-percent accuracy score, the pupils were told that if all pupils received a 100-percent score on any day, the whole class could listen to the radio for fifteen minutes.

The results showed that prior to the experimental treatment, the median number of perfect papers each week was twelve. During the free-time contingency condition, the median number of perfect papers rose to 25.5. When the group-contingency condition (listening to the radio) was included, the median number of perfect papers increased to thirty. The last phase (listening to the radio for total-class performance) was recorded for a three-week period. Although it was effective, the class was never allowed this opportunity because all pupils did not obtain a perfect score on any one day.

Although the Lovitt, Guppy, and Blattner (1969) method was obviously effective, even better results might have been achieved if the radio-listening reinforcement contingency had been set at a lower level; total class performance might have been further improved if reinforcement had been given for total class improvement rather than requiring a 100-percent score for all and even more so if both the radio listening and the free-time activity were used simultaneously.

The methods reported in the two previous studies need not be confined to improving spelling accuracy. They may also be used with other academic tasks such as increasing the amount of reading or the number of arithmetic problems done correctly. All that is required is that for a particular academic task a reliable method for measuring response must be used. If reinforcement procedures are then used appropriately, accuracy of response in any subject may be increased.

Individualizing Instruction by Using Aides

The use of the reinforcement approaches we have described above may not be enough for certain children, who may also require individual instruction. Unfortunately, large class loads make teachers unable to provide the help some students need, and restricted finances often make the use of teacher aides unrealistic. In the school itself, however, there exists great potential for developing a better educational program. One of the methods with great potential is to use as teacher aides more able pupils who are succeeding to help those who are achieving poorly. Myers, Travers, and Sanford (1965) demonstrated that pupils were able to learn the English equivalents of sixty German words by having another pupil as their teacher. The task was highly structured and involved using the pupil-teacher as a reinforcer to his subject when correct answers were given. The results of this study showed that the person in the pupil role learned about as much as those pupils who were taught by the teacher in a typical class. Since the procedure was used in grades four through eight, it appeared to have considerable applicability.

Use of this type of method will take some initial work by the classroom teacher. However, once the pupils who will serve in the teaching capacity are trained, the teacher will be free to work with a few pupils who require her help. Flash cards can serve as an excellent and easy method to allow pupils to work with their less able peers. It must be emphasized to the teacher that the pupils who will act as teacher aides learn to give praise (secondary reinforcement) to the less able pupil every time he makes a correct response.

Greater class unity and more empathy on the part of more able pupils for those who are achieving poorly is the likely result of these methods. Moreover, the able pupils may develop greater facility in learning to interact with pupils who are having difficulties, as well as obtaining learning dividends themselves.

Riessman (1965) has discussed another variation of this approach. He used sixth-grade pupils who were having reading difficulties to tutor fourth-grade pupils who also had inadequate reading skill. He found that fourth graders were able to learn from this experience, and the performance of the sixth graders also improved.

Both of these methods, using able pupils to tutor their less able peers and pupils in the upper grades to work with pupils in the lower grades, appear to have utility in the classroom. However, these methods must be used intelligently. Pupil-teacher aides must be trained to appropriately reinforce peers who are experiencing learning difficulties. If such caution is not taken, the pupil-teachers may become authoritarian with the pupils they are teaching, and pupils are likely to become resentful if they are not praised for their work.

Besides pupils as aides, parents also can be used to give individual assistance to children in the classroom. Cowen (1969) used housewives to work in a counseling-type capacity with children. The parents received nonacademic training and then worked a half day for five days a week. They were paid $5.00 for each half-day. However, in spite of the low pay of the "semi-volunteers," their motivation was high and their efforts were productive. Patterson (1969) used parents to modify deviant behavior of their own children in the classroom. Training for parents required only six hours of counselor time. The results, though minimal, showed that parents were able to have some effect in reducing disruptive behavior of their children in the classroom. A follow-up study the next school year indicated that the children who received help from their parents were performing at an adequate academic level.

It appears from the studies above that parents can provide valuable aid to students in the classroom. Combining behavioral techniques with knowledge of reading, math, social studies, etc., may make these people very valuable in an educational setting.

Chronic Misbehavior

Having discussed behavior problems directly related to academic success, we will now focus on problem behavior that may interfere not only with one child's learning but with the learning of the whole class. The chronic misbehaver is one of the greatest sources of difficulty for the classroom teacher. Although shy and withdrawn children may have more severe problems, they are not troublesome and do not often come to the attention of the classroom teacher. Obviously, the chronically misbehaving child cannot be ignored, since his behavior is disruptive and may be contagious. Children frequently like to imitate their peers, especially those who obtain attention from others.

A procedure that is useful with chronic misbehavers has been discussed by Sulzer, Mayer, and Cody (1968); it involves a time-out room, with which the reader is already familiar (see Chapter 3). It will be recalled that the assumption underlying the time-out procedure is that children tend to receive reinforcement or peer approval for certain undesirable behavior in the classroom, but when a child is placed in a time-out room, peer reinforcement of misbehavior is terminated.

Although the use of time-out usually involves placing the child alone in a room with neutral stimulus properties, this may not always be necessary. A younger child may be placed behind a partition in his classroom for a specified period of time. However, regardless of the form of time-out used, the same general principles apply. If a child continues to yell after being placed in time-out, he should be left until he exhibits ten minutes of "proper" behavior. A child should be placed in time-out as soon as the undesirable behavior occurs.

As Sulzer, Mayer, and Cody (1968) have suggested, the use of time-out not only helps to control a child's chronic misbehavior, but is also valuable in helping the pupil develop self-control. (As a matter of fact, some pupils who have insight into their emotional difficulties may ask to be placed in the time-out room until they are able to regain control.)

When a teacher uses the time-out room, she should neither scold or devalue the child nor allow anyone to speak to him. The time-out room should have neutral stimulus, being thought of by the pupils as neither a pleasant nor an unpleasant place; otherwise the procedure will not work.

Keirsey (1969, 1965) has described a similar method that appears effective with more severely disturbed children. It is called "systematic exclusion." It essentially involves a contract, since it requires an agreement between all parties to perform predetermined roles. The teacher agrees to give the child a signal to leave the room at the first instance of his misbehavior. The child agrees to be responsible for himself and to go home for the rest of the day when the teacher signals him to do so. The principal insures that the daily suspension is carried out, and will use physical force if necessary. The parents cooperate by not scolding the child or even asking him the reason for his exclusion.

The method, as Keirsey mentions, will work well if the counselor or psychologist attempts to make sure that all participants understand their roles. Parents and teachers might at first be resistant to the method since they will say that being sent home is just what the child wants. Keirsey (1969) explains to parents and teachers that almost all children like school, but some of them have not yet discovered this. Being sent home soon makes it clear to the child that misbehavior results in exclusion. Parents may also object to the exclusion on the grounds that the child will learn little while at home. Keirsey responds by indicating that the child is learning little anyway. However, if this method is used, the child will gain the self-control necessary for learning.

Keirsey (1965) indicates that this method works well with kindergarten-age children as well as seniors in high school. It is a particularly effective system with impulsive children, because they are able to predict the consequences of their behavior. Predictability allows the child to feel more security, and, as Keirsey further points out, it simplifies the environment for them.

The authors have utilized this approach and have found it effective. However, we disagree with Keirsey's (1969) view that being sent home should be made pleasurable. When we have used this method, it has been recommended to the parents that the child be placed in a room with low reinforcement value: The child's own room is not a desirable place. The child should remain in the room with no reinforcement property until the time he normally comes home from school. Thus, being sent home does not reinforce the misbehavior.

Another method for handling less intense misbehaving can be performed in the classroom. There have been some recent studies (Hall, Panyan, Rabon, and Broden, 1968; Ward and Baker, 1968; Hall, Lund, and Jackson, 1968; Thomas, Becker, and Armstrong, 1968; and Madsen, Becker, and Thomas, 1968) that have shown that if teachers ignore inappropriate behavior of students and show approval for appropriate behavior, they can reduce disruptive behavior in the classroom. However, as Madsen *et al.* (1968) point out, the task is a difficult one. When some teachers have to ignore inappropriate behavior of their students, they become upset because the classroom at first becomes worse. Madsen *et al.* suggest that a training program be instituted to help teachers tolerate the periods of misbehavior of their pupils, and help them realize how they affect the behavior of their pupils.

Ignoring misbehavior and reinforcing appropriate behavior sounds simple, but it requires a good deal of change in typical teacher behavior. To help teachers institute these changes, counselors and psychologists can observe them in the classroom and give specific feedback about behavior of theirs that might be desirably modified. If baseline data were obtained prior to instituting treatment, then a continuation of rewarding the changes occurring in the classroom would serve to further reinforce teacher behavior if the results were positive. Data that indicated the method was not working might encourage the teacher to examine his behavior more closely.

Deficiencies in Verbalization

Compared to the chronically misbehaving child discussed above, children who are reticent or who lack verbal fluency may appear to be a minor problem. But if he is to learn, this type of child is, of course, just as much in need of help. Often, the culturally deprived child has been characteristically labeled as inarticulate and nonverbal. But, as Riessman (1963) states, these children are often quite verbal in nonschool situations. Riessman believes that schools must approach these children in a different way. But there are other children reared in middle-class homes who are also very inhibited in speech. Since these children cannot participate fully in academic activities, it is desirable to use methods that establish greater fluency.

One such method that teachers can use in helping to develop verbal fluency in children is role-playing (its procedures are discussed in an excellent book by Shaftel and Shaftel, 1967). When combined with learning-theory principles, role-playing can be effectively used to change the verbal behavior of children. Role-playing may be most effectively used to enhance verbalization in situations that are not responded to as aversive stimuli. Since classrooms frequently are seen as hostile by nonverbal youngsters, it may be best introduced in a more neutral setting, such as the playground or gymnasium. Once children are engaged in role-playing, this activity can then be transferred to the classroom. Dramatic play, a form of role-playing, can also be used as a method to help children acquire concepts and become more enthusiastic about learning. Essentially, role-playing encourages children to act out things they may be learning, problems that are unresolved, or situations requiring more thorough study.

Shaftel and Shaftel (1967) list various steps to follow when role-playing is used in a class setting. The first step is getting the group "warmed-up." To achieve this, the teacher may wish to read a problem story to the children. Containing elements of human relations, the problem story provides a structured situation that readily initiates the group into role-playing. When this has been accomplished, the second step, selecting the participants for role-playing, is taken. Children should volunteer rather than be assigned to roles. Ideally, children should perform roles with which they can identify. In the third step, the teacher should have the role-players develop a very brief plan of their proposed role-playing. When these steps have been completed, the teacher prepares the audience to be participating observers. The teacher may direct the children to ask themselves questions, such as whether they think the actors would really behave that way in a similar situation and whether the roles are true to life. When certain pupils have difficulty listening, the teacher may ask each one of them to observe a particular player or to think of the consequences of the actions. The fifth step involves the actual role-playing situation. The sixth step is a discussion and evaluation. According to Shaftel and Shaftel (1967), at the close of an enactment, discussion usually is quite fast, since most students are quite enthusiastic. At this point the teacher may wish to introduce another step—further role-playing. That is, she may allow the role-players to play their roles over again, changing their interpretations in the light of some of the comments made by their peers. The final step is sharing experiences and general discussion.

It is during the sixth step of discussion and evaluation and the eighth step of sharing experiences that the teacher must be careful to reinforce children for comments they make. At first, the teacher should reinforce by extending recognition and approval of any type of comment that is made by the children. She may smile, nod her head, and perhaps say something like "That is interesting," or "I am glad you said that." After children are able to verbalize, the teacher may want to reinforce more meaningful verbal statements. It should be remembered that the teacher must be instructed by the psychologist or counselor to successively approximate more meaningful comments by the students.

The ability to increase the probability of various types of talks has been well demonstrated (Greenspoon, 1955; Verplanck, 1955; and Krasner, 1962). Using a combined approach of role-playing and selective responding, the teacher can shape up not only an increase in verbal fluency but also more meaningful discussions. Riessman (1963) claims that youngsters who participate in role-playing in school tend to improve markedly in the discussion period following the session. Riessman believes that deprived children are able to verbalize to a much greater extent about actions they have seen, rather than respond to words alone as is typical of the middle-class child.

When difficulty in speaking is limited to only a few members of the class, role-playing may still be an effective method. Instead of involving the whole class, individuals can be worked with after class. Hosford (1969) worked with a sixth-grade girl who experienced great anxiety when talking before her classmates. The child was seen by a counselor once a week for six weeks. At that time she was requested to role-play giving a report in class. Each session involved a greater degree of report-giving behavior. For example, in the first session, the child practiced getting up out of her seat and going to the front of the room. She also read a short paragraph aloud from her seat. Each week the child gave a longer report.

The classroom teacher worked with the counselor to increase the amount of talking the child did in class. The child was assigned to a social-studies committee that had to give oral presentations every week. The child was told by the teacher to participate only when she was able to do so without any tension. The child gradually participated to a greater degree and was reinforced by both the teacher and her peers. By the end of the school year the child was able to speak in front of not only her own class but other classes as well. It was also reported that she began to volunteer to give oral reports to the class.

Role-playing is, of course, not the only way to increase verbalizations. Hart and Risley (1968) attempted to teach disadvantaged preschool children the use of descriptive adjectives in their speech. They found that the traditional methods were ineffective in changing the infrequent use of descriptive adjectives during free play. The traditional methods involved direct teaching of adjectives and providing social interaction with peers and teacher praise when a child used descriptive adjectives. It was decided to focus on increasing color-noun combination of words. Teachers were instructed to withhold materials the children usually used until the child asked for them by using a color to describe the materials. During the first three days the methods were employed, teachers prompted the child to use both the name of the object he wanted and the color. After the third day, a child had to use both the name of the object and the color without being helped by his teacher. The results showed a significant increase in the color-noun combination during free play.

With basically the same type of approach, Reynolds and Risley (1968) made teacher attention and allowing a four-year-old disadvantaged child to use materials contingent upon verbalizations. When the child requested the use of materials, the teacher would question her and require further verbalizations. The child had to respond to at least one question before receiving the materials. This combination (teacher attention and materials) proved effective in increasing the child's spontaneous verbalizations. Prior to treatment, the child rarely talked. If attention and materials were given when the child did not verbalize, her talking decreased to its former level. Reinstatement of the contingency quickly increased the talking to its previous high level. When the content of the child's verbalizations was analyzed, the increase was found to be only in terms of repeating requests for materials, but little increase in other types of verbalizations to the teacher or to other children. Reynolds and Risley (1968), however, were optimistic, believing that this procedure could be further used to require the child to exhibit different types of speech contingent upon teacher attention and materials.

Inappropriate Talking

While children of the type we discussed in the last section talk too infrequently, there are others who talk too much, and who some teachers spend a great deal of time reprimanding. Classroom disruption because some children are talking not only makes it difficult to teach the other children, but causes a great deal of frustration and tension in the teacher. A technique that has been suggested by Smith and Smith (1966) will help to reduce this type of classroom problem.

To use this technique, a frequency count of the instances of talking should be taken by the teacher or counselor. One method of doing this recommended by Smith and Smith is to record the frequency of occurrences of talking that goes on in a ten-minute period for each of three days. When these baseline observations are completed, the following procedure can be implemented.

The teacher should set aside a ten-minute period each day for at least two weeks. During the ten minutes the children are given an assignment which they will be able to complete by themselves, such as doing math or reading or doing their workbook. After the teacher gives the assignment, she should tell the students, "During the next ten minutes you are to work by yourselves. I will not answer any questions. There will be one rule: No talking."

The teacher must be careful during the ten minutes not to respond to any of the nontalking behaviors exhibited by the children. If a child sits and stares out the window, raises his hand, or gets up from his seat frequently, this behavior should be ignored. That is, the teacher should not respond to such behavior by looking at the child or speaking to him. The only time the teacher should respond to a child is when the child breaks the rule of no talking. All the teacher should say is "The rule please—no talking," or something similar.

Smith and Smith (1966) state that the teacher will notice a sharp rise in limit-testing and other irrelevant behavior. However, if the teacher is consistent, these behaviors will extinguish themselves and pupils will work on the task. It is important that in order to evaluate the results of this method, the teacher keep a record of the children's talking behavior.

If this method is used consistently for at least a two-week period, the teacher will notice that the behavior will generalize to other subjects and for a longer period of time. In addition, this technique demonstrates to teachers the importance of ignoring irrelevant behavior as a means of extinguishing it (Smith and Smith, 1966).

A similar method for dealing with excessive talking is presented by Hunter (1967). First, identify the behavior that needs to be changed (talking) and the desired new behavior (listening). This identification process should take place with the child, who has to be told that his talking behavior is inappropriate; he is also told that each time he talks, a tally mark (negative reinforcement) will be placed on the board. However, only the talker should know why. According to Hunter (1967), this will generally suppress the talking of most children. Once there has been a reduction in talking, listening should be reinforced. There are several ways this may be done: The child can be praised for not talking, a note may be sent home commending him, or he may be allowed to go home first at dismissal time.

Hunter (1967) emphasizes the necessity of constantly reinforcing listening so that it becomes stronger than inappropriate talking behavior. Once listening becomes stronger than talking, an intermittent schedule can be used. At first, the number of times listening behavior is not reinforced is small. Gradually, there must be an increase in the number of listening responses that have to occur before the teacher praises the child. As we have noted before, intermittent reinforcement of behavior makes it resistant to extinction.

Barrish, Saunders, and Wolf (1969) discuss still another technique to reduce inappropriate talking. Their method was employed in a regular fourth-grade class to reduce talking-out behavior and out-of-seat behavior. The class was told that they would play a game during their math period. The teacher divided the class into two groups based upon rows and seats. Children were told that one or both teams could either win or lose. The team(s) that won would obtain special privileges. The privileges were wearing a victory tag, obtaining a star by one's name, being first to line up for lunch, and thirty minutes of free time at the end of the day.

The class was told that the way they could earn the privileges would be to have team members avoid talking out or being out of their seats. Every time one of these rules was violated, the team got a check mark. To win, the team needed the fewest check marks. However, both teams could win if they had no more than five marks each.

The results showed a sharp decrease in talking-out and out-of-seat behavior during the math class. The experimenters then decided to apply the game method during reading and discontinue it temporarily during math. This procedure resulted in a decrease in the talking-out and out-of-seat behaviors during reading but a recovery of its former level during math. The game was then applied during both math and reading. These two periods were combined and treated as one long period. Disruptive behavior remained at its low level during reading and declined to its former low level during math.

Barrish *et al.* (1969) report a problem that arose when these methods were employed. Two students announced to the class that they would not go along with the rules. The teacher simply excluded their names from the teams and kept a separate score. If during the free-time activity either child refused to work he was kept after school.

The studies in this section clearly illustrate that a common behavior problem such as talking without permission can be effectively reduced. The same methods might be applied to any other disruptive behavior occurring in the classroom.

Reducing Negative Effects of Peer Reinforcement

In the last section we discussed a study by Barrish *et al.* (1969) that used peer pressure to reduce talking-out and out-of-seat behavior. In some instances, peer pressure or attention can, of course, be quite negative to the classroom teacher who may be attempting to extinguish a child's behavior. Although approval may be withheld because of a child's deviant behavior, he may be getting approval from his peers. This problem will tend to increase as the child gets older, since he will not rely on secondary reinforcement (praise) from adults; instead he will look more to his peers for reinforcement. Obviously, to promote the type of behavior desired, reinforcement administered by peers must be systematically applied or brought under teacher control.

Reducing those effects of peer influence (reinforcement) that sustain undesirable behavior can be achieved through the presentation of a positive reinforcer as well as by a response contingent on withdrawal of reinforcement. An example of this type was demonstrated by Carlson *et al.* (1968). They wished to control the behavior of a child with severe temper tantrums. It was observed that the child was receiving a good deal of attention from the school staff. Consequently, the staff members were instructed to use firmer methods with the child, such as putting her at her desk when the tantrum behavior occurred and holding her there and attempting whenever possible to ignore her deviant behavior.

But the common problem of peer attention was observed: When the child engaged in tantrum behavior, the other children looked at her. A simple method was devised to handle this problem. A primary reinforcer was used with other class members. Children were given a candy treat when they did not turn around to watch the girl who was exhibiting the deviant behavior. If a class member did attend to the deviant behavior, negative reinforcement was used by removing the candy placed at the side of each child's desk. Candy was also given intermittently to the children in the classroom so that they would not provoke the girl to have tantrums. In addition to the candy treat, the children in the classroom were allowed to have a class party when the child who had temper tantrums exhibited four half-days of nontantrum behavior. At this time, the child who had exhibited the deviant behavior distributed the candy to the rest of the class, and thus her peer acceptance was increased.

Patterson (1965b) believes that the more a behavior is valued by peers, the more that behavior is likely to elicit reinforcement. However, this can be used in constructive manners. Children depend upon peers to get their reinforcement, and increasing peer pressure can cause a child to change his behavior. Patterson used a technique similar to Carlson's *et al.* with a hyperactive child. To assist this child in improving his behavior, he told the other children in the class that the subject was having trouble learning and sitting still; they were made part of the experiment to teach the child more appropriate behavior. They were told that the hyperactive child would earn a piece of candy from time to time, and when he accumulated enough candy it would be divided up among the class. To help the hyperactive child earn candy, other class members were asked not to pay attention to him.

Another procedure for decreasing the effects of peer reinforcement in sustaining deviant behavior was mentioned earlier. Discussing the time-out procedure, Sulzer, Mayer, and Cody (1968) stated that this method removed the opportunity for a student to receive essential reinforcement from his peers. The time-out procedure can be further extended: When peers reinforce the undesirable behavior of another, both the offender and the child who reinforces the offending behavior should be placed in a time-out room. In this way, children learn to ignore deviant behavior in their peers.

If a check-mark system is being used in a classroom, as discussed earlier, points can be given to the children who do not reinforce deviant behavior in their peers. For example, when a child turns to talk to another child and the second child does not respond, the second child should be given check marks for exhibiting good pupil behavior. In the same manner, pupils who ignore a peer who is exhibiting deviant behavior can also be rewarded with bonus check marks.

Dickinson (1967) has also suggested a method to change the manner in which a child seeks reinforcement from his peers. When a child exhibits appropriate behavior for a designated period of time, he is permitted, if he so desires, to tell jokes in front of the class. It can be seen how obtaining reinforcement for joke-telling behavior might decrease the need for seeking reinforcement of deviant behavior. Also, since being able to tell jokes is contingent upon exhibiting appropriate behavior, the probability of appropriate-behavior occurring tends to increase.

The methods we have discussed show that the teacher can have control over the extent and manner in which children receive reinforcement from their peers. Counselors and psychologists can help teachers increase the number of situations in which children can produce positive effects on each other. However, it is not implied that a teacher can eliminate the total effects of peer influence on deviant behavior, but rather that she can greatly decrease the number of times the deviant behavior will occur.

Peer Rejection and Social Isolation

In some ways this section may appear to conflict with the preceding section. For here we are concerned with helping children who are shy, withdrawn, and rejected to become more desirable to their peers. Nevertheless, some of the methods discussed in the preceding section can be used. For example, the method that Patterson (1965b) used with a hyperactive child readily applies. That is, if a child exhibits socially acceptable behavior rather than deviant behavior, other class members receive a reinforcement. Such a procedure can increase the child's status with his peers.

The use of peer models (Sulzer, Mayer, and Cody, 1968) might help a child learn more desirable behavior. For example, seating a child who exhibits deviant behavior with a child who obtains positive reinforcement from his peers can be readily used in the regular classroom. The process of modeling can be greatly enhanced when the teacher praises the model for good work habits. The more specific the teacher is in defining these good behaviors, the greater will be the help to the child. However, teachers must be cautioned not to use the same child as a model consistently. The overuse of the same child as a model results in his getting disproportionate praise and being labeled as "teacher's pet." Such a label may reduce children's desires to imitate the model's behavior.

Sometimes children can learn to model the behavior of a film character. O'Connor (1969) presented a 23-minute film of a child interacting in a nursery school. Each of its eleven scenes showed the child gradually engaging in more and more social interaction followed by reinforcing consequences. The preschool children who viewed the movie increased their social interaction, while a control group showed no change.

Barclay (1967) demonstrated that the social acceptance of children who were formerly rejected could be increased by planned intervention. In his study, Barclay asked the classroom teacher to appoint the low-status children in the classroom as monitors in the hall and to have them perform errands. Teachers were further instructed to reward the low-status children for appropriate behavior and for displaying any interest in learning. Procedures were also designed in which low-status children could participate with pupils in their class as equals or superiors. Attempts were made to break up cliques in the classroom. Activities were designed that required mutual cooperation for success and were as unthreatening to the low-status children as possible. Barclay used role-playing in which low-status children played the hero roles and a spelling game in which popular and unpopular children worked together to spell words correctly and obtain rewards of candy. Although his results were not significant on all of the criteria, they did demonstrate the significant utility of his methods in changing the sociometric status of children.

Some of the methods that were suggested for use in increasing verbal fluency with children can be utilized here. That is, successive approximation may be used to encourage social participation. However, it must be used skillfully; Bandura (1967) has indicated how a teacher can mistakenly reinforce or fail to decrease the extent of a child's withdrawal behavior by utilizing well-intentioned but inappropriate reinforcement procedures: A child who is in a corner by himself and wishes no contact with his peers will often receive attention from the teacher, which can reinforce the child's withdrawal from the group. In a study cited by Bandura, a teacher reversed the process and used the principle of successive approximation. The child was only given attention by the teacher when he approximated some type of interaction with his peers. At first the child received attention (reinforcement) from the teacher when he merely looked toward a group of his classmates at play. Later on, to receive reinforcement he was required to slowly approach the group. By these successive steps, the teacher was able to integrate the child into classroom play groups.

The mistake that the teacher in the cited study made can be corrected relatively easily. At first, the teacher should be praised for his interest in the child. Subsequently, he may be told how he can use his attention in a more constructive fashion. During the teacher's initial attempts, learning how to successively approximate the appropriate terminal behavior may require considerable assistance.

Disruptive Behavior in the Cafeteria

Though not a classroom problem, the last behavior problem we will deal with in this chapter often causes difficulty for teachers. We are speaking here of disruptive behavior that occurs at lunchtime. At any one time, there are large numbers of children in the cafeteria, and lunchtime occurs after children have been confined for a long period of time. Consequently, they are naturally prone to be more active and disorderly. Yet, since a teacher's class is on public display before fellow teachers and the school principal, they feel a particular need to maintain order.

A method that may have some utility in a situation like this has been suggested by Baer (1962). Baer has demonstrated that withdrawing positive reinforcement when a certain behavior is occurring will reduce its frequency. Although Baer's method was used in a different context, the same procedures might be applied to cafeteria disorder. The principle may be appropriately applied by setting up a record player in the cafeteria, with loudspeakers, so that it can be heard by all pupils who are eating in the cafeteria; the music played should be pleasant to most children so that it has reinforcing characteristics. When the teacher in charge feels that the cafeteria noise is getting too loud, then the positive reinforcement (music) can be withdrawn. As soon as the noise is reduced, the music is continued.

Another approach that might be utilized is similar to the triangle technique mentioned in the last chapter. The teacher divides her class into groups of three. Each child in the group becomes a monitor of the other two children's cafeteria behavior. In other words, every one of the three children is observed by the other two children as well as being a monitor for the peers in his triangle. To make the technique operable, a few simple rules have to be explained by the teacher. First, the teacher should tell the class that they can earn up to four points for exhibiting good cafeteria behavior. Each child is told that he begins with a total of four points. When a child's behavior is too noisy he is informed by one of the monitors, and one point is lost. On each subsequent occasion, a point is deducted for noisy behavior. Moreover, if a pupil hits another or throws food, all four points are eliminated. Similarly, being reprimanded by a teacher for excessive talking might result in a loss of two points. When a total of twenty points has been accumulated by a pupil, he should be able to exchange the points for an activity privilege, inexpensive trinket, or even a dessert. After this procedure has been in operation for two weeks, the teacher can gradually increase the number of points required to obtain the trinket or activity privilege. To ensure some success, as soon as the pupils return to the classroom, the teacher should have them write on a piece of paper the names of the two pupils for whom they were monitors and rate them according to the points they feel these two pupils deserve. Furthermore, the pupil should rate himself as to how many points he feels he has earned in the cafeteria. If two monitors disagree, an average of the two marks should be taken. By following the latter procedure, pupils learn to discern when their behavior is inappropriate. Also, the use of pupil monitors in small groups is a way to help pupils learn responsibility.

For extreme behavior deviations in the cafeteria, a time-out procedure may be used. To make this procedure operative, individual tables or desks need to be brought into the cafeteria. They should be placed at the corner of each wall, and if necessary, one in the middle of each wall. Children who become disruptive after appropriate warning are moved to one of these tables and isolated from the rest of their peers for a ten-minute period. A second infraction of the rules might result in a two- or three-day suspension from being able to eat in the cafeteria. These students might be forced to eat in a classroom so that it is not possible to talk to other children. If, in addition, recess is made contingent on proper cafeteria behavior, the disruptive behavior may further decrease. It is important that these rules be adhered to consistently. If they are not, the child's disruptive cafeteria behavior may be reinforced on an intermittent schedule.

Potential Reinforcers

Teachers who are interested in using behavioral methods in the classroom often ask the question: "How do I determine what will be reinforcing to a child?" The only sure way is to observe children and identify these stimuli or events that increase the frequency of the response they follow. However, it is possible to discern stimuli or events that often have potential reinforcing properties for many children (see the *Appendix* for the form for determining potential reinforcers). At particular ages and grade levels certain objects, toys, activities, or events appear to be frequently selected free-choice activities.

Homme, deBaca, Devine, Steinhurst, and Rickert (1963) used some unusual reinforcing events for preschool children. They found that throwing a cup across the room, pushing an adult around in a swivel chair, and kicking a waste basket across the room were reinforcing to some children. In working with mentally retarded children, Daley (1969) used activities such as talking, coloring, swinging feet, jumping, looking out the window, dancing, and listening to records as reinforcers. Candy or food appear to be more effective than social praise with emotionally disturbed children (Levine and Simmons, 1962). Ferster and De Myer (1962) have also found tangible rewards (trinkets) to be effective as reinforcers with children who have various types of emotional difficulties.

Hewett (1968) has suggested that the monetary value of a reinforcer is relatively unimportant to its value as a reinforcer, especially with younger children. In Hewett's engineered classroom, items with values that exceed five cents are rarely used as reinforcers. If more expensive items are used, a considerable period of time is required to earn them.

With older children, the tangible reinforcers may have to be of greater value to be effective. Staats and Butterfield (1965) used such items as records, shoes, hair cream, and money as reinforcers for a culturally disadvantaged delinquent youth. The 14-year-old boy with whom they worked had an initial reading level of low second grade. A reinforcement system was devised so that for correct reading responses he received tokens that were subsequently exchanged for tangible reinforcers such as those mentioned above. He was given forty hours of instruction, with a resulting change in reading performance from low second-grade level to middle fourth-grade level. The boy's aggressive and defiant behavior greatly decreased and he began obtaining passing grades. The cost of the reinforcers during the period of instruction amounted to $20.31. This is a small sum for the results achieved.

In public schools it is not always possible and sometimes is not considered desirable to use reinforcers that have monetary value. If such circumstances exist, special privileges or activities will often serve as effective reinforcers. In a junior-high-school class, Broden, Hall, Dunlap, and Clark (1970) used tokens (points) which could be exchanged to obtain special privileges. For example, points could be exchanged for privileges such as moving their desks for one period, talking to another person for five minutes, going on a field trip, being permitted to go to lunch five minutes early, listening to records, and working on a puzzle. In addition to the token-exchange-for-a-privilege-system, points were also withdrawn for deviant behavior.

In another study with junior-high-school pupils, Nolen, Kunzelmann, and Haring (1970, p. 165) used reinforcing activities such as "...handicrafts, typing, woodworking, organized games or science units." Phillips (1968) worked with young adolescents in a home-type rehabilitation center. He found that privileges such as staying up late, watching TV, allowances, and games had substantial reinforcement property.

In some cases, it might be more effective if the teacher allows students to determine the requirements necessary to obtain a reinforcer. Lovitt and Curtiss (1969) found that when a pupil was allowed to decide the requirements to obtain special privileges for his academic responses, his rate of responding was higher than when the teacher specified the requirements. To insure realistic requirements, students would probably need teacher guidance for their decision.

The reviewed studies illustrate that observant teachers can readily identify a great variety of potentially useful reinforcing stimuli, activities, or events. To further aid teachers in identifying potential reinforcers, lists have been compiled by the writers, in Figures 11 through 14. The potential reinforcers were identified for elementary age level children by administering the form in the *Appendix* to approximately sixty children at each grade level. The data on kindergarten children were obtained in small group discussions with them. The data on junior-high and high-school level pupils are based on information supplied to us by teachers.

This chapter has attempted to illustrate ways in which counselors and psychologists can increase their effectiveness as consultants to teachers. Particular emphasis was given to the applications of learning theory to classroom instruction and child-management problems. If the counselor and psychologist can use these principles and methods effectively, they can greatly enhance the interpersonal and learning environment of the classroom.

Girls	Boys
Objects	*Objects*
small doll	candy
note pads	toy car
candy	whistles
books	colored paper
jewelry	ball
makeup kits	toy soldiers
jump rope	marbles
jacks	coloring book
play money	masks
crayons	badges
Activities	*Activities*
being read a story	finger painting
cutting pictures	holding the flag
writing on the board	blocks
coloring	pasting
playing in the doll house	being read a story
cleaning the sinks	listening to a record
felt board	writing on the board
listening to a record	going on the swings
stringing beads	playing with trucks
painting	felt board
Games	*Games*
Candy Land	Funny Faces
Lotto	farm set
dolls	Lego
picture dominoes	puppets
pegs	Play Tiles
Playschool Match-ups	Tinker toys
Funny Faces	clay
puzzles	Lotto
puppets	Picture Dominoes
clay	puzzles

FIGURE 11.   *Kindergarten. Potentially reinforcing objects, activities, and games, as determined by interviews with children and teachers.*

Girls	Boys
Objects	*Objects*

Girls	Boys
jacks	water gun
candy	comic books
eraser	small cars
pencil	toy flying planes
comic books	candy
toy rings	rubber ball
small dolls	whistles
crayons	baseball cards
coloring book	pencil
paper dolls	marbles
	clay

Activities	*Activities*
writing on the board	painting
coloring	making paper objects
cutting with scissors	taking care of pets
jumping rope	science experiments
dusting	kicking a ball
cleaning the sinks	swinging on the swings
going to the office	cleaning the board
painting	going to the office on an
working with flash cards	errand
reading	cleaning the floor

Games	*Games*
jacks	Kaboom
playing with dolls	Time Bomb
Kaboom	Spirograph
Candy Land	checkers
Pick Up Stix	puzzles
Spirograph	Clue
Slap Stick	marbles
Old Maid	Hands Down
Clue	Green Ghost
Dominoes	Slap Stick

FIGURE 12. Grades 1 to 3. Potentially reinforcing objects, activities, and games, as determined by interviews with children and teachers.

Girls	Boys
Objects	*Objects*
candy or gum	squirt gun
pencils	model planes
comic books	candy or gum
teen magazines	comics
felt pens	popcorn
paperback books	yo - yo's
notebooks	stamps (for collection)
stationery	football or baseball cards
combs	colored pencils
plastic or paper flowers	magic puzzles
Activities	*Activities*
talking to a friend	science experiments
making things for special projects	clay
drawing	drawing
teacher's helper	puzzles
puzzles	talking into a tape recorder
reading	working film strip
creative writing	looking at or feeding pet
talking into a tape recorder	looking at magazines
clay	painting
vocabulary cards	line leader
Games	*Games*
Life	Chess
Dating Game	Monopoly
Go to the head of the class	Battle Ship
Scrabble	slot cars
Twister	Clue
Easy Money	Booby Trap
Slap Stick	checkers
Spill and Spell	Scrabble
Password	Green Ghost
Hands Down	Dark Shadows

FIGURE 13.   *Grades 4 to 6. Potentially reinforcing objects, activities, and games, as determined by questionnaires given to children.*

Girls	Boys
Objects	*Objects*

Girls	Boys
records	records
teen magazines	car or sports magazines
combs	combs
pens	pens
pictures of movie stars	psychedelic posters
candy bars	candy bars
small toys for siblings or	key chain
disadvantaged children	paperback books
paperback books	hair cream
make-up	free lunch ticket
free lunch ticket	

Activities	*Activities*
talking to a friend	talking to a friend
time in class to do homework	getting out of class early
typing	working on crafts or models
looking at teen magazine	looking at a car or sports
not having to take a test	magazine
helping a younger child learn	playing chess or checkers
playing Scrabble	playing Monopoly
grading papers	puzzles (1,000 pieces)
reading a book	time in class to do homework
puzzles (1,000 pieces)	not having to take a test

Total Class Activities

listening to the radio
bringing in T.V. to watch
  special programs
class party
sitting by whomever you want to
listening to records
field trips
class debate
watching a movie

FIGURE 14. Junior high and high school. Potentially reinforcing objects and individual and class activities, as determined by interviews with teachers.

Chapter 8

Counseling with Parents

Among the child's experiences, those that have the most decisive effect upon personality development take place in the home. Parents are the most essential part of the child's learning environment and the primary determinants of what he is or will subsequently be. They are the chief dispensers of rewards and punishments, as well as the principal models upon which the child patterns his behavior. Consequently, they are an important part of the therapeutic equation.

Parental impact on child behavior is related to the child's age and developmental level. When the child is young and unable to act on or satisfy his own needs, he is completely dependent on his parents for gratification. Thus, the extent to which the parents meet his needs is instrumental in the development of a sense of security, or the lack of it; expectations he has for the future; and the means by which he learns to cope with the world. However, as he acquires more independence and his world expands, parental influences are not primary or exclusive. Other people in his milieu begin to have significant influence on his behavior. When he reaches school age, his experiences with teachers and peers, and the relative success he has at school, all have significant impact on his behavior patterns. These influences must also be considered in the therapeutic strategy.

Parental Attitudes, Expectations, and Influences

Most if not all parents are desirous of encouraging the development of healthy and effective ways of behaving in children. However, this is not to say that all parents are aware of the impact their child-rearing methods and their relationships and expectations have on their children. Many parents, sincere in their desire to perform their parental roles effectively, quite unintentionally do promote child behavior patterns that are neither effective nor healthy. It is precisely these areas that require careful analysis and the development of an effective treatment plan.

As was discussed in an earlier chapter, there are some crucial behaviors that the child must acquire for healthy development. These do not naturally blossom forth, but need to be appropriately reinforced in a facilitating learning environment. Some parents need help in properly handling various transition points in development. For example, an important transition point for most children is entry into public school. Many children, perhaps too dependent on their parents, experience this separation as a difficult developmental crisis. A little later, in about the third or fourth grade, children begin to accelerate their sex-typing activities and begin to seek identification with a same-sex peer group. For some children, these new phases of growth pose difficult problems. Still later, at about the seventh grade, girls begin to renounce some of the intimate ties in their same-sex peer group for awakening interests in boys. A multitude of new behaviors must be learned if the transition is to be made healthily and happily. Counselors must be alert to these important developmental crises and must provide help to both children and parents in navigating them.

Another area in which many parents may unknowingly create difficulties for their children is the expectations they have for them. Perhaps some parents too frequently rely on their children's achievements as a means of enhancing their own status. Inevitably, children react to excessive pressure or unrealistic standards by resistance, anxiety, or avoidance behavior.

In the life experiences of most children, it is not unusual to find episodes that leave them in certain areas vulnerable, oversensitive, phobic, and markedly inhibited. Some children have lost a parent during a developmental period essential to the health of object relationships. Others may have experienced intensely frightening punishments that lead them to fear certain types of situations or people. Still others may have experienced intense panic in an automobile accident or a storm or flood, leaving them phobic to a number of situations or events. It is important, when these situations occur, to provide immediate psychological assistance to prevent the phobic or anxiety reactions from generalizing to other situations.

Finally, it should be noted that some parents do not establish an enhancing learning environment or utilize the methods that encourage the learning of desirable behavior. Some parents fail to develop their reinforcement properties because they have not been sensitive to the child's needs, helped him with his distress, or given appropriate affectional response. Other parents administer negative reinforcement too often or do not consistently reinforce the behavior desired.

Methods of Analyzing Parent-Child Interaction and Conflict

Before launching a facilitation or change strategy, it is desirable to assess parent behavior style and parent-child interactions. Perhaps the most important reason for doing this is to determine the type and schedule of reinforcement that parents use in interacting with their children. In addition, it is desirable to obtain a developmental and medical history information for more comprehensive treatment planning.

Perhaps the most useful method of analyzing behavior style and parent-child conflict is to make observations in the family setting, thus obtaining a record of the sequence of activities and areas of conflict, the roles that each family member assumes, and the parents' reinforcement style. Unfortunately, this requires a considerable amount of time, and it is not always possible to gain access to the home when all family members are present. Consequently, this method cannot be used as often as may be desirable.

Another method that has many virtues of family observations at home is to create a situation in an office or clinic in which the family or parents and child are encouraged to interact as naturally as possible. One such way is to invite the parents and child or children into a play or activity room and observe, through a one-way window, the nature of their verbal and nonverbal interaction. In a relatively short period of time the skilled observer can quickly determine parent-child relationships, conflicts, and parent reinforcement style. Frequency counts can be kept of the number and type of deviant behaviors exhibited by the child and the reinforcement pattern of the parents.

A third method that does not have all of the merits of the two previously mentioned is a carefully conducted interview. Because of the economy of time and for other practical reasons, it is desirable to consider the parent interview at greater length.

Obtaining Essential Information

The structure and focus of any interview is dependent on the purpose or purposes it serves. Our interest is in obtaining information that a behavior-counseling strategy can be readily created to deal with. The natural starting point is the distressing behavior of the child's that we desire to change. First, to secure a history of that behavior, we must determine the circumstances in which it first appeared, how long it has been present, its frequency, and the present situations in which it is manifest. This type of information helps us to analyze *how serious a problem it is and what or who is maintaining it*. That is, it is important to know whether it appears only at home or at school and in whose presence. For example, when a parent reports that the child only has temper tantrums when the mother is present, it is possible to infer, if the information is accurate, that the mother is maintaining the behavior. If this proves to be correct, we must then discover *how* the mother is reinforcing the behavior. Armed with these data, we are able to develop effective extinction procedures.

As we make inquiries about distressing or disturbed behavior, we encourage the parents to report the *actual behavior,* not vague generalizations. A parent report that "Johnny is mean," has little value. Rather, we want the parent to make observations in behavioral terms. For example, "Johnny strikes his sister when she refuses to share her toys."

It is important to discover not only who is maintaining a specific disturbed behavior in a child, but also the typical kinds of interaction that take place between parents and child. Do parents consistently use positive or negative reinforcement? What parent has the greatest reinforcement properties? Obviously, if one wishes to promote specific behavior in a child, it is crucial to involve the parent who is most able to provide positive reinforcement. An excellent method for assessing parent-child interaction is to have the parents select a particular day in the week and have them describe all of the activities that take place between them and the child on that particular day. By using this method, one is able to identify the nature of the conflicts between parents and child and aspects of behavior about which the parents are most concerned. Inevitably, one discovers areas of high conflict that provide a good place to intervene in order to get immediate change in the child.

As we have noted before, it is also desirable to make a systematic analysis of parental aspirations and expectations. If conflict is present between parents and child, it is certain to be manifest in this area. Also, we can only change or shape those behaviors that are within the child's capacity to perform. If parental expectations and aspirations are unrealistic, a child soon stops trying to meet the expectations and may become hostile or develop varied aversive or avoidance reactions. Moreover, if we change unrealistic parent expectations, we have changed the amount of negative reinforcement a child will receive.

Parental expectations and aspirations for a child are readily revealed by direct questioning. However, if one wishes to help a parent gain better perspective on the appropriateness of his expectations, a very simple procedure can be used. The parent is first asked to describe, as completely as possible, "How would you like your child to behave and what would you like him to be?" When the parents have finished responding to this question, a second question is asked: "Describe to me what his present behavior is." Parents typically perceive the disparity between what they expect of the child and what his present behavior is. With a little assistance in discussing the discrepancies, the parents are able to adjust their expectations so they are more realistic. It is often desirable to ask a third question: "Indicate how you attempt to encourage in the child the behavior you consider desirable." This question quickly reveals the manner in which the parents attempt to control or coerce the child, the type of discipline used, and the type of reinforcement typically employed.

Another type of information to obtain is the child's relationships and progress at school. The reinforcements the child receives in school and from the people there assume a prominent role in his behavior. If he is doing poorly in school or has a teacher who expects too much or employs inappropriate reinforcement, adjustments need to be made. Also, when a child's performance at school is enhanced, the amount of positive reinforcement a child receives from many sources—particularly parents—greatly increases.

As we indicated in Chapter 5, a medical history is obtained to make certain the child does not have health problems that require treatment and to make necessary adjustments at school for chronic and serious ones. The importance of the physical status and medical history is well illustrated by the case of a child who one of the authors worked with several years ago. A girl, age seven, was referred because of her poor adjustment at school. When the child was first seen it was noted that she appeared to have some type of visual and/or perception problem. Even though she wore glasses, which had been fitted within the previous year, it seemed advisable to have a more definite examination by an ophthalmologist. The ophthalmologist immediately referred her to a neurologist. The neurologist discovered that the child had cancer of the optic nerve. Though it was first feared that the cancer was inoperable, an operation was performed, saving her life, but not saving her from blindness, which followed. But fortunately, the condition had been discovered in time to save the child's life; a delay of six months would have resulted in her death.

Finally, we should again note the usefulness of investigating the nature of the activities, stimuli, objects, and events that are reinforcing to the child and may be used to promote the behavior that is desirable. While expressed interests or reported activities in which the child freely engages may identify potential reinforcers, they may not work as such. As we defined it in Chapter 1, a reinforcer is a stimulus that increases the probability that a specific behavior or response will occur. It is difficult to determine whether a stimulus has these qualities until one observes that it increases the frequency of a response it follows. Of course, if we want to be on safer ground, we can use a primary reinforcer until we obtain more definitive information about secondary ones. To accomplish this task, there is no substitute for observing the child and empirically testing the reinforcement properties of various stimuli.

It is important to find a variety of secondary reinforcers, because they are more easily utilized at school and at home. Also, fewer people object to their use. Then, too, schools appear not to have great affinity for the notion of using taxpayers' money to buy candy, cookies, and other edibles as learning incentives.

Reality Appraisal

Up to now in this section, we have discussed ways of obtaining important information to help parents change the behavior of their children.

There are some parents, however, who do not recognize that their children have any real problems. The reality-appraisal technique may be used to deal with such parents. The method requires the cooperation of those who deal with the child—in a school setting, the cooperation of the teacher and the psychologist or counselor. The first step in using this method requires the counselor or psychologist to have the teacher define as specifically as possible the behaviors that he feels are deviant in the child. When this has been done, the child should be observed in the classroom. A period of at least 30 minutes should be used. Ideally, the counselor or psychologist should observe the child for six different thirty-minute segments at randomly selected times during the week. A frequency count should be kept of the amount of disruptive behavior that the child exhibits.

When these data have been obtained, the information is presented to the parents. If the parents believe that it is not their child who is the cause of the disturbed behavior, an additional investigative method can be used. This method requires the counselor or psychologist to initial an "I" for child-initiated contacts with his peers and an "R" when he is the recipient of their contact. In this way, parents can be shown who is initiating the misbehavior. A written record of the child's misbehavior makes it difficult for most parents to deny the validity of information presented to them.

This information should be presented to the parent in as unthreatening a form as possible. The information should not be used coercively or to arouse guilt in the parent. Rather, the psychologist or counselor should present the data to the parents in a matter-of-fact way and then ask them how they might cooperate with him to change the child's behavior and improve his general functioning at school and home.

Methods for Working with Parent and Child

There are several methods by which behavior change may be promoted in a child. First, some form of therapy may be conducted directly with the child. These methods have been discussed in Chapter 6. Second, because change that the therapist is able to promote in parent behavior will often change the child's behavior as a result, therapy may be conducted directly with the parents without any assistance being given to the child. And, as the child begins to change his behavior, it serves as a reinforcer to maintain the changes that have taken place in the parents (Zeilberger, Sampen, and Sloan, 1968). Third, both parents and child may be counseled concurrently to help resolve psychological problems in each.

In this section, methods of working with both parent(s) and child will be considered. Later in the chapter, methods of working with only the parents will be presented. Both types of strategies are applied to problems that occur in the home.

Parent-Child Conflict

Besides the numerous specific problem behaviors for which parents often seek assistance, there are areas of parent-child tension and conflict of a more general nature, which arise because of ineffective child-rearing methods. Such difficulties may not always develop into well-defined symptoms or problem behaviors, but frequent conflict because of ineffective child-rearing methods. What is often required is appropriate assistance in dealing with the high-tension or conflict areas. Sometimes it is necessary to instruct parents how to respond appropriately to their children.

A method that appears to have considerable promise in dealing with parent-child conflict situations has been described by Straughan (1964). The method required two therapists, each performing specific but supporting roles. One therapist worked with the child in the playroom, while the second explained to the parent the procedures that were being used with the child. After a period of time, the mother was placed in the playroom for short periods. It was assumed that the mother's presence in that relaxed atmosphere would tend to countercondition the mother-child conflict. In the first session, the mother sat quietly and did not respond to the child. But, with each successive session, the length of time the mother spent in the playroom, as well as her involvement, gradually increased. As the mother's involvement in the play situation increased, the therapist's decreased, though when the situation required it, he pointed out how the mother's pressure or coercive behavior led to frustration in the child.

In the sessions in which both mother and child participated, several elements were stressed. The mother was encouraged to establish simple rules, to understand the meanings of the problems the child experienced in play, and to attend carefully to the child's reactions when she communicated something important to him. In addition, the necessity of setting limits, and their importance in maintaining the child's security were carefully explained to the mother.

Although only five sessions were conducted, positive therapeutic effects were obtained. A follow-up eight months after the sessions were conducted revealed that the therapeutic gains had been maintained. The results of the therapy sessions also seemed to generalize to school. The teacher reported that the child was more relaxed and better able to deal with her peers.

As Straughan suggests, several principles were operating to produce therapeutic gain. The anxiety that the child felt toward the mother was counterconditioned by placing the child in a pleasant situation and slowly moving the mother into a more active role. As the mother realized that the child acted in a happy relaxed way when she was not present, she was able to accept the fact that some of her own actions were affecting the child. Therefore, she learned that her own behavior was a stimulus to which the child responded, and the child's behavior served as a discriminative stimulus for her. Imitation learning also appeared to be operating. Also, because siblings were not present in the play sessions, it was easier for the mother and the child to learn appropriate behavior.

Though these procedures appear to have much utility, it should be noted that they are most effective when mother-child conflict is involved, and the mother must be willing to understand and change her behavior.

A modified form of Straughan's approach has been used successfully by one of the writers. Eight sessions were required. The mother was placed in the playroom with her child. She wore earphones and was instructed by the therapist, who was behind a one-way window, how to respond to the child. The mother was verbally reinforced when she responded correctly to the child, but was encouraged to "try again" when her behavior to the child was inappropriate. Positive gains were obtained, and, according to the child's mother, the communication by earphones added to the effectiveness of the procedure.

All of the above studies seem to show that parents can be taught ways of reducing conflict with their children. It appears from these studies that one of the most effective methods is to provide an adult model for the parent to observe. When the parent also observes his own child and views the model as being effective, he becomes more aware that his own behavior may be causing, or at least maintaining, the conflict. Needless to say, parents must be reinforced for any successful approximation that leads toward conflict reduction.

There are other types of parent-child difficulties that require a therapist to deal with both the child and one or both parents. These problems may not be due to a conflict between the parent and the child, but rather to an inability of the parent to control his child's behavior.

Demanding Behavior

Many parents seem to experience excessive difficulty dealing with the demands of their children. Rather than being able to control their children, they are controlled by them. Some children often set up their own rules, and parents appear to comply with them. One often gets the impression that the parents are afraid to get angry, and consequently become objects that are skillfully manipulated by the children.

A method for dealing with parent-child problems of this type has been reported by Wahler, Winkel, Peterson, and Morrison (1965). In their therapeutic procedure, both the parents and child are involved. The mother and child are first placed in a play situation (before treatment is begun) to classify the child's deviant behavior and to determine the reinforcement contingencies that maintain it. Rather than have the mother observe the therapist working with the child (as was done by O'Leary *et al.,* 1967; Straughan, 1964; and Russo, 1964), the parent is given instructions before and after the therapy session with his child. While in the playroom with the child, the mother is signaled with a light when to respond to the child.

If such a signal is not given, she is instructed to sit and read a book and make neither nonverbal nor verbal comments to the child. If the mother is able to discriminate when to reinforce or when to ignore her child, the light system is used as a feedback mechanism as well as a way for her to obtain reinforcement when responding correctly.

Wahler *et al.* successfully used the procedure with a six-year-old boy who controlled the time he went to bed, the food he ate, and the activities he performed in the house. Apparently, the parents were unable to refuse any of the child's demands. When attempts were made to handle the child's demanding behavior, the child's crying and shouting led the parents to concede to the demands.

Application of the methods previously described extinguished the child's demanding behavior. To determine whether the mother's new response to the child had changed his behavior, the mother was asked to reinstate the methods she had used before the therapeutic program was begun. The return of the child's demanding behavior indicated that it was the mother's behavior change that had promoted the therapeutic change in the child. However, when she reinforced cooperative behavior, the child's cooperative behavior increased to a high rate.

Wahler *et al.* treated another child with behavior similar to that just described. The child was extremely stubborn, ignored the mother's commands, and would often do just the opposite of the mother's request. However, ignoring the child's oppositional behavior and verbally rewarding cooperative behavior did not appropriately change the behavior. Consequently, the mother was instructed to use time-out whenever an oppositional behavior appeared. When this procedure was added, cooperative behavior increased markedly.

The results from studies such as Wahler *et al.* show that ignoring deviant behavior and reinforcing positive and incompatible behavior can often bring the desired improvements. However, when the problem has persisted for a long time, the parents often need a counselor or psychologist to observe them and to point out what behaviors to ignore and which ones to reinforce. Sometimes, just ignoring a child's negative behavior will not be sufficient. Additional procedures such as time-out may have to be introduced.

Parents may also need instruction, as well as observation of their behavior, for other types of problems. In some cases, parents may not be aware that they are affecting their child's or children's behavior. This lack of awareness often occurs in situations in which a parent does not interact directly with his child.

Sibling Rivalry

Sibling conflict, which appears to be a natural occurrence in most families, often creates tension in the home. Usually the severity of the difficulties between the siblings is not so great that it warrants therapeutic intervention, but in some cases parents seek help from a counselor or psychologist.

O'Leary, O'Leary, and Becker (1967) have demonstrated how parents can be taught to greatly reduce sibling rivalry. The procedures they used were somewhat unusual in that the therapist went into the home to help the parent to control the deviant sibling interactions. It will be seen how these methods might be necessary in some cases and will probably result in maximum treatment effects.

Before the treatment procedures were initiated, a baseline rate of cooperative behavior was recorded. When these observations were completed, the therapist rewarded the children with candy and praise each time cooperative behavior was exhibited. Cooperative behaviors were defined as saying "Please" and "Thank you." Also, answering each other's questions and playing together constituted cooperative play. This procedure continued for two days; on the third and fourth days, reinforcement was changed to a variable-ratio schedule. On the fifth day, the children were informed that candy could be earned only if they exhibited certain specified behavior. The expected behaviors were carefully explained to them. For each successive day during the experimental period, the behaviors for which candy could be earned were described to the children. Also on the fifth day, the children were given check marks in addition to the candy. On a blackboard each child's name was placed in a column, which received a checkmark for each instance of cooperative behavior; at the same time, the children were told who received it. Check marks were exchanged for reinforcers, such as candy, kites, comic books, etc. Gradually, the number of check marks required to receive a reinforcer was increased.

To determine the effectiveness of the experimental procedures, a second baseline observational period was initiated, executed by an observer in the therapist's absence. The results showed that the deviant behavior rose to its pre-treatment level. When the second experimental period was begun, only two days were required to increase cooperative behavior to the rate obtained in the first experimental period.

At this time, the mother was taught to implement the experimental procedures. The time-out procedure was used when the children displayed physical aggression or engaged in name-calling. The therapist remained in the home to instruct the mother when token or time-out procedures were to be used. As the mother became able to employ the procedures effectively, the therapist gradually assumed a less active role. Ultimately, the parent was able to administer the procedures independently.

A time-out procedure was added because the check-mark system did not appear to be effective enough to eliminate all of the aggressive behavior. The bathroom was used as the time-out room, where the children were required to remain for at least five minutes. If the child displayed deviant behavior in the time-out room, the behavior had to subside for at least three extra minutes before the child was permitted to leave the room. These procedures proved very effective during the second experimental period, and the mother obtained highly cooperative behavior.

It is of interest to note that an older child's deviant behavior was not entirely eliminated. The child continued to display some aggressive behavior at school. However, both the teacher and parents indicated that the child had made considerable progress during the year.

A variation of the approach cited by O'Leary *et al.* (1967) might be to combine the number of check marks each child obtains. In this way, the focus would be on developing cooperation. A predetermined number of check marks could be exchanged for trips to the zoo, movies, ball games, etc.

Methods for Enhancing Parent Impact on Child Behavior

Changes in child behavior may be produced without working directly with a child. It has already been shown that when a parent and child are seen together in a therapeutic situation and parent behavior changes, positive effects occur in the child. Consequently, direct work with parents is an important and economical therapeutic intervention strategy. It is most successfully employed when parents are intellectually and emotionally able to profit from and implement certain prescribed procedures.

Approaches of this type may be conveniently classified into two categories. In the first, the parent is given specific instructions for changing a particular child behavior. A second approach requires the instruction of the parents in using learning-theory principles for handling a variety of child problems. The writers have found that a minimum of ten sessions are required to teach the parents the basic concepts of behavior modification. It must be emphasized that parents will still need help transferring methods from one situation to another. There are, though, some excellent books available to assist the counselor or psychologist in performing these instructional tasks. We wish to mention two that are especially helpful: (1) Smith and Smith's *Child Management: A Program for Parents,* and (2) Patterson and Gullion's *Living with Children.* These books are simple but well-written and do not barrage the parent with an excessive number of sophisticated concepts that tend to be difficult and confusing to them.

In this section, we wish to discuss methods that are useful in helping parents solve problems that occur frequently in the home. Although some of the methods to be discussed have been mentioned in other chapters, effort has been made to reduce duplication. However, if a method has special utility in dealing with particular child problems in the home, its application in this context is discussed. Obviously, some methods can be employed in a number of different situations.

Since these methods do not involve a therapist to observe parent-child interaction, a caution should be noted. Parents need highly specific instructions for dealing with each behavior problem they wish to modify. In their work with parents, both of the authors have found that without guidance parents are unable to transfer a technique used in one situation to another.

Bedtime Problems

Problems that appear at or involved with bedtime tend to create much concern and distress in parents. At the end of the day and as bedtime approaches, the energy and emotional resources of both parents and children are considerably depleted. When a child is resistant to going to bed, much conflict and tension can be produced between parents and child as well as between the parents. Because such conflicts are not particularly conducive to restful sleep or pleasant dreams, it is important to help the parents solve them.

Wolf, Risley, and Mees (1964) have discussed how a disturbed child's bedtime problems were solved, by a relatively simple procedure. At bedtime the disturbed child was placed in his bed with the door of his room left open. If the child got out of bed, he was instructed to return to bed and go to sleep or the bedroom door would be closed. If a temper tantrum occurred, the door remained closed until the child ceased his tantrum. When the child returned to bed, the door was opened and remained so as long as he complied with the request.

Wolf *et al.* found that the child had considerable difficulty for five nights because he did not comply with the request to stay in bed. The child exhibited quite violent behavior during this period. On one occasion, a temper tantrum lasted more than an hour. However, by the sixth evening, the procedure proved successful and the child rarely exhibited bedtime problems from that time on.

With a little ingenuity, this basic procedure can be modified and used with most bedtime problems. While opening and closing a door will work, a light or a child's favorite blanket may be used. That is, a light in the child's room is either left on or turned off according to the behavior he exhibits; or the child's favorite blanket—or toy or teddy bear—can be removed until he behaves properly.

It can be seen that this method utilizes negative reinforcement as well as response-contingent withdrawal of reinforcement. An aversive stimulus is removed (the door is opened) when the child exhibits the specified behavior: negative reinforcement is being used. When a favorite blanket or toy is removed because an undesirable behavior is exhibited, response-contingent withdrawal of reinforcement is being used.

A word of caution must be given here. Sometimes when parents are attempting to reduce bedtime problems, other problems can interfere with the procedures being used. In a study mentioned in an earlier chapter, Williams (1959) encouraged parents of a young child to use methods to reduce the child's demand for their attention at bedtime. It will be recalled that the method required putting the child to bed in a leisurely manner and closing the door. The child's screaming was to be ignored. Although the parents would have been able to use the method successfully, the child's aunt reinforced his bedtime problems by refusing to leave the child's room until he went to sleep. The procedures had to be reinstated without the aunt by the parents for almost as long as it took to extinguish the behavior the first time. The same problem can develop with a grandmother or a well-meaning babysitter who is not aware of the rationale behind the method.

Eating Problems

Much like bedtime or sleeping problems, eating problems are a source of considerable distress to parents. Middle-class parents seem especially upset by these problems and desirous of effective action, because they are much aware of the desirability of proper diet and table manners.

A child of one of the present writer's had a problem with eating. After some analysis, the author discerned that the problem appeared as a result of excessive negative attention to the child's eating. Consequently, a regime was instituted in which the manner of eating as well as the quantity eaten was ignored. However, this procedure did not appear to change the behavior, and a second procedure was implemented. When the child exhibited the undesirable behavior, she was dismissed from the table and placed in a time-out room. This procedure was equally ineffective. Finally, a method that employed both primary and secondary reinforcement proved to be successful.

The child was rated on a scale from one to four by the amount of food she ate. One point was obtained for merely touching the food, two points were received for eating half of the meal, three points were received for a portion somewhat greater than half, and four points were received for eating the whole meal. A reasonable time limit was given for eating, followed by an evaluation. Initially, each point earned was paired with candy. To make candy a potent reinforcer, it was withheld at other times during the day. When the child had accumulated enough points, she was able to exchange them for a small toy. The toys were chosen in advance by the child and she did not receive them until the specified number of points had been earned.

The number of points required to earn a toy was initially small, but gradually increased. Highly valued activities were also used as reinforcers. Points could be exchanged for a trip to the zoo, amusement park, etc. In addition, the child was given a small "bonus toy" when four points were earned. This "bonus toy" was always paired with praise and given on a variable basis when she earned four points for any one meal.

The child's eating increased to a level satisfactory to both parents. After the first week, the child was able to score her own eating behavior. Although this procedure was used for the supper meal only, it had its effects on lunch and breakfast.

To determine whether the reinforcers were in fact influencing the behavior, the procedure was terminated for a one-month period. For almost
two weeks the child's eating behavior was equivalent to that attained during the experimental period. The eating behavior appeared to be maintained as a result of the child's grading herself at dinnertime. During the
third and fourth weeks, a sharp decline in appropriate eating behavior was
noted. A reinstatement of the procedures quickly increased the child's eating habits to the level of the first experimental period. The child was eventually placed on a variable schedule and her eating behavior is now
satisfactory to her parents.

Sometimes a child's eating problems may involve throwing food or
deliberately spilling a drink. The use of time-out procedures or removing
the child from the table for brief periods of time can effectively reduce
this behavior (Williams, 1962). Parents must be warned that when their
children exhibit this problem, they will have to take the child away from
the table many times before the procedure is successful.

Sloppiness

Sloppy, messy, or disorderly behavior cannot be considered very serious, but, like bedtime and eating problems, is irritating to parents; it can
be unlearned if parents are given effective assistance. Patterson and Gullion (1968) recommend a method used by Lindsley for dealing with such
problems. The method involves the use of a "Saturday box." Parents
simply explain to their children that when articles of clothing are found
lying around the house they will be placed in the Saturday box. Once the
clothes are deposited in the Saturday box, they cannot be worn until the
box is opened on Saturday.

To make the method work effectively, the children should be extended
the same opportunity to deposit the parents' clothes in the Saturday box
when found lying around. By giving the children the same rights as the
parents, some of the negative aspects of the method are mitigated. As
with most methods, consistency is essential. That is, if something is placed
in the Saturday box, it should remain there until Saturday. This could
mean that a child might have to wear two different-colored socks to
school some day.

Although this simple method seems to work reasonably well in changing behavior appropriately, its effectiveness may be enhanced by additional procedures. Parents might be encouraged to improvise on the
"Saturday box" method. One such way would be to give a "bonus" to a
child who does not have any item in the box on Saturday. For extremely
sloppy children, a daily "bonus" might have to be used for a few months
before switching to the weekly method. With older children, a small fine
(a nickel, for example) may be used for each item in the box on Saturday.

Patterson and Gullion (1968) have described another method that can
be used to reduce sloppiness. By this system a child will receive a point
for picking up his clothes in a particular room. Once he is adequately

complying with the parent's request, he is told that he can earn additional points by picking up his clothes in another room. When the child's behavior attains a desirable level, this procedure is extended to other rooms and the points that can be obtained are increased. This procedure allows the parents to successively approximate the ultimate goal, helping the child to put all of his things in their proper places. When the child is able to put away his clothes and is earning sufficient points, the number of days required to earn points can be increased or the amount of work can be increased to earn the same number of points. The earned points may be exchanged for a toy or a special privilege.

Although sloppy or disorderly behavior is not a severe problem, changing the behavior greatly reduces parent irritation. Equally important, in mastering this problem, parents will have learned a method that can be applied to changing other undesirable child behavior.

Tantrum Behavior

Unlike other behaviors discussed in this chapter, temper tantrums in children are not only a source of irritation to the parent, but they can often cause a good deal of embarrassment when other people are present. Parents sometimes accidently reinforce this behavior in their children. For example, if a child asks for ice cream and responds to his parents' refusal of his request by throwing a tantrum, the parents might decide to buy him the ice cream, in an effort to stop the tantrum behavior, thereby teaching the child that persistence or tantrum behavior will be followed by reinforcement.

Most parents who realize that their child is controlling them through tantrum behavior will attempt to ignore it. Unfortunately, many of these parents will not be consistent and will occasionally give the child what he requests when a tantrum occurs. Such behavior intermittently reinforces the child and makes the behavior more resistant to extinction.

Wolf, Risley, and Mees (1964) discuss the use of behavioral methods for a child displaying such severe tantrum behavior as head-banging, hair-pulling, face-slapping, etc. An autistic boy, he was first hospitalized to bring his behavior under control, and later cared for at home by his parents, who had been taught the professional methods of control. A time-out procedure was used when the child had a tantrum. He was placed in his room and the door remained closed until the tantrum was stopped. But ward attendants seem to have unknowingly reinforced a temporary increase in tantrum behavior. They talked to the child and tried to explain and even apologize to him for placing him in the room. To reduce the effects of the attendants' reinforcement (attention), a minimum of ten minutes in the room was required when tantrums occurred. Parents were later taught the methods for handling the tantrums at home. A follow-up study six months after the child returned home revealed that there were no further tantrums.

The ten-minute period in the time-out room used above has been found effective by the present authors. However, the child must exhibit ten minutes of nontantrum behavior in the time-out room before he is released. Whenever avoidable, the child's own room should not be used, since toys, television, and other reinforcing stimuli are often present. Rather, it is more appropriate to use the parent's bedroom or the bathroom as a time-out room. The light in the room should be left on. A darkened time-out room may be frightening to young children and may not produce the desired result.

Occasionally, a child may refuse to stay in the time-out room. If this does occur, a head-on clash or the use of physical force should be avoided. Locking the door seems to be the most effective procedure. With the implementation of this measure, the severity of the tantrum subsides and the behavior is eventually extinguished.

Dependent and Fearful Behavior

A child's dependency on the parent is another form of deviant behavior that, as we stated in our discussion of the temper tantrum, can be taught by the parents unknowingly. It often appears as if the child's dependency meets an important need of the parents'. But as the child gets older and the dependency becomes obviously inappropriate, the parents become aware of the desirability of changing it.

One applicable method of change discussed earlier is to reinforce independent behavior and ignore manifestations of dependent behavior. Patterson and Gullion (1968) recommend the procedure, but suggest that independent behavior be encouraged in small steps. Each minor manifestation of independent behavior (such as dressing and undressing oneself) must be consistently reinforced. First, it may be desirable to reinforce a child for finding his shoes. The child is then reinforced for putting them on. A few days later, the child may be reinforced for finding other articles of clothing. Gradually, by successive approximation, the child is encouraged to perform the appropriate terminal behavior. As the child makes progress, his achievements are proudly announced to the other family members. This announcement is not only reinforcing to the child but effectively involves other family members in helping the child learn the desirable behavior.

For some children, the dependent behavior is much too strongly entrenched for such a method to be effective. A child may be fearful of leaving mother at all and is unable to involve himself in play with his peers. With such children, a method described by Patterson (1966) appears applicable. A certain period of the day is set aside to encourage the desirable behavior. The child is given a small cup and each time he makes an attempt to interact with his peers, candy is placed in the cup. At first, the child is reinforced for merely looking at his peers, later for interacting with them.

Interaction is greatly facilitated if his peers are reinforced for initiating interactions with him. When they do, a piece of candy is taken from the child's cup and given to the peer. In this way, the fearful child is encouraged to initiate interaction with his peers and his peers have an additional incentive to interact with the fearful child.

As the child begins to display social interaction, the parent gradually moves into the background. It may be best to move away a few feet at first, and then gradually extend the distance. When this is achieved, the mother tells the child that she must go into the house for a minute and will return in a short time; the frequency and duration of her stays in the house are gradually increased.

With children whose dependent and fearful behavior is severe, it is desirable to use additional procedures. Since these children cannot be "talked out" of their fear, it is necessary to teach unfearful behavior (Patterson and Gullion, 1968). To do this, a child must be encouraged to perform behavior that is incompatible with fear. Patterson and Gullion illustrate the concept by using an example of a child who is fearful of going into the water. It is suggested that the parents give the child candy for spending a few seconds sitting in the water without crying. Since eating candy cannot occur while the child is crying, the two behaviors are usually incompatible. To the extent that the candy is a potent reinforcer, the child, by successive steps, is encouraged to give up the fear of water. Dealing with a similar problem, Bentler (1962) had the child's mother slowly introduce the child to larger and larger amounts of water while the mother was in close contact with the child. In addition, toys the child frequently played with were present. This last procedure is a form of reciprocal-inhibition therapy, discussed in an earlier chapter.

Many fears can be overcome with the use of similar principles described by Patterson and Gullion (1968) and by Bentler (1962). In a gradual manner, the parent reinforces the child's bravery for remaining in the fearful situation. At first, the child is encouraged to stay in the fearful situation for a short period of time. When he does, he is reinforced and the length of time is extended. To increase the child's desire to remain in the fearful situation, favorite objects such as a teddy bear or toy can be placed in the situation. The child is permitted to play with it as long as he remains in the situation that frightens him; it is withdrawn when he does not.

For some children, fear of separation from parents poses very difficult problems. Such a child may be assisted to conquer the fear by first being made to go outside with another adult in whom he has confidence. The mother may step just outside the door, remain for a few minutes, and reenter the house. This series of events is repeated several times the first day it is initiated. Of course, each time the child remains outside and does not cry, his adult companion immediately reinforces the child. If the child cries while the mother is inside, the mother should wait until the child stops crying before returning. This point must be emphasized to the mother, because her reappearance while the child is crying reinforces the crying behavior and not the independent behavior.

Working with parents of dependent and fearful children, the authors have found it extremely important to give praise (secondary reinforcement) to parents for efforts they make in reducing their child's dependent behavior. This seems to be necessary because the dependence of the child may satisfy some parental needs. To help the parents understand these needs and allow the child more independence may require skillful counseling.

Unfinished Homework

Most clinicians do not consider unfinished homework as a serious problem. However, because parents become very upset when their child has this problem and are anxious to correct it, referrals of this type are very common in the school setting. Phillips (1968) worked with three delinquent boys ranging in age from 12 to 14 years, to increase their preparation for classroom assignments and homework. All were in a residential treatment center for children with delinquent behaviors. The children were asked to carry with them a small index card on which their school assignments were written. The assignments were divided into five equal parts, and each part was scored independently. To earn reinforcements, the completed assignments had to be 75-percent accurate. Three types of reinforcers were used at various times throughout the experiment. The boys could earn one-fifth of the total points, money, or time for each assignment that had less than 25-percent error.

Money was first used to motivate the children to complete their assignments. The boys were given the choice of receiving the money either at the end of the day or at the end of the week. A second type of reinforcer was the earning of "late time," up to an hour of time that a boy could stay up later than usual, which, like the money reinforcer, could be used on the day it was earned or saved for the weekend. Earned points were used to obtain privileges such as riding a bike, watching TV, etc. The price of these particular privileges tended to vary, but usually one of them could be earned for completing all of the assignments with 75-percent accuracy for two days.

When the types of reinforcement were compared, the point system had proved most effective. Daily late time, though also effective, was less so, and money, interestingly enough, was least effective. At first it was thought that the ineffectiveness of money resulted from the boys' lack of experience with it, so they were given a weekly allowance for seven weeks, after which money was again used as a reinforcer. However, its reinstatement did not result in any better performance by the boys.

Reinforcement for homework completion and correctness has great applicability to a home situation. The parents might request the classroom teacher to write out the homework assignments on the child's card. If there is no homework for that day, this should also be noted on the card. In this way, parents will have an accurate account of the amount of work that is required to be completed at home each day. The parents can check the correctness of the child's work and reinforce appropriately. If the parents are unable to do this, reinforcement is given as a result of the teacher's rating. As was true of Phillips' study, it may be desirable to deduct points if assignments are not done. Inaccurate homework should not result in losing points unless the parent believes that the child did not make any attempt at being accurate. Penalties, if used, should be realistic, and parents must consistently enforce the rules.

Patterson and Gullion (1968) have suggested a technique for enhancing the child's ability to do homework. They suggest that parents should ask about and display interest in the child's homework. At first the child is reinforced for working on his homework for a short period of time (ten or fifteen minutes). Gradually, the amount of time devoted to homework is increased. A point system or praise may be used as reinforcers. All criticism by parents (*e.g.,* work is messy) should be avoided. Such methods are aversive and lead the child to avoid homework.

Patterson and Gullion (1968) recommend that reinforcement for grades on a semester report card is not effective. Rather, reinforcement, which must be immediate, should be given for successive approximations of the final goal. It is much more effective to give pennies for a series of specific behaviors than to give a dollar for a final grade.

Both methods seem effective. We would, however, recommend the Patterson and Gullion technique for younger children and Phillips' method with older children. With either system, it is important to explain to the parents how and why tangible reinforcers effectively change behavior. Since parents may object to extrinsic rewards, it is important to point out that reinforcement may ultimately lead to intrinsic satisfactions in doing homework.

Difficulty with Household Chores

Most parents expect and consider it desirable for children to do household chores. Yet relatively few parents feel they are successful in getting children to perform them properly. In some instances these difficulties may relate to the unreasonableness of parent expectations. If so, appropriate adjustments have to be made. It may be helpful in this regard to encourage parents to check with other parents who have children of similar ages to see what is considered reasonable.

In cases in which parental expectations are reasonable but children do not carry out their chores, an approach suggested by Smith and Smith (1966) may be helpful. They suggest that for each chore assigned to a child, a reasonable time limit should be set. This may be done by specifying the time in minutes or by making it impossible to participate in a desired activity—watching TV, playing baseball, etc.—until the chore is performed. It is also absolutely essential that the chore request be enforced during the time specified. It may be desirable, for example, to turn off the TV until the child has completed the assigned task of carrying out the garbage. Since a request of this type may anger the child, it is essential that the parents do not respond negatively to the child's anger. A temper tantrum should be ignored and the request enforced.

The Smith and Smith method invokes negative consequences when an assigned task has not been performed. That is, the child will perform the task to prevent the occurrence of an undesirable event. The approach of Smith and Smith is very similar to the contingency-management procedures of Homme, discussed previously. However, with Homme's procedures, choices of positive activity are given when a desirable behavior is performed.

There is no reason why a reinforcement-menu approach would not work equally well in the home. The child could be told that when he completes his chore, he can choose one of five activities. These activity choices should be things the child enjoys doing (watching TV, calling a friend, staying up fifteen minutes later, eating a snack, playing a game, etc.). New choices should be added occasionally and other choices should be temporarily terminated. This is done to prevent satiation.

Another method of helping parents with this problem is to use a monetary-reward system. The allowance a child might normally get for the week is paid for completing chores; it is not simply given, but is earned by the child. The system can be made more attractive by making it possible to earn money by completing special "bonus" tasks. Such a system not only increases the frequency with which chores are done, but it also teaches the child the appropriate use of money. It may also give the child a sense of pride for doing "his work" like grownups. For the little time that is required in record keeping, parents may find themselves greatly rewarded.

Infraction of Rules

At the risk of being repetitious, this section deals with the establishment and enforcement of rules. Some of the points discussed here are similar to those mentioned above in the preceding section. The authors believe, however, that this section needs to be included so that counselors and psychologists can help parents when their children will not obey established rules.

Before any assistance can be attempted, the reasonableness of the rules must be carefully analyzed with the parents. Also, it must be determined whether the rules are too numerous—some of them perhaps unnecessary. Rules should be established only when they are important to the functioning of the family, are effective in reducing tensions, and promote the desired behavior.

Smith and Smith (1966) suggest that when a parent establishes a rule, it should be stated as a rule, not as a question. For example, a parent should not ask a child: "Do you want to go to bed?" when only one reply is possible. Obviously, the child is likely to say, "no." Rules must be stated as rules. As with chores, rules must be defined so that a child knows what is expected of him. A rule should not be established if it cannot be enforced.

Smith and Smith suggest that when an infraction of a rule occurs, parents should first ask the child for a restatement of the rule. This tends to decrease the probability that the rule will be broken again. Although simple, this method seems to be highly effective. It is most effective when the rule cannot be corrected at the time it is broken. For example, if a child comes home later than requested, restatement of the rule is an effective procedure. In other cases, an infraction of the rule should be corrected by requiring the child to repeat the desired behavior correctly immediately after the infraction.

When a rule is being enforced, irrelevant behavior should be ignored. That is, even though a child has a tantrum, it is ignored, but the child must perform the behavior specified by the rule. Similarly, consistency in enforcement is essential. For example, if a rule has been set regarding dinner time and a child arrives late for dinner he gets no dinner.

As most parents know, children are experts at putting rules to the test. Once the rules have been consistently enforced for a time, the rule-testing greatly decreases. Rules make the environment orderly and predictable and are a basis for promoting security in a child.

In addition to the methods described by Smith and Smith, enforcement of rules can be greatly enhanced by the use of positive reinforcement. If obeying rules has been a particularly difficult problem, it may even be desirable to use primary reinforcement (candy, ice cream, etc.). For example, Phillips (1968) combined both negative and positive reinforcement to enhance a delinquent's ability to obey rules. When a rule was broken, the child was fined. When a rule was obeyed, the child received points that could subsequently be exchanged for special privileges. Such a system proved to be useful.

It is likely that many methods will work in enforcing rules or correcting infractions. However, it is probably true that most methods work because of one essential ingredient: They are consistently enforced in combination with a positive reinforcement system.

The problems we have discussed and the learning-theory principles we have applied to them are only a few of the many possible ones. Our hope is that the applications we have described will open up new vistas to the practitioner who desires to enhance and promote a happier and more productive future for every child. Subsequent research and more rigorous testing in clinical and natural settings may greatly extend their utility. We will greet such developments with open arms, since we know very well the great number of child clients who wait restlessly for help with their struggles.

A Method for Identifying Potential Reinforcers with Children

The form listed below may be used to identify potential reinforcers that *may be* useful with children. Whether a stimulus has reinforcement properties can only be determined empirically. That is, if a stimulus increases the probability that a response reoccurs, it is a reinforcer. The form listed below may be used to interview younger children who are not able to respond in writing or, for older children, the form may simply be given to the child to complete.

Name: Age:

School: Grade:

                               Boy or Girl (Please circle one)

1. If you were going into a store to buy three games that you would like, what would they be?

2.   What three special things do you like to work with or play with in the classroom?

3.   What are three jobs in this classroom you like to do the most?

4.   If you went to a store and had 25¢ to spend on whatever you wanted, what would you buy?

5.   What things that you did not mention above do you like to do in your classroom or while you are at school (in the building or playground)?

References

Addison, R.M., and Homme, L.E. The reinforcing event (RE) menu. *National Society for Programmed Instruction Journal,* 1966, *5,* 8-9.

Allen, K.E., Hart, B.M., Buell, J.S., Harris, F.R., and Wolf, M.M. Effects of social reinforcement on isolate behavior of a nursery school child. *Child Development,* 1964, *35,* 511-518

Ayllon, T., and Michael, J. The psychiatric nurse as a behavioral engineer. *Journal of Experimental Analysis of Behavior,* 1959, *2,* 323-334.

Azrin, N.H., and Holz, W.C. Punishment. In W.K. Honig (Ed.), *Operant behavior: areas of research and application.* New York: Appleton-Century-Crofts, 1966, pp. 380-447.

Baer, D.M. Laboratory control of thumbsucking by withdrawal and representation of reinforcement. *Journal of Experimental Analysis of Behavior,* 1962, *5,* 525-528.

Baer, D.M., and Sherman, J.A. Reinforcement control of generalized imitation in young children. *Journal of Experimental Child Psychology,* 1964, Vol. 1, 37-49.

Bandura, A., Ross. D., and Ross, S.A. Transmission of aggression through imitation of aggressive models. *Journal of Abnormal and Social Psychology,* 1961, *63,* 575-582.

————. Imitation of film-mediated aggressive models. *Journal of Abnormal and Social Psychology,* 1963, *66,* 3-11.

Bandura, A., and Walters, R.H. *Social learning and personality development.* New York: Holt, Rinehart and Winston, Inc., 1963.

Bandura, A. Behavior modification through modeling procedures. In L.P. Ullmann and L. Krasner (Eds.), *Research in behavior modification.* New York: Holt, Rinehart and Winston, 1965, pp. 310-340.

————. Behavioral psychotherapy. *Scientific American,* March 1967, pp. 78-86.

————. *Principles of behavior modification.* New York: Holt, Rinehart and Winston, 1969.

Barclay, R., Jr. Effecting behavior change in the elementary classroom: An exploratory study. *Journal of Counseling Psychology,* 1967, *14,* 240-247.

Barrett, B.H. Reduction in rate of multiple tics by free operant conditioning methods. In L.P. Ullmann and L. Krasner (Eds.), *Case studies in behavior modification.* New York: Holt, Rinehart and Winston, 1965, pp. 255-263.

Barrish, H., Saunders, M., and Wolf, M.M. Good behavior game: Effects of individual contingencies for group consequences on disruptive behavior in a classroom. *Journal of Applied Behavior Analysis. 2,* 79-84.

Bentler, P.M. An infant's phobia treated with reciprocal inhibition therapy. *Journal of Child Psychology and Psychiatry,* 1962, *3,* 185-189.

Bijou, S. Implications of behavioral science for counseling and guidance. In J.D. Krumboltz (Ed.), *Revolution in counseling.* Boston: Houghton Mifflin Co., 1966, pp. 27-48.

Blackham, G.J. Strategies for change in the child client. *Elementary School Guidance and Counseling,* 1969, *3* (March), 174-181.

Bloom, B.S. (Ed.) *Taxonomy of educational objectives, the classification of educational goals handbook: cognitive domain.* New York: David McKay Co., 1956.

Broden, M., Hall, R.V., Dunlap, A., and Clark, R. Effects of teacher attention and token reinforcement system in a junior high school special education class. *Exceptional Children,* 1970, *36,* 341-349.

Browning, R.M. Behavior therapy for stuttering in a schizophrenic child. *Behaviour Research and Therapy,* 1967, *5,* 27-35.

Bugelski, B.R. *The psychology of learning applied to teaching.* Indianapolis: Bobbs-Merrill Co., 1964.

Burns, B. Jim: The case of an effeminate boy. Unpublished manuscript. Tempe Elementary Schools, 1970.

Bushell, D., Jr., Wrobell, P.A., and Michaelis, M.L. Applying "group" contingencies to the classroom study behavior of preschool children. *Journal of Applied Behavior Analysis,* 1968, *1,* 55-61.

Campbell, D.T., and Stanley, J.C. Experimental and quasi-experimental designs for research on teaching. In N.L. Gage (Ed.), *Handbook of research on teaching.* Chicago: Rand McNally, 1963, 171-246.

Carlson, C.S., Arnold, C.R., Becker, W.C., and Madsen, C.H. The elimination of tantrum behavior of a child in an elementary classroom. *Behaviour Research and Therapy,* 1968, *6,* 117-119.

Cohen, J. *Operant behavior and conditioning.* Chicago: Rand McNally, 1969.

Coleman, J.C. *Abnormal psychology and modern life* (2nd Ed.). Chicago: Scott, Foresman and Co., 1956.

Cowen, E. Mothers in the classroom. *Psychology Today,* 1969, *3,* 36-39.

Daley, M.F. The reinforcement menu: finding effective reinforcers. In J.D. Krumboltz and C.E. Thoresen (Eds.), *Behavioral counseling, case studies and techniques.* New York: Holt, Rinehart and Winston, 1969, 42-45.

Daley, M.F., Holt, G., and Vajanasoontorn, N.C. Reinforcement menus in the instruction of mentally retarded children. Paper presented at the Conference on Instructional Methods and Teacher Behavior, Berkeley, California, November, 1966.

Deese, James. *The psychology of learning.* New York: McGraw-Hill Book Co., 1958.

Dickinson, D.J. An operant conditioning program for children who will not complete their school assignments. Unpublished manuscript, Las Vegas, Nevada, 1967.

Dollard, J., and Miller, N.E. *Personality and psychotherapy.* New York: McGraw-Hill Book Co., 1950.

Erikson, E. *Childhood and society* (2nd Ed.). New York: W.W. Norton and Co., 1963.

Ferster, C., and DeMyer, M. A method for the experimental analysis of the behavior of autistic children. *American Journal of Orthopsychiatry,* 1962, *32,* 89-98.

Flanagan, B., Goldiamond, I., and Azrin, N.H. Operant stuttering: The control of stuttering behavior through response-contingent consequences. *Journal of Experimental Analysis of Behavior,* 1958, *1,* 173-177.

Ford, D.H., and Urban, H.B. *Systems of psychotherapy: a comparative study.* New York: John Wiley, 1963.

Gagné, Robert M. *The conditions of learning.* New York: Holt, Rinehart and Winston, 1965.

Gewirtz, J.L., and Baer, D.M. Deprivation and satiation of social reinforcers as drive conditions. *Journal of Abnormal and Social Psychology,* 1958, *57,* 165-172.

Gittelman, M. Behavioral rehearsal as a technique in child treatment. *Journal of Child Psychology and Psychiatry,* 1965, *6,* 251-255.

Gladstone, R. *A set of principles of teaching derived from experimental psychology.* (2nd Ed.), Stillwater, Okla.: Oklahoma State University, 1967.

Goldstein, A.P., Heller, K., and Sechrist, L.B. *Psychotherapy and the psychology of behavior change.* New York: John Wiley, 1966.

Graziano, A.M., and Kean, J.E. Programmed relaxation and reciprocal inhibition with psychotic children. *Behaviour Research and Therapy,* 1968, *6,* 433-437.

Greenspoon, J. The reinforcing effect of two spoken sounds on the frequency of two responses. *American Journal of Psychology,* 1955, *68,* 409-416.

Grunbaum, A. Causality and the science of human behavior. In R. Ulrich, T. Stachnik, and J. Mabry (Eds.), *Control of human behavior.* Glenview, Ill.: Scott-Foresman and Co., 1966, pp. 3-10.

Hall, R.V., Lund, D., and Jackson, D. Effects of teacher attention on study behavior. *Journal of Applied Behavior Analysis,* 1968, *1,* 1-12.

Hall, R.V., Panyan, M., Rabon, D., and Broden, M. Instructing beginning teachers in reinforcement procedures which improve classroom control. *Journal of Applied Behavior Analysis,* 1968, *1,* 315-322.

Haring, N.G. *Attending and responding.* San Rafael, California: Dimensions Publishing Co., 1968.

Harris, F.R., Wolf, M.M., and Baer, D.M. Effects of adult social reinforcement on child behavior. *Young Children,* 1964, *20* (1), 8-17.

Hart, B.M., Allen, K.E., Buell, J.S., Harris, F.R., and Wolf, M.M. Effects of social reinforcement on operant crying. *Journal of Experimental Child Psychology,* 1964, *1,* 145-153.

Hart, B.M., and Risley, T.R. Establishing use of descriptive adjectives in the spontaneous speech of disadvantaged preschool children. *Journal of Applied Behavior Analysis,* 1968, *1,* 109-120.

Havighurst, R.J. *Human development and education.* New York: Longmans, 1953.

Hawkins, R.P., Peterson, R.F., Schweid, E., and Bijou, S.W. Behavior therapy in the home: amelioration of problem parent-child relations with the parent in a therapeutic role. *Journal of Experimental Child Psychology,* 1966, *4,* 99-107.

Hewett, F. *The emotionally disturbed child in the classroom: A developmental strategy for educating children with maladaptive behavior.* Boston: Allyn and Bacon, 1968.

Hewett, F.M. Educational engineering with emotionally disturbed children. *Exceptional Children,* 1967, *34,* 459-467.

Hewett, F.M., Taylor, F.D., and Artuso, A.A. The Santa Monica project: Evaluation of an engineered classroom design with emotionally disturbed children. *Exceptional Children,* 1968, *35,* 523-529.

Holland, C.J. Elimination by the parents of fire-setting behavior in a seven-year-old boy. *Behaviour Research and Therapy,* 1969, *7,* 135-137.

Holt, E.B. *Animal drive and the learning process.* Vol. 1. New York: Holt, 1931.

Homme, L.E., deBaca, P.C., Devine, J.V., Steinhurst, R., and Rickert, E.J. Use of the Premack principle in controlling the behavior of nursery school children. *Journal of the Experimental Analysis of Behavior,* 1963, *6,* 544.

Hosford, R.E. Overcoming fear of speaking in a group. In J.D. Krumboltz and C.E. Thoresen (Eds.), *Behavioral counseling, case studies and techniques.* New York: Holt, Rinehart and Winston, 1969, pp. 80-83.

Hunter, M. *Reinforcement theory for teachers.* El Segundo, California: Tip Publications, 1967.

Jones, M.C. The elimination of children's fears. *Journal of Experimental Psychology,* 1924, *7,* 383-390.

Kagan, J. Acquisition and significance of sex typing and sex role identity. In M.L. Hoffman and L.W. Hoffman (Eds.), *Review of child development research,* Vol. 1. Hartford, Conn.: Russell Sage Foundation, 1964.

Keirsey, D.W. Transactional casework: a technology for inducing behavioral change. Paper presented at the Convention of California Association of School Psychologists and Psychometrists, San Francisco, 1965.

————. Systematic exclusion: eliminating chronic classroom disruptions. In J.D. Krumboltz and C.E. Thoresen (Eds.), *Behavioral counseling, case studies and techniques.* New York: Holt, Rinehart and Winston, 1969, pp. 89-113.

Keller, F.S. *Learning: reinforcement theory.* New York: Random House, 1954.

Kennedy, W.A. School phobia: Rapid treatment of fifty cases. *Journal of Abnormal Psychology,* 1965, *70,* 285-289.

Krasner, L. The therapist as a social reinforcement machine. In H.H. Strupp and L. Luborsky (Eds.), *Research in Psychotherapy, Vol. II.* Washington, D.C.: American Psychological Association, 1962, pp. 61-94.

Krathwohl, D.R., Bloom, B.S., and Masia, B.B. *Taxonomy of educational objectives, handbook II: affective domain.* New York: David McKay Co., 1964.

Kushner, M. The reduction of long-standing fetish by means of aversive conditioning. In L.P. Ullmann and L. Krasner (Eds.), *Case studies in behavior modification.* New York: Holt, Rinehart and Winston, 1965, pp. 239-242.

Lal, H., and Lindsley, O.R. Therapy of chronic constipation in a young child by rearranging social contingencies. *Behaviour Research and Therapy,* 1968, *6,* 484-485.

Lazarus, A.A. The elimination of children's phobias by deconditioning. In H.J. Eysenck (Ed.), *Behavior therapy and the neuroses,* New York: Pergamon Press, 1960, pp. 114-122.

————. Group therapy of phobic disorders by systematic desensitization. *Journal of Abnormal and Social Psychology,* 1961, *63,* 504-510.

Lazarus, A.A., and Abramovitz, A. The use of "emotive imagery" in the treatment of children's phobias. *Journal of Mental Science,* 1962, *108,* 191-195.

Levin, G., and Simmons, J. Response to praise by emotionally disturbed boys. *Psychological Reports,* 1962, *11,* 10.

Lovaas, O.I., Freitag, A., Gold, V.J., and Kassorla, I.C. Experimental studies in childhood schizophrenia: analysis of self-destructive behavior. *Journal of Experimental Child Psychology,* 1965(a), *2,* 67-84.

Lovaas, O.I., Schaeffer, B., and Simmons, J.O. Building social behavior in autistic children by use of electric shocks. *Journal of Experimental Research in Personality,* 1965(b), *1,* 99-109.

Lovibond, S.H. The mechanism of conditioning treatment of enuresis. *Behaviour Research and Therapy,* 1963, *1,* 17-21.

Lovitt, T.C., and Curtiss, K.A. Effects of manipulating an antecedent event on mathematics response rate. *Journal of Applied Behavior Analysis,* 1968, *1,* 329-333.

————. Academic response rate as a function of teacher- and self-imposed contingencies. *Journal of Applied Behavior Analysis,* 1969, *2,* 49-53.

Lovitt, T.C., Guppy, T.E., and Blattner, J.E. The use of a free-time contingency with fourth graders to increase spelling accuracy. *Behaviour Research and Therapy,* 1969, *7,* 151-156.

Lundin, R.W. *Personality: an experimental approach.* New York: Macmillan Co., 1961.

Madsen, C.H., Jr. Positive reinforcement in the toilet training of a normal child: A case report. In L.P. Ullmann and L. Krasner (Eds.), *Case studies in behavior modification.* New York: Holt, Rinehart and Winston, 1965, pp. 305-307.

Madsen, C.H., Jr., Becker, W.C., and Thomas, D.R. Rules, praise and ignoring: elements of elementary classroom control. *Journal of Applied Behavior Analysis,* 1968, *1,* 139-150.

Mager, Robert F. *Preparing instructional objectives.* Palo Alto: Fearon Publishers, 1962.

Mallick, S.K., and McCandles, B.R. A study of catharsis of aggression. *Journal of Personality and Social Psychology,* 1966, *4,* 591-596.

Maslow, A. *Motivation and personality.* New York: Harper and Bros., 1954.

McKenzie, H.S., Clark, M., Wolf, M.M., Kothera, R., and Benson, C. Behavior modification of children with learning disabilities using grades as tokens and allowances as back-up reinforcers. *Exceptional Children,* 1968, *34,* 745-752.

Michael, J., and Meyerson, L. A behavioral approach to counseling and guidance. In R.L. Mosher, R.F. Carle, and C.D. Kehas (Eds.), *Guidance: an examination.* New York: Harcourt, Brace and World, 1965, pp. 24-48.

Miller, N.E., and Dollard, J. *Social learning and imitation.* New Haven: Yale University Press, 1941.

Myers, K.E., Travers, R.M., and Sanford, M.E. Learning and reinforcement in student pairs. *Journal of Educational Psychology,* 1965, *56,* 67-72.

Myrick, R.D. The counselor-consultant and the effeminate boy. *Personnel and Guidance Journal,* 1970, *45,* 351-361.

Neale, D.H. Behavior therapy and encopresis in children. *Behaviour Research and Therapy,* 1963, *1,* 139-143.

Nighswander, J.K., and Mayer, G.R. Catharsis: A means of reducing elementary school student's aggressive behaviors? *Personnel and Guidance Journal,* 1969, *47,* 461-466.

Nolen, P.A., Kunzelmann, H.P., and Haring, N.C. Behavior modification in a junior high learning disabilities classroom. *Exceptional Children,* 1967, *34,* 163-168.

O'Connor, R.D. Modification of social withdrawal through symbolic modeling. *Journal of Applied Behavior Analysis,* 1969, *2,* 15-22.

O'Leary, D.K., and Becker, W.C. Behavior modification of an adjustment class: a token reinforcement system. *Exceptional Children,* 1967, *33,* 637-642.

O'Leary, D.K., O'Leary, S., and Becker, W.C. Modification of a deviant sibling interaction pattern in the home. *Behaviour Research and Therapy,* 1967, *5,* 113-120.

Patterson, G.R. A learning theory approach to the treatment of the school phobic child. In L.P. Ullmann and L. Krasner (Eds.), *Case studies in behavior modification.* New York: Holt, Rinehart and Winston, 1965(a).

——. An application of conditioning techniques to the control of a hyperactive child. In L.P. Ullmann and L. Krasner (Eds.), *Case studies in behavior modification.* New York: Holt, Rinehart and Winston, 1965(b).

——. Teaching parents to be behavior modifiers in the classroom. In J.D. Krumboltz and C.E. Thoresen (Eds.), *Behavioral counseling, case studies and techniques.* New York: Holt, Rinehart and Winston, 1969, pp. 155-161.

Patterson, G.R., and Brodsky, G.D. A behavior modification program for a child with multiple problem behaviors. *Journal of Child Psychology and Psychiatry,* 1966, *7,* 277-295.

Patterson, G.R., and Gullion, M.E. *Living with children: new methods for parents and teachers.* Champaign, Illinois: Research Press, 1968.

Pavlov, I.P. *Conditioned reflexes.* (translated and edited by G.V. Anrep), New York: Dover Publications, 1960. (First published in 1927.)

Peterson, D.R., and London, P. A role for cognition in the behavioral treatment of a child's eliminative disturbance. In L.P. Ullmann and L. Krasner (Eds.), *Case studies in behavior modification.* New York: Holt, Rinehart and Winston, Inc., 1965, pp. 289-295.

Peterson, R.F., and Peterson, L.R. The use of positive reinforcement in the control of self-destructive behavior in a retarded boy. *Journal of Experimental Child Psychology,* 1968, *6,* 351-360.

Phillips, E.L. Achievement place: token reinforcement procedures in a home-style rehabilitation setting for "pre-delinquent" boys. *Journal of Applied Behavior Analysis,* 1968, *1,* 213-224.

Premack, D. Toward empirical behavior laws: I. positive reinforcement. *Psychological Review,* 1959, *66,* 219-233.

Quarti, C., and Renaud, J. A new treatment of constipation by conditioning: a preliminary report. In C.M. Franks (Ed.), *Conditioning techniques in clinical practice and research.* New York: Springer Publishing Co., Inc., 1964, pp. 219-227.

Reese, E.P. *The analysis of human operant behavior.* Dubuque, Iowa: Wm. C. Brown, 1966.

Reynolds, N.J., and Risley, T.R. The role of social and material reinforcers in increasing talking of a disadvantaged preschool child. *Journal of Applied Behavior Analysis,* 1968, *1,* 253-262.

Riessman, F. The culturally deprived child: A new view. *The Education Digest,* 1963, *29,* 12-15.

————. The helper therapy principle. *Social Work,* 1965, *25,* 27-32.

Risley, R. The effects and side effects of punishing the autistic behaviors of a deviant child. *Journal of Applied Behavior Analysis,* 1968, *1,* 21-34.

Ritter, B. The group desensitization of children's snake phobias using vicarious and contact desensitization procedures. *Behaviour Research and Therapy,* 1968, *6,* 1-6.

Ruch, F.L. *Psychology and Life* (6th ed.).Chicago: Scott, Foresman and Co., 1963.

Russell, J.C., Clark, A.W., and Sommers, P.V. Treatment of stammering by reinforcement of fluent speech. *Behaviour Research and Therapy,* 1968, *6,* 447-453.

Russo, S. Adaptations in behavioral therapy with children. *Behaviour Research and Therapy,* 1964, *2,* 43-47.

Sarbin, T.R. Role theoretical interpretation of psychological change. In P. Worchel and D. Byrne (Eds.), *Personality change.* New York: John Wiley, 1964, 176-219.

Schrupp, M.H., and Gjerde, C.M. Teacher growth in attitudes toward behavior problems of children. *Journal of Educational Psychology,* 1953, *44,* 203-214.

Shaftel, F.R., and Shaftel, G. *Role-playing for social values: decision-making in the social studies.* Englewood, Cliffs, N.J.: Prentice-Hall, 1967.

Shostrom, Everett. *Man, the manipulator.* New York: Bantam Books, 1968.

Skinner, B.F. *Science and human behavior.* New York: Macmillan Co., 1953.

————. Freedom and the control of men. In R. Ullrich and J. Mabry (Eds.), *Control of human behavior.* Glenview, Ill.: Scott, Foresman and Co., 1966, pp. 11-20.

————. *The technology of teaching.* New York: Appleton-Century-Crofts, 1968.

Smith, J.M., and Smith, E.P. *Child management: A program for parents and teachers.* Ann Arbor, Michigan: Ann Arbor Publishers, 1966.

Staats, A.W., and Butterfield, W.H. Treatment of nonreading in a culturally deprived juvenile delinquent: an application of reinforcement principles. *Child Development,* 1965, *36,* 925-942.

Staats, A.W., and Staats, C.K. *Complex human behavior.* New York: Holt, Rinehart and Winston, 1963.

Straughan, J.H. Treatment with child and mother in the playroom. *Behaviour Research and Therapy,* 1964, *2,* 37-41.

Sulzer, B., Mayer, A.R., and Cody, J.J. Assisting teachers with managing classroom behavioral problems. *Elementary School Guidance and Counseling,* 1968, *3,* 40-48.

Tate, B.A., and Baroff, A.S. Aversive control of self-injurious behavior in a psychotic boy. *Behaviour Research and Therapy,* 1966, *4,* 281-287.

Thomas, D.R., Becker, W.C., and Armstrong, M. Production and elimination of disruptive classroom behavior by systematically varying teacher's behavior. *Journal of Applied Behavior Analysis,* 1968, *1,* 35-45.

Travers, R.W.M. *Essentials of learning.* New York: Macmillan Co., 1963.

Tyler, V.O., Jr. Exploring the use of operant techniques in rehabilitation of delinquent boys. Paper read at the American Psychological Association Convention, Chicago, September, 1965.

Ullmann, L.P., and Krasner, L. (Eds.), *Case studies in behavior modification.* New York: Holt, Rinehart and Winston, 1965, pp. 1-63.

Valett, R.E. *Programming learning disabilities.* Palo Alto: Fearon Publishers, 1969.

Verplanck, W.S. The control of the content of conversation: reinforcement of statements of opinion. *Journal of Abnormal and Social Psychology,* 1955, *51,* 668-676.

Wagner, M.K. Reinforcement of the expression of anger through role-playing. *Behaviour Research and Therapy,* 1968, *6,* 91-95.

Wahler, R.G. Oppositional children: A quest for parental reinforcement control. *Journal of Applied Behavior Analysis,* 1969, *2,* 159-170.

Wahler, R.G., Winkel, G.H., Peterson, R.F., and Morrison, D.C. Mothers as behavior therapists for their own children. *Behaviour Research and Therapy,* 1965, *3,* 113-124.

Ward, H., and Baker, B.L. Reinforcement therapy in the classroom. *Journal of Applied Behavior Analysis,* 1968, *1,* 323-328.

Watson, J.B., and Raynor, R. Conditioned emotional reactions. *Journal of Experimental Psychology,* 1920, *3,* 1-14.

Werry, J.S., and Quay, H.C. Observing the classroom behavior of elementary school children. *Exceptional Children,* 1969, *35,* 461-470.

Whiting, J.M. Resource mediation and learning by identification. In I. Iscoe and H.W. Stevenson (Eds.), *Personality development in children.* Austin: University of Texas Press, 1960.

Wickes, I.G. Treatment of persistent enuresis with the electric buzzer. *Archives of Disease in Childhood,* 1958, *33,* 160-164.

Wickman, E.K. *Children's behavior and teacher's attitudes.* New York: Commonwealth Fund, 1928.

Wickramaserkera, I. The application of learning theory to the treatment of a case of sexual exhibitionism. *Psychotherapy: Theory, research and practice,* 1968, June, *5* (2), 108-112.

Williams, C.D. The elimination of tantrum behavior by extinction procedures. *Journal of Abnormal and Social Psychology,* 1959, *59,* 269.

––––––. Extinction and other principles of learning in the treatment and prevention of children's disorders. Paper read at the American Psychological Association Convention, St. Louis, September, 1962.

Wolf, M.M., Giles, D.K., and Hall, V.R. Experiments with token reinforcement in a remedial classroom. *Behaviour Research and Therapy,* 1968, *6,* 51-64.

Wolf, M.M., Risley, T.R., and Mees, H.L. Application of operant conditioning procedures to the behavior problems of an autistic child. *Behaviour Research and Therapy,* 1964, *1,* 305-312.

Wolf, M.M., and Risley, J. Analysis and modification of deviant child behavior. Paper read at the American Psychological Association Convention, Washington, D.C., September, 1967.

Wolpe, J. For phobia, a hair of the hound. *Psychology Today,* June 1969, *3,* 34-37.

Wolpe, J., and Lazarus, A.A. *Behavior therapy techniques: a guide to the treatment of neuroses.* Oxford: Pergamon Press, 1966.

Zeilberger, J., Sampen, L.E., and Sloane, H.N., Jr. Modification of a child's problem behaviors in the home with the mother as therapist. *Journal of Applied Behavior Analysis,* 1968, *1,* 47-53.

Zimmerman, E.H., and Zimmerman, J. The alteration of behavior in a special classroom situation. *Journal of the Experimental Analysis of Behavior,* 1962, *5,* 59-60.

Zinzer, O. Imitation, modeling and cross-cultural training. Aerospace Medical Research Laboratories, Aerospace Medical Division, Wright-Patterson Air Force Base, Ohio, September, 1966.